Intersectionality of Race, Ethnicity, Class, and Gender in Teaching and Teacher Education

Advances in Teaching and Teacher Education

VOLUME 3

Scope

Advances in Teaching and Teacher Education is an international book series that aims to provide an important outlet for sharing the state-of-the-art research, knowledge, and practices of teaching and teacher education. The series helps promote the discussion, improvement, and assessment of teachers' quality, teaching, and instructional innovations including technology integration at all school levels as well as through teacher education around the world. With no specific restriction to disciplines, the series strives to address and synthesize different aspects and stages in teaching and teacher professional development both within and across disciplines, various interactions throughout the process of instructional activities and teacher education from various theoretical, policy, psychological, socio-cultural, or cross-cultural perspectives. The series features books that are contributed by researchers, teacher educators, instructional specialists, and practitioners from different education systems.

The titles published in this series are listed at *brill.com/atte*

Intersectionality of Race, Ethnicity, Class, and Gender in Teaching and Teacher Education

Movement toward Equity in Education

Foreword by Geneva Gay

Edited by

Norvella P. Carter and Michael Vavrus

BRILL

SENSE

LEIDEN | BOSTON

All chapters in this book have undergone peer review.

The Library of Congress Cataloging-in-Publication Data is available online at http://catalog.loc.gov

Typeface for the Latin, Greek, and Cyrillic scripts: "Brill". See and download: brill.com/brill-typeface.

ISBN 978-90-04-36518-6 (paperback)
ISBN 978-90-04-36519-3 (hardback)
ISBN 978-90-04-36520-9 (e-book)

Contents

Foreword: Considering Another View of Intersectionality

Geneva Gay

The authors of *Intersectionality of Race, Ethnicity, Class, and Gender in Teaching and Teacher Education* provide compelling profiles, persuasive arguments, and substantiating evidence that marginalized individuals and groups in the U.S. experience many different oppressions and exploitations simultaneously, or they routinely encounter multiple, interconnected, and inseparable marginalities. They give functional meaning to the Critical Race Theory idea that racism and other multiple forms of oppression toward disadvantaged groups in U.S. society are structurally pervasive, persistent, and normative. Individually and collectively the chapter authors recommend that educational policies, programs, and practices designed to liberate and empower marginalized populations include a deeper understanding of and response to these interconnected oppressions. They also offer some viable suggestions for how these goals can be accomplished. I suggest that another viewpoint be added to the discourse on intersectionality, not to distract attention away from the necessity of or diminish the power of those presented by the authors in this book but to complement and join them by analyzing the empowering dynamics of the resistance, resilience, and transcendence marginalized groups engage in opposition to oppression and exploitation. These acts of empowerment like the oppressive and restrictive practices that often catalyze them, are multimodal, multifocal, and interactive. That is, intersectionality is as evident in transformative and transcendent actions as it is in oppression and exploitation, and should be subjected to thorough analysis in these contexts as well.

Intersectionality is both a commonsensical idea and a compelling analytical framework. In most instances its primary *raison d'être* is to offer multi-based analyses and transformative possibilities of negative perceptions and experiences of disenfranchised groups due to oppression, exploitation, discrimination, marginalization, and other forms of inequity. But analyses of intersectionality also can include positive possibilities generated from resistance, resilience, and transcendence. In fact there are many interconnections between negative consequences of various forms of imposed marginality and how victimized populations navigate them. Invariably, multiple perspectives, constituent issues, and methodologies are included in these transformative navigations.

A case in point is how literary authors of color create counter narratives to multiple forms of oppression, and reconstruct their multiple identities as racialized, cultured, gendered, and classed individuals. For example, the protagonist in Ralph Ellison's *Invisible Man* deals simultaneously with his own individual racial, gender, cultural, ethnic, and economic marginalization, and those of the various groups to which he belongs. In fact, individual and group issues, identities, resistance, and resilience are interconnected. Another example is the poetry of Maya Angelou (such as "Still I Rise" and "Phenomenal Woman") and Nikki Giovanni (i.e., "Ego Tripping") who use poetry to name various oppressions and discriminations African Americans encounter, resist, and transcend. The stories they tell speak about challenges to their individual ethnic, racial, class, physical appearance, gender, and performance abilities as well as those of their ethnic group (African American). These texts also attest to how some forms of courage, resistance, perseverance, resilience, and transcendence of African Americans are interconnected with their oppression, discrimination, and exploitation. Implicit in these analyses are undercurrents of human complexity and multi-dimensionality, and that their performance capabilities will be cultivated and enhanced to the extent that these interactive multiplicities are understood, respected, evoked, and promoted.

In trying to manage human interrelated dimensionalities and complexities the tendency is to compartmentalize them. Thus, educators may emphasize the intellect; religious and moral leaders may focus on spirituality and ethics; healthcare professionals may concentrate on physical well-being; and psychologists may target emotionality. Other common ways of sectionalizing human complexity is by age, gender, race, ethnicity, class, residence, and status. Yet, there is no such thing as one-dimensional human beings; nor is it possible to disconnect the various parts of their identities without distorting and even destroying the quality of human life. Therefore, intersectionality can be viewed simultaneously as a curse and a blessing; an aberration and a normalcy; a problem and a potential; a reality and a mission.

While the need to manage human complexity by compartmentalizing it may be understandable, it is untenable because it is impossible to accomplish in reality without distorting humanity. People simply cannot suspend some aspects of their humanity at will, and even when others attempt to impose this upon them it is still impossible to do. Therefore, it is ironic that many teachers attempt to ignore their students' race or ethnicity or gender by being colorblind and culturally mute, while claiming to be committed to maximizing these students individual and human potential. Or, they claim to *not* be personally present, on multiple levels, in their own teaching. These claims ignore a fundamental fact of the humanity of teachers and students, as well as the act of teaching itself. That is, humans, their beliefs and behaviors, are multidimensional and complex. Simply put, teachers and students cannot separate their role functions in educational contexts and practices from their human intersecting multiplicities. People are comprised of many selves that are always operating simultaneously and interactively. To attempt to ignore or deny this reality is a practice in futility, and the results are likely to diminish the human worth, value, and integrity of both students and teachers, and minimize their performance possibilities.

My appeal to educational researchers, scholars, and practitioners is to not view intersectionality only through the more common paradigm of multiple interactive marginalities. The challenge is to give credence to positive aspects of intersectionality without diminishing or distracting attention away from the negatives. To reiterate, intersectionality is inherent to humanity, and it is present in all human interactions all the time, whether these are constructive, destructive, or ambivalent. Educators must understand, accept, and act on this reality to more effectively meet the needs of students from different identity categories. Thus, second generation immigrant Latinx students with a learning disability are, at the same time, male and/or female; of a certain age; live in a given residential context; have a language heritage; have a variety of background experiences; have worthy competencies and capabilities in other aspects and locations of living and learning outside of schools; and so on. In other words, they are complex human beings, and they should not be simplified and reduced to one dimension, such as their language, race, or residence. To do so would be an insult to and an assault on their human dignity. Genuine responsive and high quality educational programs and practices have to be multidimensional and complex to interface effectively with the *human* multidimensionality and complexity of different marginalized individuals and groups. No simple solution, quick fix, best practices for all, or default to individuality will do!

Historical records show that regardless of the magnitude and severity of the dehumanizing, oppressive, and marginalizing practices imposed upon individuals and groups of color they never allowed them to be the totality of their being; nor did they concede entirely to the impositions. Under the most demeaning, demoralizing, and restrictive conditions, and in the absence of some of the most basic human resources, various marginalized people not only survived but many thrived; they resisted; they persevered; they created; and they produced (as they continue to do). The generative creativity that evolved in these acts of resistance, resilience, and transcendence deserve more prominence in comprehensive analyses of intersectionality.

So, what's to be done about this human complexity and multidimensionality in educational situations, especially those involving students and teachers who are ethnically, racially, culturally, socially, gender, and economically dissimilar from each other. Stated more simply, what's to be done in U.S. schools about honoring and evoking the human complexity of students and teachers since the lens through which humanity are filtered are increasingly more divergent than convergent, yet addressing students' needs are more segmented than holistic. Despite the frequently evoked claims in discourse about cultural diversity that "humans are more alike than different," the differences that do exist are significant and should be deliberately and comprehensively engaged in teaching and learning.

The apparently easy and simple, though actually difficult and complex, answer is to "teach the whole child," from comprehensive perspectives. This does not necessarily mean that teachers need to address every conceivable aspect or dimension of students' humanity simultaneously. That may be impossible to do. But, whatever dimension is the focal point at any given time should always be maintained, analyzed, and addressed in the context of and interaction with other components, perspectives, issues, and experiences. For example, the educational needs of African American girls need to be understood and addressed by being cognizant of how their race, gender, ethnicity, living environment, cultural heritage, structural inequities, social class, and so on interact with learning opportunities and real and possible outcomes. This is necessary because all Black girls are not the same Black girl!

My ultimate point is that the idea of interactive multi-dimensionalities that underlie intersectionality is more fundamental than just promoting viable educational justice and empowerment agendas for marginalized and disenfranchised groups, even though these are desirable goals. It speaks to the essence of humanity. People are multi-dimensional beings comprised of many different things, all of which have their own function, but they interact simultaneously with each other. Education should complement, not contradict this human reality. This means, at a minimum, they should stop trying to address only one part or component of students' identity while ignoring all others, or looking for an easy way out. To make the point, while improving academic performance for various individuals and groups of color is paramount, to try to do so by focusing on only academics will never be adequate.

Instead, understanding and employing the intersectionality of students' human multiplicities is a more viable course of action to pursue. In doing so educators interacting with culturally, ethnically, racially, and socially diverse students should remember (and act accordingly),

My Multiple Me

The more you see of me
The more there is of me for you to see
My complexity may at first mystify

But at closer study it will clarify
Who I am and what I can be
For it's the foundation of my potentiality.
Don't diminish my humanity
By simplifying my complexity
Instead, embrace and cultivate my multidimensionality
Without it I cannot be
All of my possibility.
For me to be more of me
My education must routinely see
All of my multiplicity.

Acknowledgement of Reviewers

We wish to express our deep gratitude to the following individuals who provided a careful review of initial drafts of chapters and feedback for authors:

Juanita Johnson-Bailey
Terah Venzant-Chambers
Jon Davis
Phyllis Esposito
Leslie Flemmer
Terry Ford
Brandon Fox
Lisa Hobson
Patricia J. Larke,
Petra Robinson

We also appreciate the comprehensive review of the entire manuscript and subsequent recommendations by anonymous reviewers.

The professional and thoughtful assistance of this entire group of scholars served to enrich this book.

Notes on Contributors

Norvella P. Carter

is Professor and Endowed Chair in Urban Education at Texas A&M University (TAMU). Dr. Carter is Executive Editor of the National Journal for Urban Education and Practice and served as the past-director of the Center for Urban School Partnerships at TAMU. Dr. Carter's scholarship has been published widely in research journals, books and teaching manuals. As a scholar, she was invited to give expert testimony on "Closing the Achievement Gap for Children of Color," at a Congressional Hearing on Capitol Hill in Washington DC sponsored by the Children's Caucus in congress. Her national and international research agenda include urban education, equity pedagogy, African American children and urban programs for university settings.

Warren L. Chalklen

has a Ph.D. from Texas A&M University and serves as a Data Associate at Educators For Excellence, a national non-profit organization advocating for equity centered education policy, based in New York City. His research interests include critical race theory and Ubuntu philosophy. More specifically, he examines how the intersection of race, class and gender operate in urban school settings. He is a co-author of the chapter "Re-Rooting Roots: The South African Perspective" in *Reconsidering Roots* (University of Georgia Press, 2017).

Julia Daniel

is a doctoral student in the School of Education at the University of Colorado, Boulder. Having worked in organizing Florida around issues of racial, gender and economic justice, she is committed to community organizing. Most of her organizing centered on ending the schoolhouse-to-jailhouse pipeline for Black and Latino students in Miami by working with impacted young people in demanding alternatives such as restorative justice. She researches and writes on issues of education with respect to racial, gender and class equity, focusing on disparate discipline practices and community schools.

Kelly Ferguson

is currently serving as clinical assistant professor at Loyola University-Chicago and teaches undergraduate and graduate courses in the School of Education. Kelly's passion for and commitment to social justice, particularly for that of marginalized groups, can be found in her research focus on Black male education. Kelly's research and life's work are committed to supporting practitioners in their understanding of and work with Black male students and providing learning environments responsive to their educational needs.

Geneva Gay

is Professor of Education at the University of Washington-Seattle where she teaches multicultural education and general curriculum theory. She is the recipient of many awards for Distinguished Scholarship in the Field of Education. She is known for many seminal publications such as *Culturally Responsive Teaching: Theory, Research, and Practice* (Teachers College Press). She is nationally and internationally known for her scholarship in multicultural education, particularly as it relates to curriculum design, staff development, classroom instruction, and intersections of culture, race, ethnicity, teaching, and learning. Her professional service includes membership on several national editorial review and advisory boards. International consultations on multicultural education have taken her to Canada, Brazil, Taiwan, Finland, Japan, England, Scotland, and Australia.

Willie C. Harmon, Jr.

is a doctoral student in Curriculum and Instruction (Urban Education) at Texas A&M University. He has ten years' experience working with youth (K-16) from urban and suburban school districts in various capacities. His research interests include resiliency in students of color, equity in urban schools, youth organizing/activism, and the use of African American history in critical pedagogy.

John P. Hopkins

holds a Ph.D. in the Social & Cultural Foundations of Education from the University of Washington. He serves as the Associate Dean of Students and Director of Service & Diversity Initiatives at Saint Martin's University in Lacey, WA. He also teaches courses in Communication Studies and Social Justice. His academic interests include the philosophy of education, multicultural education and theory, and Indigenous philosophy of education.

Marlon C. James

is an Assistant Professor of Urban Education and the Co-Director of the Collaborative for Advancing Urban School Excellence at Texas A&M University. His research and teaching explores urban teacher preparation, school reform, and organizing African American community resources for improving student development and success.

China M. Jenkins

has a Ph.D. in Educational Human Resources and Development. She is currently the manager of Faculty Development Services for the Houston Community College System. Her research interests are culturally responsive teaching in higher education, intercultural communication, and faculty development.

Kevin L. Jones

is earning a doctorate in Curriculum and Instruction, with an emphasis in urban education, in the Department of Teaching, Learning and Culture at Texas A&M University (TAMU). He has a master's degree in music education from Florida State University. He teaches multicultural education classes at TAMU and also serves as a research assistant. His research interests are curriculum and instruction, urban education, African American males and music education

Victoria L. Carter Jones

is earning her doctorate in Educational Administration and Human Resources at Texas A&M University (TAMU). She has a master's degree in Curriculum and Instruction from TAMU and currently serves as a research assistant in her department. Her research interests include leadership, curriculum and instruction, culturally responsive pedagogy, social justice and the preparation of leaders for urban school districts.

Chi Yun Moon

is doctoral student in the Department of Teaching, Learning, and Culture in the College of Education and Human Resource Development at Texas A&M University in College Station. She is currently working on the development of her dissertation proposal that explores the socio-political challenges in understanding the "receivement gap" and social justice tenets.

Mónica Vásquez Neshyba

is a Clinical Assistant Professor at Texas A&M University. She teaches courses on second language acquisition and assessment, English as a Second Language methodology, the Latino learner, multicultural education, and teaching behavior. She has presented at various local, state, national and international conferences on a variety of topics concerning English learners, including literacy, second language acquisition, gifted and talented education, and cultural and linguistic diversity. Dr. Neshyba received her Ph.D. from the University of Texas at Austin in Curriculum and Instruction with a specialization in Bilingual and Bicultural Education.

Quinita Ogletree

is a lecturer in the Department of Teaching, Learning, and Culture in the College of Education and Human Resource Development at Texas A&M University (TAMU). She earned her master's degrees from Virginia Union University in religion and University of Houston in Educational psychology and her Ph.D. from TAMU in curriculum and instruction. Her research interest, publications and presentations focus on urban, multicultural and early childhood education.

Amy J. Samuels

earned her doctorate in Educational Leadership from the University of South Florida. She is an assistant professor of Leadership at University of Montevallo. Her research interests include application of critical race theory, critical Whiteness, critical pedagogy, and culturally responsive teaching in instructional and leadership practices.

Dawn Tafari

is a visiting assistant professor in the Department of Education at Winston-Salem State University in North Carolina. Areas of specialization include Black male students and teachers, hip-hop feminism, and composite counterstorytelling.

Michael Vavrus

is the author of *Diversity and Education: A Critical Multicultural Approach* and *Transforming the Multicultural Education of Teachers: Theory, Research, and Practice.* His invited book chapters, research, and book reviews have appeared in a variety of professional journals and research handbooks/encyclopedias. Dr. Vavrus is the past-president of the Association of Independent Liberal Arts Colleges for Teacher Education and the Washington state chapter of the American Association of Colleges for Teacher Education. He is professor emeritus of interdisciplinary studies (education, history, & political economy) at the Evergreen State College in Olympia, Washington.

Gwendolyn C. Webb-Hasan

is an Associate Professor in the departments of Educational Administration and Human Resource Development and Teaching, Learning and Culture at Texas A&M University. Her current research and scholarship examines the academic outcomes of African American girls and culturally responsive leadership in PreK-12 settings.

Terrenda White

has a Ph.D. from Columbia University and serves as an assistant professor in education foundations, policy, and practice at the University of Colorado Boulder. She studies issues of race, culture, power, and pedagogy in public schools, particularly in charter schools and other market-based education reforms. Her work in journal articles, book chapters, and conference presentations highlights the impact of reforms on students and teachers of color, as well as school working conditions, teacher turnover, and forms of teacher activism and resistance.

Denise K. Whitford

has a Ph.D. from University of Arizona and serves as an Assistant Professor of Special Education at Purdue University who specializes in school discipline disproportionality as it relates to underreported student populations. She is involved in research that includes (a) the investigation of disproportionality patterns, (b) examination of the effects of disproportionality on student achievement, post-academic outcomes, and emotional well-being, and (c) determining methods for decreasing disproportionality in K-12 settings, particularly through the use of culturally responsive practices and educator and administrator professional development.

Kamala V. Williams

is the Editorial & Creative Services Specialist for the Minority Achievement, Creativity, and High Ability Center for the Whitlowe R. Green College of Education, Prairie View A&M University. She received her bachelor's degree from the University of North Texas and her master and doctoral degrees from Texas A&M University. She is an adjunct professor and member of the graduate faculty at Texas A&M University. Dr. Williams also serves as the Managing Editor of the National Journal of Urban Education and Practice. She has several publications in peer-reviewed journal articles, published book chapters, and is co-author of a manual used for professional development in several urban school districts.

CHAPTER 1

Introduction: Intersectionality Related to Race, Ethnicity, Class and Gender

Norvella P. Carter

In 2016, several presenters at the American Educational Research Association annual meeting focused on the intersectionality of race, ethnicity, class and gender. The presentations were unique, because the scholars applied an intersectionality approach that investigated the schooling effects of identification based on race, ethnicity, class, and gender in relation to teaching and teacher education. The presenters translated their work into this volume. Rather than an emphasis on theorizing models of intersectionality, this research collection brings together scholarship that has applied an intersectionality methodology to conditions that affect public school children, teachers and teacher educators. Therefore, this book examines teaching and learning experiences in relation to intersectionality of group identities that include interactions with institutional systems of power and privilege.

Conceptually this book is influenced by the intersectionality scholarship of Crenshaw (1993), critical race theorist and legal scholar. Intersectionality provided chapter authors a methodology to examine group identities for their differences and experiences of oppression, and also for differences within groups that contribute to conflicts among groups (Bright, Malinsky, & Thompson, 2016). This approach allowed authors to move beyond "single-axis thinking" that "undermines legal thinking, disciplinary knowledge production, and struggles for social justice" (Cho, Crenshaw, & McCall, 2013, p. 787).

Crenshaw (1993) refers to three types of intersectionality. First, there is structural intersectionality which for our purposes, refers to the way in which students of color "are situated within overlapping structures of subordination" (p. 114). Secondly, there is political intersectionality which can refer to the way people of color or of low income are ignored in discussions about race, class or gender (Crenshaw, 1993). Finally, representational intersectionality uses race, [ethnicity, class] and gender stereotypes to frame images of people of color (1993).

Intersectionality in this collection helps complicate commonsense, one-dimensional mainstream notions of race, ethnicity, class, and gender in education by subverting standard assertions of essentialized identities.

© KONINKLIJKE BRILL NV, LEIDEN, 2018 | DOI 10.1163/9789004365209_001

Intersectionality is critical because so often these components are excluded from important conversations regarding equality and equity. Our lives are enriched by the lives and experiences of people who have multiple aspects that make up their identity. Furthermore, marginalization and oppression is both complicated and compounded when we refuse to acknowledge all of the variables that comprise one group of people.

The intersectionality research presented serves as "an analytic sensibility" to address "larger ideological structures in which subjects, problems, and solutions were framed" (Cho, Crenshaw, & McCall, 2013, pp. 791, 795). Consequently, this book examines teaching and learning experiences in relation to intersectionality of group identities that include interactions with institutional systems of power and privilege.

1   Movement toward Equity in Teaching and Teacher Education

Historically, a pivotal time in our nation's history was the *Plessey v. Ferguson* (1896) U.S. Supreme Court decision. This was a significant time, because it had been documented that people were "open-minded" to the Supreme Court's decision and were ready to accept whatever was mandated by the "law of the land." When the Supreme Court ruled that "separate, but equal" was legal, this law was implanted in the hearts of the people. Decades later, in 1954 when the ruling in the case *Brown v. Board of Education of Topeka* (1954) reversed the decision, it was too late, the hearts of the people had already accepted the discriminatory view. A movement of resistance and resentment to equity became infused throughout our society.

Currently we are still waging a battle for equity and fairness, which includes schooling and our educational process. Coleman, in his seminal study known as the "Coleman Report," helped move the concept of equality of educational opportunity forward by documenting the moral and ethical issues that were raised by group-based inequality in educational outcomes (Coleman et al., 1966). More recently Field, Kuczera, and Point (2007) generally define equity in education as a combination of fairness and inclusion. They relate fairness to ensuring that people do not encounter irrelevant obstacles toward achieving their human potential and inclusion as the existence of a minimum standard of education that is guaranteed for everyone.

According to Secada (2012), it was during the decades of the 1970s and 1980s that educators began to use the term equity. Burbules, Lord, and Sherman (1982) tracked the history, but simply referred to equity as fair or fairness in terms of treatment of others. Equity was different than equality (giving everyone the same), whereas, equity moved beyond sameness to giving everyone what they needed. The distinction is powerful when applying the concept to the classroom. Teachers who provide whatever is needed for students are much more effective than teachers who provide "the same for everyone" whether the situation calls for varied instruction, curriculum support, time or attention.

In a 1987 American Educational Research Association symposium, scholars presented on the question: "What is equity in education?" The scholars followed with a monograph that:

a Traced the historical development of notions of equity through *Brown v. Board* Supreme Court decisions;
b Considered multiculturalism as a form of equity;
c Deconstructed the continuing power of the eugenics movement to influence school texts;
d Noted how various research paradigms promote different ideals of equity; and
e Traced concerns for gender equity along the lines of inputs, processes, and outcomes of education (Secada, 1989, p. 805).

Secada (2012) refers to three major ways equity has been conceptualized: fairness, socially enlightened self-interest (engaging in a process for the benefit of society), and social justice. His definition of social justice as "interrupting current wrongs, on undoing or rectifying past wrongs, and predicting and/or avoiding potential wrongs that have been or that may be visited upon whole groups of people" (Secada, 1989, p. 806) is very inclusive in nature. It is within the acceptance of this definition that educators began to move toward meeting the needs of children in teaching and teacher education. The concept of equity is so important because it forces us to look critically into both conscious and unconscious thinking patterns, belief systems, language, and behavior of educators, which are systematically displayed by teachers in classrooms.

2 Enemies of Equity in Teaching and Teacher Education

The enemies of equity are practically limitless in number and reach into every aspect of society. For purposes of this chapter, a few are named and educators are challenged to begin the process of extinction within teaching and teacher education as a means to penetrate strongholds in our society.

2.1 *Viewing Learners through Statistical Deficits*
It is tremendously gripping that the United States in the 21st century still grapples with issues of race, ethnicity, class and gender, particularly in

teaching and teacher education. Professional development of our teachers and the preparation of teachers for our nation's children are directly concerned with one of the most important tasks facing U.S. society, educating America's youth. Theoretically and constitutionally it can be said that we are a nation that has accepted the challenge of educating all students. Yet, in reality, masses of children are not fulfilling their potential in our schools.

A brief review of literature will reveal that Indigenous students are retained almost 50% more than White students in early childhood grades (U.S. Department of Education, Office for Civil Rights, 2014a). African American learners, Latinx learners and low income learners are experiencing a disproportionate level of school failure (Delpit, 2012; Noguera, 2014; Noguera, Huertado, & Ferguson, 2011). Larke, Webb-Hasan, and Young (2017) contend that little work has been done on the academic development of African American girls. Black boys have dismal high school drop-out rates, but Black girls have the highest suspension rates of any other race or ethnicity of girls and Indigenous girls are suspended from school at higher rates than White girls or boys (U.S. Department of Education, Office for Civil Rights, 2014b).

For decades, almost any measure used to predict academic success, such as standardized test scores, college and high school Grade Point Averages (GPA), graduation and dropout rates, students of color across the nation do not achieve academically at the same rate as their European American counterparts (Banks & Banks, 2010; Carter, 2003; Howell, Lewis, & Carter, 2011; Lomotey & Lowery, 2014; Noguera, 2011). Moreover, students of color are referred to special education programs or are served in disciplinary programs at disproportionately higher levels than European American students (U.S. Department of Education, Office for Civil Rights, 2014b). In the general education environment, students of color, particularly African American learners, experience disproportionate academic failure, suspension and expulsion rates in comparison to their school representation (Williams & Carter, 2015). In special education environments African American learners are over identified in every disability category in comparison to their resident population (U.S. Department of Education, Office for Civil Rights, 2014b). Once designated to receive these "special" services, the academic failure and disproportionate exclusion patterns persist (Losen & Orfield, 2002; Carter, Webb-Hasan, & Williams, 2016).

Instead of these statistics being used to set goals for accomplishment, they have become measures of doom that imply inferiority for masses of children of color and children of low income families. Further, deficit statistics have been dramatized by media and some researchers have sought to explain these conditions through deficit theories and unchallenged stereotypes that promote racism and discrimination (Carter, Natesan, & Hawkins, 2008; Spring,

2016; Crenshaw, Ocen, & Nanda, 2015). Tragically, the home environment, family and culture have been blamed for the plight of students of color and low income children.

2.2   *Deficit Thinking, Language and Behaviors*

The great "isms," racism, classism, sexism and others are rooted and steeped in deficit thinking and behaviors that war against the concept of equity in our society. Nieto (2012) referred to deficit thinking as the assumption that some students, because of genetic, cultural or experiential differences are operating with a deficiency and are inferior to other children. Several authors in this book refer to deficit thinking because it is so ingrained in the hearts and minds of people.

Another form of deficit thinking is the acceptance that stereotypes are true. Webb-Hasan and Carter (2007) developed an instrument that was administered to 1400 teachers. Their 36-item Cultural Awareness Beliefs Inventory, helped investigate and analyze the attitudes and beliefs of urban teachers when it comes to understanding their African American students. It was later expanded to extend to other students of color, low income, special education and college students. Their findings revealed that all teachers in the study were grounded in some type of deficit thinking, but White teachers were more strongly grounded in deficit thinking (Natasan, Webb-Hasan, Walter, & Carter, 2009). For example, White teachers felt that race was not an issue that needs to be addressed in schools and most indicated they simply, do not see race in the faces of their children, they are *colorblind*.

Authors in this book also refer to the concept of *colorblindness*, meaning one who will not acknowledge the presence of race in society. Those who adopt this concept often think it is representative of their lack of racism, prejudice and bigotry. They will say "I don't see color, I only see people." Teachers bring this concept into the classroom and claim they do not see the races of their students. Ladson-Billings (1994) noted "teachers that fail to see color in children have a color-blindness mask of dysconscious racism, an uncritical habit of mind, that justifies inequity and exploitation by accepting the existing order of things" (p. 32). Gay (2014) asserted that, teachers should become critically conscious of their own cultural socialization and how it affects their perceptions, attitudes and behavior toward the cultures of other ethnic groups.

One of the more covert processes of racism is *hegemony*. Apple (1996) defines hegemony this way:

> The term hegemony refers to a process in which dominant groups in society come together to form a bloc and sustain leadership over subordinate groups. One of the most important elements that such

an idea implies is that a power bloc does not have to rely on coercion [because the subordinate groups] feel as if their concerns are being listened to. (pp. 14–15)

In other words, hegemony is a subtle, yet powerful form of discrimination in which persons are discriminated against, but they do not realize it. In addition, persons who have been discriminated against will say they have been given fair treatment, meaning in essence, they participate in their own discrimination.

In educational settings, hegemony puts students in a situation in which they have been devalued or handed an injustice, but they cannot identify the injustice because all rules have been followed and they appear to be in an environment of fairness and social justice. For example, a teacher might say democratic principles are being used and practiced in the classroom. In order to demonstrate the democratic process, the teacher calls on all of the students to voice an opinion. The student will say "yes" the teacher is using democratic principles, because all students have been given an opportunity to voice their opinion. The hegemonic behavior may be difficult to see, but it will be experienced by the students if the teacher validates the contributions of some children, but not others.

In most cases, the children who are not validated do not have values and verbal/nonverbal communication styles that are similar to their teacher. The students that have been devalued tend to believe that only a few classmates are smart, those whose contributions are consistently validated by the teacher. Therefore, hegemonic behaviors create self-fulfilling prophecies of failure on the part of the student and gives consent to the teacher to continue the practice. The irony of hegemonic behavior is that it keeps the practice going through consensual means.

Additionally, in the study by Natasan, Webb-Hasan, Walter, and Carter (2009), White teachers also felt strongly that poorer students are more difficult to teach and are not supported by their families. In interview and focus group follow-ups to the study, the White teachers supported stereotypes that their low-income students were not as bright as upper income students and their families did not care as much about their children's education. Despite research on gifted and talented students, many teachers and teacher educators do not know the literature that supports comparable brilliance, competence and potential of low income students when compared to more affluent students (Anderson, 2007; Delpit, 1995; Ford & Harris, 1999; Ladson-Billings, 1994).

2.3   *Teacher Beliefs, Efficacy and Models of Success*
Ongoing research on students of color and low-income students revealed that inadequate access to and receipt of quality instruction from teachers,

in general and special education environments, are significant factors contributing to school failure. When examining the research to improve the education of students of color, strong evidence continues to mount that teacher beliefs have a powerful impact on the academic achievement of these students (Carter, Hawkins, & Natesan, 2008; Kozleski & Artiles, 2011; Ladson-Billings, 1994, Webb-Johnson & Carter, 2007).

Beliefs are defined as "any simple proposition, conscious or unconscious, inferred from what a person says or does, capable of being preceded by the phrase, 'I believe that...'" (Rokeach, 1968, p. 113). For decades, scholars have concluded that teachers' beliefs appear to be the best predictor of teacher behavior, while also influencing teachers' perceptions and practices (Bandura, 1986; Brown, 2004; Dewey, 1933). Rosenthal and Jacobson's (1965) landmark study, *Pygmalion in the Classroom*, affirmed this concept. According to Gay (2010), teachers' assumptions and perceptions about students' intellect and behavior, affect how they treat students in the instructional settings, and impact the outcomes of student learning overtime.

In addition, an area that has major implications for teaching and functions as a tenet of multiculturalism (discussed in Vavrus' Afterword in this book) is *teacher efficacy*. A review of research associated with teacher efficacy reveals that it has been highly associated with teachers who are successful in diverse classrooms. Teacher efficacy has to do with the extent to which a teacher believes he or she can actually teach children and make a difference in their lives (Bandura, 1986; Gibson & Dembo, 1984). Other researchers state that teacher efficacy relates to a teacher's belief that students in his or her classroom can learn and that he or she can teach them (Bandura, 2001).

Teacher efficacy and expectations are "teacher characteristics" that have been consistently related to student achievement, particularly with students in diverse classrooms (Nieto, 2012). Teachers who possess a high sense of efficacy believe they can control events in the classroom, produce desired outcomes and actually spend more time planning, organizing and teaching (Carter, Webb-Hasan, & Williams, 2016). They are more open to ideas and have proven to be more willing to experiment with new methods to better meet the needs of their students (Hoy, 2004). In direct opposition to a teacher efficacy success model, the deficit model paralyzes many teachers, because they believe that circumstances in the student's life prevent learning. Teachers who are highly efficacious believe that factors beyond their control such as poverty and community environment can be overcome to achieve positive student outcomes in the classroom.

It is imperative that teachers shed deficit models and begin to embrace *models of resilience* that build on the strengths of students and focus on high expectations for all learners. Teachers and schools cannot alleviate poverty and other social ills in society that some students face on a daily basis. Therefore, it is necessary to address the challenges they can resolve in the form of policies, practices and provisions for educational environments that encourage all students to learn to the best of their ability.

Culturally responsive teaching is known as a model of success (Gay, 2014; Irvine, 2003). Phuntsog's (2001) mixed research design examined 66 elementary teachers' perceptions of the importance of implementing culturally responsive teaching within classrooms in the United States. Although culturally responsive pedagogy and teaching is becoming more widespread, none of the respondents recommended a call for fundamental curricular reforms to foster alternatives to hegemonic experiences in beliefs of prospective teachers. Furthermore, they did not suggest the importance of incorporating multicultural education into the structure, content or process of teacher education. Other researchers found similar findings in their studies (Carter, 2003; Carter, Webb-Hasan, & Williams, 2016).

Carter and Webb-Johnson (2007), developed a 36-item survey entitled "The Cultural Awareness Beliefs Inventory" (CABI). They administered the CABI to more than 1400 teachers in urban school districts. Their study, a mixed methods research design, found that a significant number of teachers of all races had biases against African American children. Some teachers indicated they did not believe African American children could learn as well as White children.

Irvine (1990) asserted that, "teachers form inaccurate impressions of student achievement especially with Black students" (p. 77). The findings of the Irvine's (1990) study suggested that teacher expectations of African American male achievement appear to be more influenced by stereotypes of African American males rather than their ability to achieve. Pohan and Aguilar (2001) found a significant relationship between preservice teachers' personal beliefs and their professional beliefs. Preservice teachers who possessed a strong bias and negative stereotypes toward students of color were less likely to develop professional beliefs and behaviors consistent with multicultural sensitivity and responsiveness.

Love and Kruger (2005) developed a survey that investigated teachers' culturally relevant beliefs and student achievement. The 48-item survey was adapted from Ladson-Billings' (1994) work reflecting culturally relevant teachers' beliefs and practices. In her study, participants endorsed items regarding communal learning environment, success for all students, teaching as giving back to the community, and the importance of students' ethnicity being correlated with higher student achievement.

Cultural therapy, developed by Spindler and Spindler (1994), encompassed critical consciousness with pedagogical skill development. As teachers become more self-aware of how their personal cultural values, assumptions, and beliefs shape their behaviors in educational settings, they are then able to recognize the cultural elements and nuances of student behavior to enhance their teaching skills (Gay, 2010). In reality, children of every race, ethnicity, class and gender are more brilliant and resilient than ever in our country's history, but we as a society of adults have failed to believe in, showcase and capitalize on their strengths (Ladson-Billings, 2009).

3   Overview of Content, Research and Theoretical Frameworks

In the work of Andersen and Collins (2012), the concept of "the matrix of domination" sets forth the importance of social structure and history and helps us to remember that race, ethnicity, class and gender affect the experiences of all groups, including those at the top and bottom of societal hierarchies. Chapters that follow set forth frameworks using intersectional approaches.

Hopkins, in Chapter 2 "Intersectionality, Colonizing Education, and the Indigenous Voice of Survivance," begins with colonization. His chapter utilizes the concept of structural intersectionality proposed by Crenshaw (1993) to examine the colonizing history of Indigenous education and its effect on Indigenous identity. The political aims of Indigenous peoples are contrasted with the Civil Rights Movement during the 1960s, followed by an analysis of how the federal government sought to dominate and control meanings of indigeneity through an assimilative system of education. The concept of survivance is utilized to illuminate how Indigenous peoples proposed nuanced meanings of Indigenous identity that both challenged colonizing education and that differed from each other. The chapter concludes by considering implications for Indigenous youth and teachers and how this research can help move a social justice agenda forward based on the concept of decolonization.

Chapter 3 by Jenkins, "Intersectional Considerations for Teaching Diversity," reminds us that teaching for diversity requires teacher educators to critically reflect not only on the way in which they teach; they must also consider the underlying messages and assumptions in their curriculum. This chapter focuses on some problematic approaches both White educators and educators of color utilize that promulgate racism while attempting to create a culturally responsive classroom. This chapter is designed to raise awareness of unintended racist practices and to challenge educators to engage in active critical reflection of the intersections of their social identities and their application of anti-racist pedagogical methods.

Williams and Ogletree examine the intersectionality of race and class in preservice teacher education and explore how teacher education can increase the capacity for educational equity in racially and economically diverse classrooms. In Chapter 4, "Intersections of Race and Class in Preservice Teacher Education: Advancing Educational Equity," the findings of their study highlight the positive effects and benefits of educational equity. Preservice teacher education is intentional in their field placement practices and expectations benefit teacher candidates assigned to classrooms that are racially and socioeconomically diverse. The complexities of race and socioeconomic status are often addressed independently however; this study examines the intersectionality of these complexities in teacher education. The chapter concludes with teacher education methodologies that can benefit all future teachers, especially those employed in schools with economically and racially diverse student populations.

The majority of the teaching population in our nation is White, while students of color continue to increase in number. Samuels in Chapter 5, "The Elephant in the Room: Approaches of White Educators to Issues of Race and Racism," examines the racial discourse of White educators to the concepts of race and racism. The notion of intersectionality is explored in relation to the interacting influences of Whiteness and professional roles as well as race-based advocacy and White privilege. The experiences of interviewees leads into a discussion of the constructive value in education curriculum for purposeful dialogue and in-depth examinations of racial tensions and disparities in U.S. public schools.

In Chapter 6 by Webb-Hasan, Jones, and Moon, "Teaching African American and Latinx Learners: Moving beyond a Status Quo Punitive Disciplinary Context to Considerations for Equitable Pedagogy in Teacher Education," the authors share lived experiences of African American and Latinx students that are recipients of punitive discipline. Their chapter focuses on how educators can and should resist the school-to-prison pipeline policies established by national and state mandates. Of particular interest is how the cultural identity perceptions and cultural consciousness of these learners intersect with their racial/ethnic identities and how these identities are understood in the school context, especially when teacher education programs prepare and develop preservice and in-service teachers.

Whitford's Chapter 7 is "Intersectionality of Ethnicity, Gender, and Disability with Disciplinary Practices Used with Indigenous Students: Implications for Teacher Preparation and Development." She introduces readers to the intersectionality of ethnicity, gender, and disability with the disciplinary practices that have been used with Indigenous students, particularly Native Americans in the United States. The chapter explores the results of a study that includes outcomes relevant to the intersection of gender and ethnicity for Native American student discipline. The chapter further examines implications for teacher preparation and professional development to improve academic, social, and emotional outcomes of Indigenous students.

In Chapter 8, "That Kind of Affection Ain't Welcome from a Black Man: The Intersections of Race and Gender in the Elementary Classroom," Tafari shares data from a qualitative study of Black, male, elementary school teachers from the Hip-Hop generation. Data are represented as a composite counterstory, a tool used by critical race theory scholars to share counternarratives of majoritarian stories. This composite counterstory acknowledges the presence and importance of *eros* in the classrooms of nine Black men who teach in U.S. public schools. Furthermore, the author challenges dominant narratives of Black masculinity and discusses the impact of heteronormativity on Black male teachers as they navigate the education profession.

James, Ferguson, Harmon and Jones in Chapter 9, "We're Not Misbehaving: Cultivating the Spirit of Defiance in Black Male Students," give insights into the behavior of African American males that may be helpful to educators. They assert that Black male students are disproportionately disciplined in schools, primarily for subjective acts of defiance. They explore how defiance is an integral force in the lives of Black males from boyhood to manhood and how schools can contribute to the development of this unique expression of resilience. They define "defiance" as a personal and collective set of resistance strategies to counter the economic, racial and social constraints unique to Black life in American society and schools. They further conclude that if defiance is channeled constructively, Black males use it to foster productive academic, social and professional lives, and to counter negative stereotypes. They write that understanding the spirit of defiance will aid teachers, schools and communities in minimizing cultural misunderstandings that lead to punitive and exclusionary disciplinary referrals.

Daniel and White in Chapter 10, "Black Girls Matter: An Intersectional Analysis of Young Black Women's Experiences and Resistance to Dominating Forces in School," share how the overuse of harsh discipline for Black and Latino students in the United States has received increased attention. However, they cite that African American female students and their experiences are largely ignored. They share how young Black female students experience multiple and intersecting forms of oppression in schools, such as racism, sexism, classism, and homophobia that can impede their academic success. Yet, little is said about them in the literature. They share insights for educators about young Black women.

In Chapter 11, "Latinx and Education: Shattering Stereotypes," Neshyba purports that Latinx students are commonly discussed in terms of achievement and graduation rates using immigration and English language proficiency as factors. However, many other factors are not included, such as intersections of race, ethnicity and gender and their implications on both schooling and teacher education. In addition to encouraging differentiation to meet the needs of culturally and linguistically diverse students, teacher educators are challenged to be purposeful in their instruction and choose their materials carefully as to avoid the perpetuation of stereotypes and deficit perspectives. This chapter provides suggestions for both teacher educators and preservice teachers on how to address these issues with their students, particularly girls, in ways that promote social justice, linguistic diversity and a culturally responsive curriculum.

Earlier in Chapter 2, Hopkins introduced readers to colonialism from a North American Indigenous perspective and Chalklen in Chapter 12, "Intersecting Histories in the Present: Deconstructing How White Preservice Teachers at Rural South African Schools Perceive Their Black Supervising Teacher and Students," shares the heinous nature of colonialism and apartheid in the country of South Africa. After a brief history of colonialism and apartheid, including the legacy of Bantu education, his study is underpinned by the intersections of race and class (Carter, Chalklen, & Zungu, 2017). He shares how White preservice teachers framed the Black African students and teachers in deficit terms and concludes with the need for deeper scrutiny of preservice education curriculum in relation to equity-based practice. Chalklen's chapter demonstrates that race, ethnicity, class and gender issues are not unique to the United States. These issues are common to other countries around the globe, which emphasizes the importance of global publications that share research internationally with other educators.

Just as this introduction to the chapters of this book, Chapter 13, "Afterword: Movement toward a 'Third Reconstruction' and Educational Equity" by Vavrus brings depth, closure and a call to action in the final chapter. Vavrus' chapter critically reflects on the implications of the research in this book as an important part of an equity movement internationally toward a Third Reconstruction for the 21st century. A look back at the First Reconstruction after the U.S. Civil War and the Second Reconstruction, or the Civil Rights Movement, gives an idea of the power of this movement toward a Third Reconstruction. Given developments captured under the tagline Black Lives Matter that spread internationally, the chapter conceptualizes a movement toward a "Third Reconstruction" through an intersectionality of race, ethnicity, class, and gender. Critical multiculturalism serves as an overarching theoretical foundation through historical inquiry in concert with the construct of intersectionality to critique rights and institutions.

4   Potential Use of the Book

This book sets forth the historical context for intersectionality of the quadrant (4) race, ethnicity, class and gender and the rationale for this intersection in teaching and teacher education. Although the setting is the United States (and South Africa, which has some commonalities), the societal experiences are applicable to any locale that struggles with our "quadrant" around the globe. Therefore, our work can be generalized across continents, because the issues that form the basis of the book are international in scope and can be justified as significant social concerns. Equity and multiculturalism as the ongoing themes intersect, cross and intermingle with our quadrant, while we identified broader definitions of terms, utilized the some of the latest research models and examined new concepts in theoretical frameworks. *Intersectionality of Race, Ethnicity, Class and Gender with Teaching and Teacher Education: Movement Toward Equity and Education* will be useful to scholars, lecturers, instructors, graduate students, K-12 practitioners, administrators, policy-makers and community leaders. However, the potential use of our book will be limitless as we work to improve the human condition in the world of education.

References

Anderson, J. D. (2007). The historical context for understanding the test score gap. *The National Journal of Urban Education and Practice, 1*(1), 1–21.

Anderson, M. L., & Collins, P. H. (Eds.). (2012). *Race, class & gender: An anthology gender & sexism* (8th ed.). Belmont, CA: Wadsworth.

Apple, M. (1996). *Cultural politics and education.* New York, NY: Teachers College Press.

Bandura, A. (1986). *Social foundations of thought and action: A social cognitive theory.* Englewood Cliffs, NJ: Prentice-Hall.

Bandura, A. (2001). Self-efficacy beliefs as shapers of children's aspirations and career trajectories. *Child Development, 72*(1), 187–206.

Banks, J. A., & Banks, C. A. (Eds.). (2010). *Multicultural education: Issues and perspectives* (7th ed.). Hoboken, NJ: John Wiley and Sons.

Bright, L. K., Malinsky, D., & Thompson, M. (2016, January). Causally interpreting intersectionality theory. *Philosophy of Science, 83*(1), 60–81.

Brown, G. T. L. (2004). Teachers' conceptions of assessment: Implications for policy and professional development. *Assessment in Education: Policy, Principles and Practice, 11*(3), 305–322.

Brown v. Board of Education of Topeka, 347 U.S. 483 (1954). Justia U.S. Supreme Court. Retrieved from https://supreme.justia.com/cases/federal/us/347/483/case.html

Burbules, N. C., Lord, B. T., & Sherman, A. L. (1982). Equity, equal opportunity, and education. *Educational Evaluation Analysis, 4*(2), 169–187.

Carter, N. P. (2003). *Convergence or divergence: Alignment of standards, assessment and issues of diversity.* Washington, DC: AACTE & ERIC Clearing House.

Carter, N. P., Chalklen, W., & Zungu, B. (2017). A critical examination of the reception of roots in South Africa. In E. Ball & K. Carter-Jackson (Eds.), *Reconsidering roots: Observations on a TV mini-series that changed the way Americans understood slavery* (pp. 165–181). Athens, GA: University of Georgia Press.

Carter, N. P., Hawkins, T., & Natesan, P. (2008). The relationship between verve and the academic achievement of African American middle school students: An examination of three urban school districts. *Educational Foundations, 22*(1–2), 29–46.

Carter, N. P., Webb-Hasan, G. C., & Williams, K. (2016). *Teaching African American children: Making it work.* West Conshohocken, PA: Infinity Publishing.

Cho, S., Crenshaw, K. M., & McCall, L. (2013). Toward a field of intersectionality studies: Theory, application, and praxis. *Signs: Journal of Women in Culture and Society, 38*(4), 785–810.

Coleman, J. S., Campbell, E. G., Hobson, C. J., McPartland, J., Mood, A. M., Weinfield, F. D., & York, R. L. (1966). *Equality of educational opportunity.* Washington, DC: Government Printing Office.

Crenshaw, K. M. (1993). Mapping the margins: Intersectionality, identity politics, and violence against women of color. *Stanford Law Review, 43*(6), 1241–1299.

Crenshaw, K., Ocen, P., & Nanda, J. (2015). *Black girls matter: Pushed out, overpoliced and underprotected.* New York, NY: African American Policy Forum and Center for Intersectionality and Social Policy Studies.

Delpit, L. D. (1995). *Other people's children.* New York, NY: The New Press.

Delpit, L. D. (2012). *Multiplication is for White people: Raising expectations for other people's children.* New York, NY: The New Press.

Dewey, J. (1933). *How we think: A restatement of the relation of reflective thinking to the educative process.* Boston, MA: D.C. Heath.

Field, S., Kuczera, M., & Point, B. (2007). *No more failures: Ten steps to equity in education.* Paris: Organisation for Economic Co-operation and Development.

Ford, D., & Harris, J. (1999). Multicultural gifted education. In J. H. Borland (Ed.), *Education and psychology of the gifted series* (pp. 1–14). New York, NY: Teachers College Press.

Gay, G. (2010). *Culturally responsive teaching: Theory, research, and practice* (2nd ed.). New York, NY: Teachers College Press.

Gay, G. (2014). Culturally responsive teaching principles, practices, and effects. In H. R. Milner & K. Lomotey (Eds.), *Handbook of urban education* (pp. 353–372). New York, NY: Routledge.

Gibson, S., & Dembo, M. H. (1984). Teacher efficacy: A construct validation. *Journal of Educational Psychology, 76*(4), 569–582.

Howell, L., Lewis, C., & Carter, N. (2011). *Yes we can! Improving urban schools through innovative education reform* (Contemporary perspectives on access, equity, and achievement). Charlotte, NC: Information Age Publishing.

Hoy, W. K., & Miskel, C. G. (2005). *Educational administration: Theory into practice* (7th ed.). New York, NY: McGraw-Hill.

Irvine, J. J. (1990). *Black students and school failure.* New York, NY: Praeger.

Irvine, J. J. (2003). *Educating teachers for diversity: Seeing with a cultural eye.* New York, NY: Teachers College Press.

Kozleski, E. B., & Artiles, A. J. (2011). Technical assistance as inquiry: Using activity theory methods to engage equity in educational practice communities. In G. S. Canella & S. R. Steinberg (Eds.), *Critical qualitative research reader* (pp. 408–419). New York, NY: Peter Lang.

Ladson-Billings, G. (1994). *The dreamkeepers: Successful teachers of African American children.* San Francisco, CA: Jossey-Bass Publishers.

Larke, P. J., Webb-Hasan, G. C., & Young, J. L. (2017). *Cultivating Achievement, Respect, and Empowerment (CARE) for African American girls in pre-K-12 settings: Implications for access, equity and achievement.* Charlotte, NC: Information Age Publishing.

Lomotey, K., & Lowery, K. (2014). Black students, urban schools, and Black principals: Leadership practices that reduce disenfranchisement. In H. R. Milner & K. Lomotey (Eds.), *Handbook of urban education* (pp. 325–349). New York, NY: Routledge.

Losen, D. J., & Orfield, G. (Eds.). (2002). *Racial inequity in special education.* Cambridge, MA: Civil Rights Project and Harvard University.

Love, A., & Kruger, A. C. (2005). Teacher beliefs and student achievement in urban schools serving African American students. *Journal of Educational Research, 99,* 87–98.

Natesan, P., Webb-Hasan, G., Carter, N. P., & Walter, P. (2011). Validity of the cultural awareness and beliefs inventory of urban teachers: A parallel mixed methods study. *International Journal of Multiple Research Approaches, 5*(2), 1–18.

Nieto, S. (2012). *Affirming diversity: The sociopolitical context of multicultural education* (6th ed.). Boston, MA: Allyn & Bacon.

Noguera, P. A. (2014). Urban schools and the Black male challenge. In H. R. Milner & K. Lomotey (Eds.), *Handbook of urban education* (pp. 114–128). New York, NY: Routledge.

Noguera, P. A., Hurtado, A., & Fergus, E. (2011). *Understanding and responding to the disenfranchisement of Latino men and boys.* New York, NY: Routledge.

Phuntsog, N. (2001). Culturally responsive teaching: What do selected United States elementary school teachers think? *Intercultural Education, 12*(1), 51–64.

Plessy v. Ferguson, 163 U.S. 537 (1896). Cornell law school legal information institute. Retrieved from https://www.law.cornell.edu/supremecourt/text/163/537#writing-ZS

Pohan, C. A., & Aguilar, T. E. (2001). Measuring educator's beliefs about diversity in personal and professional contexts. *American Education Research Journal, 38*(1), 159–182.

Rokeach, M. (1968). *Beliefs, attitudes, and values: A theory of organization and change.* San Francisco, CA: Jossey-Bass.

Secada, W. G. (1989). *Equity in education.* London: Falmer Press.

Secada, W. G. (2012). Equity, educational. In J. A. Banks (Ed.), *Encyclopedia of diversity in education* (Vol. 2, pp. 804–807). Thousand Oaks, CA: Sage.

Spindler, G., & Spindler, L. (Eds.). (1994). *Pathways to cultural awareness: Cultural therapy with teachers and students.* Thousand Oaks, CA: Corwin Press Inc.

Spring, J. (2016). *Deculturalization and the struggle for equality: A brief history of the education of dominated cultures in the United States.* New York, NY: Routledge.

U.S. Department of Education, Office of Civil Rights, and Civil Rights Data Collection. (2014a, March 21). *Data snapshot: Early childhood education* (Issue Brief No. 2). Retrieved from https://www2.ed.gov/about/offices/list/ocr/docs/crdc-early-learning-snapshot.pdf

U.S. Department of Education, Office of Civil Rights, and Civil Rights Data Collection. (2014b, March 21). *Data snapshot: School discipline* (Issue Brief No. 1). Retrieved from http://blogs.edweek.org/edweek/rulesforengagement/CRDC%20School%20Discipline%20Snapshot.pdf

Webb-Johnson, G., & Carter, N. P. (2007). Culturally responsive urban school leadership: Partnering to improve outcomes for African American learners. *The National Journal of Urban Education and Practice, 1*(1), 77–98.

Williams, K. V., & Carter, N. P. (2015). Preparing urban preservice teachers for diverse classrooms. In Y. Li & J. Hammer (Eds.), *Teaching at work* (pp. 123–144). Rotterdam, The Netherlands: Sense Publishers.

CHAPTER 2

Intersectionality, Colonizing Education, and the Indigenous Voice of Survivance

John P. Hopkins

During the Civil Rights Movement of the 1960s, racial and ethnic minority groups began to challenge the assimilationist ideology pervasive in liberal nation-states (Banks, 2009). The United States historically compelled minority groups to adopt the dominant culture and language, which in turn required them to eschew their own cultures and languages. However, the assimilationist ideology failed to accommodate these groups by structurally excluding them from full participation in the nation-state. To remedy structural exclusion, these groups collectively organized against assimilation and turned towards their cultures as sources of strength and empowerment. Rather than assimilating into the nation-state, these groups demanded "structural inclusion and the right to retain important aspects of their cultures, such as their languages, religions, and other important ethnic characteristics and symbols" (Banks, 2009, p. 12).

Similar to other racial and ethnic groups, Indigenous peoples were brought into the structural inclusion discourse of the Civil Rights Movement (Banks, 2009; Coulthard, 2014). In the 1960s and 1970s, the federal government passed key legislation that utilized a discourse of civil rights and self-determination, such as the Indian Civil Rights Act of 1968, the Indian Education Act of 1972, and the Indian Self-Determination and Educational Assistance Act of 1975 (Jaimes, 1992). This legislation sought to structurally include Indigenous peoples in the broader civil rights discourse alongside other racial and ethnic minority groups (Deloria & Lytle, 1983). The strategy to structurally include Indigenous peoples continues in recent reform efforts in American Indian education. Montana State passed the Indian Education For All act, which mandated that non-Native educators work cooperatively with tribal communities to include Indigenous cultures and histories in the mainstream curricula (Starnes, 2006).

However, Indigenous peoples historically have challenged the role modern liberal nation-states have played in creating and maintaining colonization (Smith, 2012). Colonization refers to the political, cultural, and economic power of one nation over a particular group through acts of violence, domination, and dispossession (Maldonado-Torres, 2007). Like other settler colonies such as Canada, New Zealand, and Australia, the U.S. federal government exerted domination and control over Indigenous peoples initially through invasion and settlement of Indigenous territories. This was followed by an ongoing assimilation strategy "of dismantling and erasing Indigenous society and culture, and replacing it through religious, political, and economic conversion" (DeMuth, 2012, p. 102). The political aims of Indigenous peoples are thus centered on issues specifically related to their colonization and assimilation experiences (Coulthard, 2014). Rather than seeking structural inclusion into the U.S. liberal nation-state, Indigenous peoples "have persistently and courageously fought for their continued existence as *peoples*, defined politically by their government-to-government relationship with the U.S." (Lomawaima & McCarty, 2006, p. 7).

This chapter utilizes the concept of structural intersectionality (Crenshaw, 1993) to examine the colonizing relationship between Indigenous peoples and the nation-state. Structural intersectionality offers a framework to analyze the ways Indigenous peoples have remained entangled in the U.S. system of education, a system that has sought—and continues to seek—control and domination over meanings of indigeneity. Structural intersectionality illuminates a more complicated story of Indigenous identity. Indigenous peoples have survived and resisted colonization, what the Indigenous studies literature calls *survivance* (Vizenor & Lee, 1999). Survivance is an Indigenous counter-discourse to the nation-state's colonizing agenda in an attempt to remain sovereign over their lands, cultures, and education. Survivance reveals that Indigenous peoples have not only challenged their colonizing experiences and proposed nuanced meanings of indigeneity, they have also differed from each other in what those meanings entail.

1   Structural Intersectionality and Indigenous Peoples

Structural intersectionality provides a useful lens to interpret the colonizing history of Indigenous education and its effect on Indigenous identity. Crenshaw (1993) introduced the concept of structural intersectionality to examine the lives of women of color in how they "are situated within overlapping structures of subordination" (p. 114). Davis, Brunn-Bevel, and Olive (2015) extend Crenshaw's analysis of women of color and refer to the concept of *matrix of domination* to describe the impact of intersectionality on marginalized identities. The authors focus on "the importance of social structure and history...for understanding how the intersection of race, class, and gender manifest differently in individual lives" (p. 3). According to Jones (2015), intersectionality research centers "on the lived experiences of individuals," complicates "both individual and group identity," explores "identity salience as influenced by systems of power and privilege," and advances "a larger goal of promoting social justice and social change" (p. xi). This chapter utilizes structural intersectionality research as a framework to analyze the different ways individuals have been entangled in overlapping social systems that shape their identities and lived-experiences (Davis, Brunn-Bevel, & Olive, 2015).

In the context of Indigenous peoples, structural intersectionality analyzes how colonizing history and education systems – federal Indian policies and laws and the practices and policies of off-reservation boarding schools and public education – impacted the various ways that Indigenous peoples were differently colonized and assimilated into acceptable forms of U.S. citizenship. These differences in colonization and assimilation reflect particular experiences of subordination in the individual lives of Indigenous peoples. According to Reyes (2014), intersectionality research of Indigenous peoples "calls attention to the coexistence of multiple, overlapping systems of oppression and privilege within society as well as to the coexistence of multiple, layered identities that become differently salient to individuals within different contexts" (p. 46). Structural intersectionality critically assesses how colonizing history and education have constructed one-dimensional meanings of indigeneity, which in effect fail to recognize Indigenous peoples as a complex group whose "identities have...been shaped by other experiences and entities, such as colonization, cultural connectivity, and nationhood" (Reyes, 2014, p. 46).

Federal Indian policies and laws have dictated the overall life-chances of Indigenous peoples and communities. As Deloria and Lytle (1983) explained, "[T]he lives of American Indians are interwoven with the federal government... [and] as a general rule much of Indian life falls under the federal umbrella and is subject to its changes" (p. 25). The entangled, colonizing relationship between the federal government and Indigenous peoples is not relegated to events in the past, but rather reveals an ongoing, sustained process of colonization in contemporary Indigenous life. Colonization and assimilation are so pervasive in tribal experience that, in fact, "American Indians fail to recognize that we are taking up colonialist ideas when we fail to express ourselves...about who and what we are supposed to be, how we are supposed to behave...and be within the larger population" (Brayboy, 2005, p. 431).

Some scholars interpret the colonizing history of Indigenous peoples and the federal government as random shifts in Indian policy (Bruyneel, 2007). Described as a pendulum theory, these scholars refer to the shifts in federal Indian policy as a back and forth process between anti-and pro-tribal sovereignty. For example, in one era the federal government minimized the Indigenous sovereign right to exist, only to overturn that right in a subsequent era. However, Lomawaima and McCarty (2006) argue that the pendulum theory only describes colonizing history rather than explains it, proposing instead a *safety zone theory*. Safety zone theory "traces the swings of policy to the ongoing struggle of cultural difference and its perceived threat or benefit" (Lomawaima & McCarty, 2006, p. 6). According to the safety zone theory, the federal government has not randomly swayed back and forth in its dealings with Indigenous peoples, but has created and promoted laws and policies that coherently distinguished between acceptable and unacceptable forms of Indigenous identity.

The U.S. system of education became a site to control which Indigenous identities were deemed safe and which were deemed too dangerous. The boarding school system that prevailed during the late 19th and early 20th centuries sought to eradicate Indigenous languages, cultures, and traditions in favor of an Americanized identity. However, in certain cases Native students were allowed to act out their so-called 'uncivilized' cultural expressions within these assimilative schools. These cultural expressions of Indigenous identity can be explained as a deliberate attempt by the federal government to create "its national self-image as an exceptional, divinely ordained democracy by juxtaposing its 'civilization' against its assumptions of an Indigenous 'primitive'" (Lomawaima & McCarty, 2006, p. 4). Boarding schools neutralized those Native cultural expressions that were deemed too threatening for White, mainstream culture by controlling which Indigenous identities "might be considered benign enough to be allowed, even welcomed, within American life" (p. 6).

The safety zone theory describes the structural intersectionality of Indigenous peoples in colonizing history and education. The U.S. system of education entailed an intentional and systematic process to dominate and control meanings of indigeneity. The process of assimilative education was not meant to erase Indigenous peoples, but rather to determine safe from unsafe Indigenous identities. This process continues into the contemporary educational experiences of Indigenous youth (Lomawaima & McCarty, 2006). Thus, even during eras that sought to structurally include Indigenous peoples into the dominant culture or education system – the Civil Rights Movement and present-day Indigenous education reforms, such as the Montana Indian Education For All act – the liberal nation-state continues its ongoing domination and control of Indigenous identity.

2   The Indigenous Voice of Survivance

Indigenous peoples have not been passive recipients of colonization. They have resisted and survived a colonizing agenda that attempted to reduce

Indigenous peoples to one-dimensional meanings of indigeneity. The Indigenous studies literature calls this survivance (Vizenor & Lee, 1999). "Survivance," explains Vizenor and Lee (1999), "means a native presence, the notion of sovereignty and the will to resist domination" (p. 93). *Presence* refers to a Native experience, one that is distinctively Indigenous in relationship to land, culture, and tradition. *Survivance* refers to the continual realization by Indigenous peoples to assert their sovereign right to remain Indigenous, as the original inhabitants of this land. Emerging through the utilization of personal narratives drawn from tribal cultures, epistemologies, and traditions, the Indigenous voice of survivance reveals how Indigenous peoples have countered the federal government's control of Indigenous identity, but also how they have differed from each other.

Structural intersectionality of Indigenous peoples within the U.S. system of education can be seen in each federal Indian policy era. This chapter examines multiple survivance voices during the Self-Determination era (1960s-1980s). This era included meanings of Indigenous identity that resonated with the rights and structural inclusion strategies articulated during the Civil Rights Movement. However, the Indigenous voice of survivance interrogated and challenged these strategies by offering more complex meanings of indigeneity.

2.1   *From Assimilation to Self-Determination*

In an effort to assimilate American Indians into mainstream society, Congress passed the Termination Act of 1953 and the Relocation Act of 1956 (Jaimes, 1992). These laws sought to "subject [American Indians] to the same laws and entitled [them] to the same privileges and responsibilities as are applicable to other citizens of the U.S." (Gover, 2007, p. 193). These laws also sought to relocate Indigenous peoples into metropolitan areas. The government promised adequate housing, jobs, and services needed for city dwelling; however, many of these promises failed to materialize. Those entering urban life faced the same high rates of unemployment and poverty as they had experienced on reservations. They found themselves in similar conditions as other disenfranchised groups, e.g., living in similar neighborhoods and taking on low-wage jobs. As Wilma Mankiller, the first female chief of the Cherokee Nation, recalled, "Besides the poverty and prejudice we encountered, I was continually struggling with the adjustments to a big city that seemed so foreign and cold to me" (Mankiller & Wallis, 1993, p. 102).

Relocation and termination policies established meanings of Indigenous identity that became pervasive during the Self-Determination era. As more Indigenous peoples moved into cities, differences between urban and reservation Indians became more significant. Urban Indians established broader meanings of Indigenous identity beyond reservation experiences, which "fostered a growing pan-Indian identity and a determination to preserve

Indian community and heritage" (Calloway, 2004, p. 414). Far removed from their reservations, urban Indians created a shared sense of being "Indian" – or an urban pan-Indianism – that cut across tribal lines and affiliations. Ignatia Broker, a Native woman who wrote about her urban experiences, described the pan-Indian phenomena: "[Those] born and raised in the cities...do not make any distinctions as to their tribes. They do not say, 'I am Ojibway,' or 'I am Dakota,' or 'I am Arapaho,' but they say, 'I am Indian'" (cited in Calloway, 2004, p. 445).

Urban Indians created and gathered in specific American Indian community spaces. As Wilma Mankiller described, "[Everything] seemed brighter at the Indian Center. For me, it became an oasis where I could share my feelings and frustrations with kids from similar backgrounds" (Mankiller & Wallis, 1993, p. 111). These spaces not only engendered a sense of community among urban Indians, they also engendered political advocacy to support Indian issues. Pan-Indianism, in effect, led to more political organization. Urban Indian experiences created multiple American Indian activist movements such as the American Indian Movement (AIM), National Indian Youth Council (NIYC), and United Indians of All Tribes (UIATF). Housing and employment discrimination, high poverty and low education rates, and police harassment and brutality led many urban Indian youth to question and challenge their conditions, even criticizing Indigenous leaders (Bruyneel, 2007). Clyde Warrior, a founding member and the president of the NIYC, challenged both federal and tribal governments: "We are not free. We do not make choices... these choices and decisions are made by federal administrators...and their 'yes men,' euphemistically called tribal governments" (Calloway, 2004, p. 550).

2.2   *Education and Self-Determination*

Education during the Self-Determination era challenged the safe and acceptable boundaries of Indigenous identity constructed in the U.S. system of education. Growing numbers of urban Indians engendered greater interest in Indigenous issues among those Indigenous youth from cities who were attending predominately White colleges. The first American Indian Studies (AIS) programs emerged as a result of urban Indian students demanding more Indigenous representations in their classes. However, university administrators misunderstood these demands. As AIS programs forged pathways into higher education, administrators viewed them as another ethnic studies program. According to Champagne (2010), "These programs reflected the social movement and social change trends of the 1960s and 1970s by efforts to bring more inclusion to members of historically excluded and disadvantaged groups" (p. 17). AIS programs were not satisfied with being classified as another ethnic studies program. These AIS programs vied to be seen as a "movement toward self-determination...assertion of political and cultural autonomy..., [and] greater community control and decision-making" (Champagne, 2010, p. 17).

Leaders from AIM were not only concerned with challenging the political structure of American society. They were also concerned with the education of urban Indians. The *Kennedy Report* described the context of American Indian education: "Drop-out rates are twice the national average in both public and federal schools...[achievement] levels of Indian children are 2 to 3 years below those of white students" (as cited in Reyhner & Eder, 2004, p. 253). To address these educational issues, AIM leaders worked with Native parents in Minneapolis and St. Paul to establish survival schools (Davis, 2013). Because the educational experiences of Native children in these cities were no different from the national context, survival schools "diverged from the public school model that had alienated many Native children" (Davis, 2013, p. 101). These schools immersed urban Indian children in Indigenous languages, cultures, spiritualties, and identities. Survival schools provided alternative educational experiences for Native children, connecting their urban Indian identities to homelands and reservations far removed from their daily life.

The pan-Indian Indian identity during the Self-Determination era illuminates an Indigenous voice of survivance, in how Indigenous peoples as a group countered the federal government's aim to reduce them to another racial minority. Despite these aims by the federal government, Indigenous peoples found ways to survive and resist these policies by forming Indigenous-centered communities and promoting political activism. Termination and relocation produced "exactly the opposite of what the government relocation program intended to achieve" (Calloway, 2004, p. 414). Pan-Indian identity during this era also survived and resisted the colonizing practices and policies promoted by education institutions, creating Indigenous-specific educational spaces in higher education and establishing survival schools that preserved and regenerated traditional cultures, languages, and values.

Vine Deloria, Jr. serves as an individual example of survivance during the Self-Determination era. Deloria advocated for an Indigenous identity centered on political organization and action of tribes. A member of the Standing Rock Sioux Tribe, Deloria attended reservation schools in his early years, eventually earning a bachelor's degree in science from Iowa State University and two graduate degrees, one in sacred theology and another in law. "Through all this 'white' education," stated Wilkinson (2005), "Deloria never strayed far from his Indian roots" (p. 107). Deloria utilized his education to become a significant influence in Indigenous scholarship and activism during the Self-Determination era, beginning with his first text published in 1969 *Custer Died for Your Sins: An Indian Manifesto* (see Deloria, 1969/1988).

Deloria tackles the problem of Indigenous identity in America, deconstructing the binary relationship between the ways Indigenous identity has been constructed in the White imagination and the lived-realities of tribes. "To be an Indian in modern America," observed Deloria (1969/1988), "is in a very real sense to be unreal and ahistorical" (p. 2). Challenging the classic American Indian stereotypes of the savage warrior, the unknown primitive, the instinctive animal, and the Indian princess, he argued that White Americans have mythologized Native peoples to ahistorical meanings of indigeneity. They have constructed an American Indian in their own image but have failed to understand the modern circumstances of tribal peoples.

In contrast to the mythological and ahistorical American Indian constructed in the White imagination, Deloria (1969/1988) argued that being Indigenous in the modern sense is to be resilient against colonizing structures. Furthermore, Deloria explained, "The best characterization of tribes is that they stubbornly hold on to what they feel is important to them and discard what they feel is irrelevant to their current needs" (p. 16). The survival of tribal peoples is due to their creative organization against colonization, particularly when they have "[banded] together to make themselves heard" (p. 17). Deloria's view of American Indian identity is firmly rooted in the present as a culturally and politically empowered agent, whose power arises from the idea that Indigenous peoples are the original, sovereign inhabitants of the land. The existence and survival of Native peoples entails further realization of tribal sovereignty, which will require "the public at large to drop the myths in which it has clothed us for so long" (p. 27). Deloria argues for nationhood, a political position in which Native peoples assert "the government-to-government U.S.-indigenous relationship while affirming the need to renew indigenous collective identity and agency through resistance to American colonial rule" (Bruyneel, 2007, p. 140).

2.3   Problematizing Civil Rights Discourse

Deloria's idea of nationhood problematizes the Civil Rights Movement discourse prominent during the Self-Determination era. Juxtaposing the different political positions and aims of African Americans and Native peoples in relation to the liberal nation-state, Civil Rights leaders and their liberal allies sought to combine "all people with darker skin in the same category of basic goals, then develop their programs to fit these preconceived ideas" in contradistinction to the specific needs of tribal peoples (Deloria, 1969/1988, p. 170). Civil Rights leaders interpreted the needs of tribal peoples through the lens of the Black struggle for equal rights. Deloria (1969/1988) resisted this equal rights discourse: "Equality became sameness" (p. 179). Significant historical differences and realities exist between Blacks and Natives that prevents their

histories and identities from being understood in the same way. The individual
rights discourse proved to be yet another imposition by the liberal nation-state
to usurp land and define Native peoples out of existence.

Rather than embracing pan-Indianism of urban Natives, Deloria's
survivance voice involves tribal peoples drawing from their present cultural
strength and community resources to oppose colonization and reassert their
sovereign, political status. The strength of tribes derives from Native peoples'
belonging to specific homelands. Deloria (1969/1988) argued that land is the
basis on which to determine tribal identity and nationhood. Because "certain
lands are given to certain people," it is Native peoples "who can flourish, thrive,
and survive on the land" (p. 177). To be American Indian in the modern sense
is to belong to a specific homeland with an identifiable cultural practice and
identity. Deloria helped Indigenous peoples recognize that the basic problem
between them and the federal government is their legal status as sovereign
nations and peoples. The urgency with respect to political organization and
activism centers on maintaining the relations to their homelands without
colonial interference.

3   Decolonial Implications for Indigenous Youth and Teachers

This chapter concludes by proposing what this historical analysis and structural
intersectionality research reveal for Indigenous youth and teachers and how
they can move a social justice agenda for equity forward in the Montana Indian
Education For All act. Much of what counts as American Indian education
in public schools centers on preparing Indigenous youth for conventional
citizenship. Cajete (2012) explained that "contemporary American Indian
education is based on teaching academic skills and content, in order to
prepare students to compete in the American mainstream workforce" (p. 146).
The Montana law is challenging this approach to American Indian education.
The strength of the law is that it seeks to address the educational equity gaps
between Indigenous and non-Indigenous youth by including tribal histories,
cultures, and voices into the mainstream curriculum. The law's requirement
for teachers to instruct this curriculum in a culturally responsive manner
"[reduces] the cultural dissonance Indian students feel between home and
school environments, easing their alienation and encouraging staying in as
opposed to dropping out" (Carjuzaa, 2012, p. 6).

However, the Montana law's emphasis on curricular inclusion needs to
embrace an Indigenous social justice agenda based on survivance in order
to fully challenge the contemporary context of American Indian education.
As critical as it is for Indigenous youth to see themselves reflected in the

mainstream curriculum, these students require a curriculum that teaches them how to live and think from within their cultural, traditional, and epistemological frameworks (Brayboy, 2005). Doing so enables Indigenous youth to develop the capacity to challenge colonization and interrogate the ways meanings of indigeneity remain embedded in the broader society, public schools, and their lived-experience.

To achieve an Indigenous social justice agenda, the Montana law needs to promote decolonization. Decolonization articulates an Indigenous worldview in contradistinction to the historic civil rights discourse or contemporary inclusion strategies in Native education. A direct and active response to colonization, decolonization entails political strategies that challenge the domination and exploitation of Indigenous lands and peoples. As Waziyatawin and Yellow Bird (2012) describe, decolonization is the "meaningful and active resistance to the forces of colonialism that perpetuate the subjugation and/or exploitation of our minds, bodies, and lands...[it] is engaged in the ultimate purpose of overturning the colonial structure and realizing Indigenous liberation" (p. 3). Decolonization seeks freedom from the colonizing discourses that have controlled meanings of Indigenous identity and have prevented tribal peoples from expressing their cultures, languages, and values (Battiste, 2013; Grande, 2004).

Smith (2012) contends that decolonization "is about centering our concerns and world views and then coming to know and understand theory and research from our own perspectives and for our own purposes" (p. 39). This suggests the need to incorporate a curriculum centered on decolonization. A decolonizing curriculum transforms American Indian education to reflect the interests and aims of Indigenous peoples and thus empowers Indigenous youth to engage in cultural, linguistic, and political revival strategies. At the center of decolonizing curriculum is the survivance voice. Survivance voices serve as the curricular content for Indigenous youth to learn how to interrogate, challenge, and dismantle, i.e., how to resist and survive, ongoing colonizing control over what it means to be Indigenous in the broader society and public education.

Decolonizing curriculum cannot be promoted through structural inclusion strategies as proposed during the Civil Rights Movement. Structural inclusion smooths over the deleterious effects of liberal, individualistic citizenship policies promoted by the federal government that ignores Indigenous political struggles to further sovereignty (Coulthard, 2014). Nor can it be addressed through managed multicultural strategies, which "can result in blithe calls for celebration of diversity and tolerance in the face of localized racist exclusions" (Vavrus, 2002, pp. 51–52) and serves to maintain a school's control over meanings of indigeneity. The Montana law, in fact, risks promoting managed multiculturalism by emphasizing inclusion rather than decolonization. The law seeks to include Indigenous perspectives into the curriculum without transforming the colonizing power structure inherent in public schools. Montana's schools remain embedded in Euro-American culture, beliefs, and epistemologies at the expense of Native ways of knowing and being. These inclusive strategies refuse the decolonizing aims of Indigenous peoples and thus reproduce colonization in public schools.

By contrast, a decolonized curriculum emphasizes the ways tribal peoples organize and interpret reality and human experience. A decolonizing curriculum realizes greater educational equity not by including tribal cultures and histories into the curriculum, but by explicitly teaching Indigenous youth to begin the steady process of dismantling colonizing ways of thinking and being, which they have internalized throughout their public schooling experience (Brayboy, 2005). As Grande (2004) claimed, "[T]hinking in one's own cultural referents leads to conceptualizing in one's own world view which, in turn, leads to disagreement with and eventual opposition to the dominant ideology" (p. 56). A decolonized curriculum promoted in Montana's public schools would create an equitable space for Indigenous youth to explore and learn what is central to the political and cultural aims of Indigenous peoples and liberation: the ongoing struggle to remain Indigenous on these lands and in these places.

Centering the schooling experience of Indigenous youth on a decolonizing curriculum has significant implications for teachers in promoting education equity in Montana's public schools. Teachers need to resist reproducing an unacknowledged ongoing colonizing agenda to control meanings of indigeneity in the curriculum. "Educators must reject colonial curricula that offer students a fragmented and distorted picture of Indigenous peoples," Battiste (2013) contends, "and offer students a critical perspective of the historical context that created that fragmentation" (p. 186). Survivance voices not only offer a critical perspective of the historical violence and ongoing process of colonization: they reveal pathways on how to dismantle it. Two strategies become important. First, teachers need to introduce survivance voices into the mainstream curriculum. Doing so allows Indigenous youth to contrast how Indigenous thinkers, activists, scholars, artists, and leaders differ from the dominant group's ongoing control of Indigenous identity. Second, teachers need to engage the survivance voices themselves, such that survivance claims of tribal sovereignty and Indigenous worldviews challenge their preconceptions of who Indigenous peoples have been and continue to be in the liberal nation-state. These strategies move a social justice agenda forward by creating an education system by Indigenous peoples and for Indigenous youth, facilitating their liberation from the domination and control over meanings of indigeneity deeply embedded in society and public education.

References

Banks, J. A. (2009). Multicultural education: Dimensions and paradigms. In J. A. Banks (Ed.), *The Routledge international companion to multicultural education* (pp. 9–30). New York, NY & London: Routledge.

Battiste, M. (2013). *Decolonizing education: Nourishing the learning spirit.* Saskatoon: Purich Publishing.

Brayboy, B. M. (2005). Toward a tribal critical race theory in education. *Urban Review: Issues and Ideas in Public Education, 37*(5), 425–446.

Bruyneel, K. (2007). *The third space of sovereignty: The postcolonial politics of US-Indigenous relations.* Minneapolis, MN: University of Minnesota Press.

Cajete, G. (2012). Decolonizing indigenous education in a twenty-first century world. In Waziyatawin & M. Yellow Bird (Eds.), *For indigenous minds only: A decolonization handbook* (pp. 145–156). Santa Fe, NM: School for Advanced Research Press.

Calloway, C. (2004). *First peoples: A documentary survey of American Indian history* (2nd ed.). Boston, MA: Bedford/St. Martin's.

Carjuzaa, J. (2012). The positive impact of culturally responsive pedagogy. *International Journal of Multicultural Education, 14*(3), 1–17.

Champagne, D. (2010). The rise and fall of Native American studies. In S. Lobo, S. Talbot, & T. Morris (Eds.), *Native American voices: A reader* (3rd ed., pp. 16–25). Upper Saddle River, NJ: Prentice Hall.

Coulthard, G. (2014). *Red skin, White masks: Rejecting the colonial politics of recognition.* Minneapolis, MN: University of Minnesota Press.

Crenshaw, K. (1993). Beyond racism and misogyny: Black feminism and 2 live crew. In M. J. Matsuda, C. R. Lawrence III, R. Delgado, & K. W. Crenshaw (Eds.), *Words that wound: Critical race theory, assaultive speech, and the first amendment* (pp. 111–132). Boulder, CO: Westview Press.

Davis, D., Brunn-Bevel, R. J., & Olive, J. L. (2015). Introduction. In R. Brunn-Bevel, D. J. Davis, & J. Olive (Eds.), *Intersectionality in educational research* (pp. 1–15). Sterling, VA: Stylus Publishing.

Davis, J. L. (2013). *Survival schools: The American Indian movement and community education in the Twin Cities.* Minneapolis, MN: University of Minnesota Press.

Deloria, V. (1988). *Custer died for your sins: An Indian manifesto* (2nd ed.). Norman, OK: University of Oklahoma Press. [Original work published 1969.]

Deloria, V., & Lytle, C. M. (1983). *American Indians, American justice.* Austin, TX: University of Texas Press.

DeMuth, S. (2012). Colonization is always at war. In Waziyatawin & M. Yellow Bird (Eds.), *For indigenous minds only: A decolonization handbook* (pp. 99–102). Santa Fe, NM: School for Advanced Research Press.

Gover, K. (2007). Federal Indian policy in the twenty-first century. In G. P. H. Capture, D. Champagne, & C. C. Jackson (Eds.), *American Indian nations: Yesterday, today, and tomorrow* (pp. 187–209). Lanham, MD: AltaMira Press.

Grande, S. (2004). *Red pedagogy: Native American social and political thought.* Lanham, MD: Rowman & Littlefield.

Jaimes, M. A. (1992). *The state of Native America: Genocide, colonization, and resistance.* Boston, MA: South End Press.

Jones, S. (2015). Forward. In R. Brunn-Bevel, D. J. Davis, & J. Olive (Eds.), *Intersectionality in educational research* (pp. ix–xii). Sterling, VA: Stylus Publishing.

Lomawaima, K., & McCarty, T. L. (2006). *"To remain an Indian": Lessons in democracy from a century of Native American education.* New York, NY: Teachers College Press.

Maldonado-Torres, N. (2007). On the coloniality of being: Contributions to the development of a concept. *Cultural Studies, 21*(2–3), 240–270.

Mankiller, W., & Wallis, M. (1993). *Mankiller: A chief and her people.* New York, NY: St. Martin's Press.

Reyes, N. A. (2014). The multiplicity and intersectionality of Indigenous identities. In D. Mitchell, C. Simmons, & L. A. Greyerbiehl (Eds.), *Intersectionality in higher education* (pp. 45–54). New York, NY: Peter Lang Publishing, Inc.

Reyhner, J., & Eder, J. M. O. (2006). *American Indian education: A history.* Norman, OK: University of Oklahoma Press.

Smith, L. (2012). *Decolonizing methodologies: Research and Indigenous peoples* (2nd ed.). London: Zed Books; Dunedin: University of Otago Press.

Starnes, B. A. (2006). Montana's Indian education for all: Toward an education worthy of American ideals. *Phi Delta Kappan, 88*(3), 184–192.

Vavrus, M. (2002). *Transforming the multicultural education of teachers: Theory, research, and practice.* New York, NY: Teachers College Press.

Vizenor, G., & Lee, R. (1999). *Postindian conversations.* Lincoln, NE: University of Nebraska Press.

Waziyatawin & Yellow Bird, M. (2012). Introduction: Decolonizing our minds and actions. In Waziyatawin & M. Yellow Bird (Eds.), *For Indigenous minds only: A decolonization handbook* (pp. 1–14). Santa Fe, NM: School for Advanced Research Press.

Wilkinson, C. (2005). *Blood struggle: The rise of modern Indian nations.* New York, NY: W.W. Norton & Company.

CHAPTER 3

Intersectional Considerations for Teaching Diversity

China M. Jenkins

The rapid growth of populations of color and international students in American secondary and postsecondary schools impacts the direction of programs, policies and teaching approaches within those learning environments. Traditional methods of meeting students' needs may fail to support students from varying racial and cultural backgrounds. The challenge of meeting the needs of diverse learners is especially prevalent in classrooms where the instructional styles of the teachers are incompatible with their students' learning styles (Donkor, 2011). Many students of color will attend classes with teachers who do not understand them or their learning needs. The necessity that teachers understand the intersectionality of race, culture, and identity of their students becomes paramount.

Therefore, there is a need for teacher educators to develop an awareness of how racial and cultural differences impact the teaching and learning processes so they may equip preservice teachers to meet the learning needs of their students. Ginsberg and Wlodkowski (2009) noted since people have different racial identity development processes, epistemologies, and cultural belief systems, it is important for educators to know and understand their students' cultural differences and how those differences impact their students' learning. Educators must themselves be culturally competent to effectively impart multicultural skills to their students (Vescio, Bondy, & Poekert, 2009).

To complicate matters, students and teachers have multiple identities that intersect and present within the classroom setting. Hardiman, Jackson, and Griffin (2013) argue because each of us have overlapping identities that can either be privileged or marginalized depending on context, it is impossible to fully understand how a person might understand or make meaning of an experience. They further state, "Intersectionality suggests that markers of difference do not act independent of one another. Instead, our various social identities interrelate to negate the possibility of a unitary or universal experience or any one manifestation of oppression" (p. 30). In other words, teachers cannot examine one social identity (either their student's or their own) without looking at how the other identities interact with it.

In this chapter, I highlight some of the problematic approaches teacher educators may employ in "diversity" (also described as multicultural, intercultural, or culturally relevant) education that support the dominant discourse on intercultural and interracial relations and perpetuate racist ideologies. I also point out mistakes of this nature that are common to White educators and educators of color. Furthermore, I recommend practices for teacher educators to recognize and steer clear of these detrimental approaches. This chapter has several implications for practice in education programs in colleges and universities, adding to the literature of culturally responsive teaching and teaching for transformation. It is hoped teacher educators and faculty development specialists who encourage educators to become culturally responsive will have a deeper understanding of the complexities of diversity and will be mindful of the pedagogical strategies used in training educators.

1   White Educators

Much has been written regarding White teachers being out of sync and not culturally sensitive to the lived realities or approaches to learning of their culturally, linguistically, and ethnically diverse students (Ginsberg & Wlodkowski, 2009; Sleeter, 2017). A widely established theme in the scholarship of culturally responsive teaching is the necessity and importance for White educators to adopt culturally responsive teaching due to the negative impact hegemonic Eurocentric ideologies can have on marginalized students. Even if White educators have good intentions, they can encounter difficulties in the classroom if they are not familiar with their students' cultures, experiences, and communities. This is a common dilemma, even among education professors who teach multicultural education classes.

Other issues that complicate the dynamic between White teachers and students of color from lower socioeconomic backgrounds are mismatched cultural mores, misunderstandings in communication, an inability to teach students efficiently, lower teacher expectations, teachers' negative racial attitudes, teachers' beliefs about racially and socioeconomically diverse students, and low motivations of both students and teachers (Kohli, 2016; Nieto, 2000; Sleeter, 2017). These challenges are magnified when White teachers are unaware and unresponsive to the intersection of various forms of discrimination, racism, oppression, poverty, and other social and societal problems their students may encounter; problems that the teachers themselves may have never personally encountered.

2   Educators of Color

White educators are not the only educators that face challenges in teaching learners of diverse backgrounds. Teachers of color can also marginalize the very students they are trying to empower. Kohli (2014) noted many educators of color received an education in a racially oppressive environment that promoted white cultural values, resulting in being socialized to see non-white cultural knowledge as inferior to that of the dominant culture. Peterson (1999) reported African American educators can impede the learning of their African American students by such practices as enforcing mainstream beliefs about the use of Ebonics and harboring resentment towards lower class Blacks perceived to represent the stereotypes associated with African Americans. Philip, Rocha, and Olivares-Pasillas (2017) state teachers of color can cause "friendly-fire racism" in which they hinder the learning of their students by engendering "deficit understandings" of race. Teachers of color can also fail to recognize the intersectional difficulties their students of color may face, especially when there are differences in culture, socio-economic status, and family background between teacher and students.

Educators of color often hold views that endorse White supremacy. This is due largely in part to internalized racism at work. According to Flynn (2000), Norrington-Sands (2002), and Speight (2007), internalized racism is the unconscious adopting of negative racist messages, attitudes, and behaviors into the psyche of people of color as a result of living in a racialized society. It could be argued that internalized racism and its effects on teachers of color are not researched as much in literature because it may be viewed as a shortcoming or weakness of people of color instead of what it is: a natural result of racism (Pyke, 2010). Internalized oppression affects both educators and learners of color; therefore, it should be acknowledged and addressed especially when it comes to creating an equitable classroom and curriculum.

3   Critically Examining Approaches to Diversity Education

Since White teachers and teachers of color both have gaps of understanding concerning education inequities and interracial discourse, it is vital to examine how these factors may influence racist practices in the classroom. The following pedagogical errors educators use to unwittingly support racism and other forms of oppression have been classified into three approaches: individual, others, and deficit.

3.1   *Individual-Focused Approaches to Teaching for Diversity*

One of the ways educators can create classes that reinforce dominant ideologies is by focusing only on the individual. Individualized diversity education weakens the effort towards equity because it relies on changing hearts without changing the dominant systems that disseminates hegemony. In the past, those who were teaching for diversity focused on the experiences of learners of color, but they rarely mentioned the motivations of Whites. To this day, many teach the desired behavior for all students is colorblindness by emphasizing meritocracy and self-determination. Gordon (2005) asserted colorblindness is not an inability to see one's skin color; rather, it is the strong resistance to acknowledging race-based power differentials exist in our society. Those who are "colorblind" tend to believe people of color can easily achieve social and economic goals if they work hard enough. This mindset does not consider the intersection of structural racism and classism that stand as real obstacles for people of color. Therefore, if these programs focus solely on the individual, it can be ineffective in helping people to understand the disparities in society.

Individualizing diversity issues prohibits Whites' capacity to shift their awareness of a real situation away from the personal to constructively examine the systemic foundations and institutions that underpin racial discrimination. The continuation of self-focus, Whites' reaction of uneasiness, culpability, and anger acts to ensure there is little room to deal with the needs of marginalized groups whose reality is trapped in subjugation and injustice (Solomon, Portelli, Daniel, & Campbell, 2005).

Another way used to individualize teaching for diversity is to focus on learners of color. Some educators may choose to propagate narratives of individual resistance as a method for uplifting marginalized students and instilling a positive self-esteem. It is important to be mindful that, although resistance has a place in rising above oppression, if the educational stance taken is not balanced, it can have harmful effects. First, it is very easy for the educator to use "model resistor" stereotypes most commonly seen in stories like Harriet Tubman and Rosa Parks, which are used to present the example of someone who is so strong they are unaffected by societal oppression. As stated by Pyke (2010),

> Even though the construction of the non-White subject as strong and ever-resistant provides political capital for an identity politics, it is a distortion that obscures the *injuries* of racism and thus the extent of racial oppression. Herein is the appeal to the White dominant group of controlling images that cast the oppressed as impervious to pain, ever-resilient, and possessing a virtually superhuman ability to endure

hard-ship. If the oppressed feel no pain, the oppressors can easily deny
its infliction. (p. 563)

Educators must be careful not to present people of color as so strong in the
face of racism, its impact is insignificant. Teaching in this manner will cause
students of color to believe as though they should easily get over the racial hurt
that was inflicted upon them and not express their hurt. Subsequently, if White
students never see the pain people of color feel, they may believe the impact of
racism is small or nonexistent.

Secondly, resistance is problematic if it is taught as the sole means
of overcoming racism because it does not allow for the existence of
accommodation, collusion, and the propagation of oppression (Schwalbe
et al., 2000). Educators of color can run the risk of propagating another form
of meritocracy by emphasizing self-determination without mentioning how
marginalized people moved to a better social status through certain privileges
or by complying with hegemonic practices. For example, successful teachers
of color did not reach their positions because they aggressively resisted all of
the norms and oppressive obstacles they faced. They learned how to operate
within the "system" and carefully choose their battles with their subordinates,
peers and superiors.

Not only does concentrating solely on resistance take the focus off of the
oppression and racism, it ignores those representing truly oppressed groups
who are invisible. Those who are at the lowest level of subordination do not
have the means for resistance; thus, their voices are silenced. Additionally, a
resistance-only focus is divisive because renders those who do not vehemently
struggle against oppression on all sides as unauthentic or "sell-outs."

3.2   Others-Focused Approaches to Teaching for Diversity

Another popular approach to teaching for diversity is to create curricula
designed to celebrate the differences of other cultures. Although acknowledging
the contributions of people of color can be educationally valuable, it can also
become problematic for two reasons. First, this allows White educators and
learners to separate themselves from the part Whiteness plays in reproducing
the power structure. In this setting, racism is caused only by White ignorance
of the other cultures and not by the intersection of oppression, imperialistic
agendas, and White control forced upon people of color. The act of centering
on the systemic factors that trigger racism is ignored while paying tribute to
the achievements and contributions of minorities (Solomon et al., 2005).

When marginalized groups become the "Other" and mainstream White
culture is centered as the norm, diversity education supports the status quo.
According to Solomon et al. in reference to multicultural programs for teachers

note, "the continued failure to implicate Whiteness in discussion of societal change enables the teacher candidates to effectively remove themselves from the change process, thereby re-entrenching the normalcy and centrality of Whiteness and White reality systems. This enables White privilege and dominance to remain unchecked and unchallenged" (2005, p. 159). Ignoring Whiteness and its advantages over people of color is a form of denial that rejects implicating White people in their oppression, subjugation, and abuse of minorities in this country. This can happen even in discussions about White privilege if conversation only focuses on how people of color are impacted by it. The focus then shifts from the subject to the object of racism.

Another aspect to the others-focused approach causes educators of color to focus only on White oppression without looking within themselves. There is some research concerning the need for educators of color who need to learn about diversity. For instance, Hill (2003) mentioned, in the majority of her diversity classes, the African Americans tended to focus singularly on White oppression and did very little, if any, self-reflection. Hill made the case people of color are deeply and negatively impacted by internalized racism but will not address it. She listed three reasons for concentrating only on Whiteness. First, people of color want to present a united front as a protective stance in front of Whites, so in a multicultural setting, they will not disclose anything that will make them look weak and divided. Second, they may not be comfortable doing any sort of self-examination that would expose a flaw White people could use to gain leverage against them. Third, she stated many people of color believe they cannot be racist. Hill argued if one follows the philosophy that only those in power are racist, then it denies the complex and varying levels of oppression among racial groups, and it prevents people of color from doing the self-inquiry needed to become a critical educator. This form of "othering" does not present the full view of oppression and its expressions in various social settings.

3.3   Deficit Approaches to Teaching for Diversity

The third approach in which educators can support the status quo is by using deficit theory to describe the differences between the dominant group and the marginalized. Views based upon deficit theory rationalize people of color are marginalized because of their inherent incompetence and their intellectual and moral deficiencies instead of explaining the institutional and structural power imbalance that prevails over society (Gorski, 2008). Deficit theory spotlights stereotypes are endorsed and advanced by the mainstream media in order to problematize the oppressed population rather than the oppressors (Shields, Bishop, & Mazawi, 2005). If marginalized populations can be seen as responsible for their plight, then it removes the responsibility of privileged people to develop ways to create more access to social leverage (Gorski, 2008).

As a result, students of color are understood as needing to be "fixed" and made into the image of the "good" citizens with middle-class mainstream values. Ruby Payne (2005), known for her book, *A Framework for Understanding Poverty*, is a fitting example of deficit theory framed in intercultural education. One of the biggest critiques concerning Payne is she teaches generalities about poor people of color that have no empirical support (Bomer, Dworin, May, & Semingson, 2008; Gorski, 2008). The central point of her framework is poor people are lacking the qualities needed to be successful in society. It neglects to mention how the intersection of unequal school conditions, corporations, and society at large play a direct role in keeping people in poverty. Most important, she portrays classism as nonexistent. Unfortunately, her brand of deficit-riddled pedagogy has been used as a canonical training text for professors and teacher around the nation for decades.

Another deficit approach in teaching for diversity is a practice called "defensive othering." Schwalbe et al. (2000) coined this phrase to describe the disassociations that marginalized people make to separate themselves from harmful stereotypes about their group in order to identify with the dominant group. Often educators of color may use defensive othering to present themselves as being equal to the Whites or they may favor high achieving minority students placing them as role models for other students. Defensive othering puts people of color in a double bind. Gilman (1986) termed the phrase "double bind" to describe what happens when a marginalized group tries to associate with the dominant group.

A person of color will accept the governing ideals, structures and beliefs that keep him or her oppressed but it is a double bind because it is a false promise of escaping his or her "otherness" by rejecting their individual dissimilarities the dominant group declared to be "with." Even though it is not true, the subordinated group believes if they become like the dominant group, they will be accepted. When a subordinate group is divided due to defensive othering, the deviant subset of that group will be seen as the cause of oppression instead of institutional racism and other forms of systemic oppression.

Although Pyke (2010) documented defensive othering as a natural extension of internalized racism, using this technique is problematic for two reasons. First, it confirms the negative beliefs about stereotypical racial characteristics. Second, defensive othering is divisive because it decenters racism and places in-group tensions in the center. Teachers who engage in defensive othering or accept it from their students can inadvertently confirm the targeted group's inferiority.

4   Pedagogical Transformation through Critical Self Reflection

Growth as a culturally responsive educator does not take place without a personal and professional transformation. According to Mezirow (2000), the leading scholar on transformative theory, transformation is simply "the process by which we transform our taken for-granted frames of reference" (p. 6), which happens when one has the opportunity to critically reflect on an issue through candid dialogue with others in a safe environment.

An aspect of transformational learning is it irreversibly expands the creation of meaning and broadens one's conception of self (Cranton & King, 2003; Poutiatine, 2009; Tolliver & Tisdell, 2006). This position asserts a person cannot choose to "unknow" what he or she has learned without intentional denial. Once a paradigm has been expanded and rearranged, the framework from which the world is viewed is foundationally and permanently transformed (Poutiatine, 2009).

Consequently, in the case of culturally responsive educators, it is common for people to begin the process of transformation when they experience an event that invokes critical reflection (Canniff, 2008; Howard, 2003). Many scholars encourage critical self-reflection as the means for developing a sociocultural consciousness because it challenges preconceived ideas and beliefs (Gay & Kirkland, 2003; Villegas & Lucas, 2002b). Based upon the literature, I recommend teacher educators engage in critical reflection in at least three areas: their assumptions and beliefs, their histories and the histories of others, and the hegemonic social structures that impact themselves and their students (Canniff, 2008; McCalman, 2007; Vescio et al., 2009).

4.1   *Critical Reflection of Assumptions and Beliefs*
One of the first steps in engaging in critical reflection for culturally responsiveness begins with examining how cultural belief systems influence the experiences of learners and teachers' beliefs about their students (Canniff, 2008; McCalman, 2007). According to Smolen et al. (2006), flawed assumptions and inaccurate beliefs can permeate a professor's instruction and curriculum. They asserted even professors' self and cultural identities can impact their ability to encourage pre-service teachers towards becoming culturally competent.

Gere, Buehler, Dallavis, and Haviland (2009) conducted a study in which they collected data on fifteen pre-service students in a Teach for Tomorrow program as they responded to multicultural reading assignments. They found in their efforts to make their students more race conscious, the instructors themselves discovered how their own races, in interacting with their students, brought out stereotypes and influenced the nature of the class assignments and the responses of the students. Other scholars have found critical reflection to be a key component towards cultural competence. Garmon (2004) gleaned from his case study, which focused on the attitudinal transformation of one student towards diversity, critical reflection was a major component of her change in beliefs. Over the course of ten hours of interviews, he also discovered openness and a commitment to social justice were critical dispositions one needed to possess.

4.2   *Critical Reflection of Histories*

Culturally responsive teacher educators should also examine their personal histories, the histories of others, and how each person's history has shaped his or her beliefs and outcomes in society (Richards, Brown, & Forde, 2007; Vescio et al., 2009). Richards et al. (2007) discussed the importance of teachers examining their ancestral background in order to understand why they view themselves as raced or non-raced individuals. They argued when teachers comprehend the historical foundations of their beliefs, they are able to better relate in their interactions with others. Conversely, educators that do not examine their histories fail to understand how they have been privileged or disadvantaged by society.

It is important for educators to study how their culture shaped their lives because as Ladson-Billings (1992) noted, culture both "constructs and constricts" the perspectives through which they view society. Therefore, they should seek to understand not only who they are and how they think, but to challenge their notions of knowledge, question their assumptions, and to perceive the framework from which they are teaching. Moreover, McKenzie, and Scheurich (2004) affirmed those who do not understand how cultural, racial, and ethnic differences are constructed will view their learners as having deficits.

It has been found that the sharing and examining personal histories are valuable in creating open-mindedness towards others. Canniff (2008) explained how she used a class assignment that centered on her pre-service teachers' educational history to help them understand how past educational policies impacted their families. She directed her pre-service teachers to reflect upon how their families' social identities shaped the direction of their educational journeys. When the teachers learned how certain laws in the past benefitted some students' families and disadvantaged others, they realized the intersections of their social identities (race, gender, and class) played an important role in the quality of education, as well as the level of education, attained in their family. They also learned there are other ways of determining intelligence and success than solely relying on academic achievement. This study demonstrated one way in which critical reflection aids teachers in the process of becoming culturally responsive.

4.3   *Critical Reflection of Social Structures*

Along with self-reflection and personal historical inquiry, teacher educators learn to analyze the hegemonic social constructions that undergird social norms, which impacts people within and outside of our education system. Villegas and Lucas (2002b) stated teachers "need to understand that social inequalities are produced and perpetuated through systematic discrimination and justified through a societal ideology of merit, social mobility, and individual responsibility" (p. 22). Critical reflection is vital to becoming culturally responsive in that reflection forces educators to understand how his or her positionality impacts the relationships with their students (Canniff, 2008). To that end, several scholars have advocated educators should acknowledge and take responsibility for his or her dominant group membership and work from within that membership (McKenzie & Scheurich, 2004; Quezada & Romo, 2004). For teacher educators to grow in cultural competence, they have to examine themselves and acknowledge both their biases as well as their privileges. An important factor in critical self-reflection surfaces when educators realize there are social and political forces at work in everything they do and take an account of their actions. Cochran Smith (2004) asserted they must then ask themselves, "How are we complicit-intentionally or otherwise-in maintaining the cycles of oppression that operate in our courses, our universities, our schools, and our society" (p. 83)?

McCalman (2007) suggested the first step towards becoming culturally responsive is becoming culturally conscious, or in other words, understanding one's own culture and how it affects his or her interaction with others. Being culturally responsive does not come naturally; it is an ability that must be cultivated over time and is the result of introspection, self-inquiry, and transformative learning. These characteristics are necessary precursors to developing cultural consciousness leading to cultural responsiveness.

5   Conclusion

Teacher educators should examine the foundational principles upon which they develop their teaching philosophies because it will inform them about the degree to which they are actually committed to creating equity in the classroom. They must ask themselves the hard questions like, "Do I support diversity as long as it does not change the stability of the current social powers or my own privilege?" or "What are my beliefs about my race, the race of my students and how it affects the teaching and learning process" (Gorski, 2008)? An educator's belief influences his or her teaching.

Educators who teach for diversity or who strive to be culturally responsive in the classroom need always to consider whether they are teaching in a way that empowers each student to become stronger in the things they value. Any curriculum, program or agenda that does not have at its core the intention of restoring equity is a tool for maintaining hegemonic practices (Gorski, 2008).

As a result, educators who teach for diversity should be willing to move beyond black and white thinking to engage the gray, complex intersectionality of racial and cultural dynamics in the classroom. This is neither simple nor painless because it may mean confronting some deep-seated beliefs that fall in line with the mainstream psyche. Nevertheless, the role of diversity education is to diminish educational, and social inequities; therefore oppressive ideologies should not be given credence over the ideologies of those who are marginalized (Gorski, 2006). One needs to use a critical lens to deconstruct the underlying messages that are transmitted in multicultural education.

References

Blum, L. (2000, April). *Reflections of a White teacher teaching a course on racism.* Paper presented at the Annual Meeting of the American Educational Research Association, New Orleans, LA.

Bomer, R., Dworin, J. E., May, L., & Semingson, P. (2008). Miseducating teachers about the poor: A critical analysis of Ruby Payne's claims about poverty. *Teachers College Record, 110*(12), 2497–2531.

Canniff, J. G. (2008). A cultural memoir of schooling: Connecting history and critical reflection to the development of culturally responsive educators. *Teaching Education, 19*(4), 325–335. doi:10.1080/10476210802436476

Cochran-Smith, M., Davis, D., & Fries, K. (2004). Multicultural teacher education: research, practice, and policy. In J. Banks & C. Banks (Eds.), *Handbook of research on multicultural education* (pp. 931–975). San Francisco, CA: Jossey-Bass.

Cranton, P., & King, K. P. (2003). Transformative learning as a professional development goal. *New Directions for Adult and Continuing Education, 98*, 31–38.

Donkor, A. K. (2011). Higher education and culturally responsive teaching: A way forward. *The Journal of Multiculturalism in Education, 7*, 1–29.

Flynn, K. (2000, July 20). Internalized racism can destroy one's soul. *Share, 23*, 9. Retrieved from http://search.proquest.com/docview/345074363

Garmon, M. A. (2004). Changing preservice teachers' attitudes/beliefs about diversity what are the critical factors? *Journal of Teacher Education, 55*(3), 201–213.

Gay, G., & Kirkland, K. (2003). Developing cultural critical consciousness and self-reflection in preservice teacher education. *Theory into Practice, 42*(3), 181–187.

Gere, A. R., Buehler, J., Dallavis, C., & Haviland, V. S. (2009). A visibility project: Learning to see how preservice teachers take up culturally responsive pedagogy. *American Educational Research Journal, 46*(3), 816–852. doi:10.3102/0002831209333182

Gilman, S. L. (1986). *Jewish self-hatred: Anti-semitism and the hidden language of the Jews*. Baltimore, MD: Johns Hopkins University Press.

Ginsberg, M. B., & Wlodkowski, R. J. (2009). *Diversity and motivation: Culturally responsive teaching in college*. New York, NY: John Wiley & Sons.

Gordon, J. (2005). Inadvertent complicity: Colorblindness in teacher education. *Educational Studies, 38*(2), 135–153. doi:10.1207/s15326993es3802_5

Gorski, P. C. (2008). Good intentions are not enough: A decolonizing intercultural education. *Intercultural Education, 19*(6), 515–525.

Hardiman, R., Jackson, B. W., & Griffin, P. (2013). Conceptual foundations. In M. Adams, W. J. Blumenfeld, C. Castaneda, H. W. Hackman, M. L. Peters, & X. Zuniga (Eds.), *Readings for diversity and social justice* (3rd ed.). New York, NY: Routledge.

Hill, R. A. (2003). Seeing clearly without being blinded: Obstacles to Black self-examination. *Journal of Negro Education, 72*(2), 208–216.

Howard, T. (2003). Culturally relevant pedagogy: Ingredients for critical teacher reflection. *Theory into Practice, 42*(3), 195–202.

Kohli, R. (2014). Unpacking internalized racism: Teachers of color striving for racially just classrooms. *Race Ethnicity and Education, 17*(3), 367–387. doi:10.1080/13613324.2013.832935

Kohli, R. (2016). Behind school doors: The impact of hostile racial climates on urban teachers of color. *Urban Education* [Online]. doi:0042085916636653

Ladson-Billings, G. (1992). Culturally relevant teaching: The key to making multicultural education work. In C. A. Grant (Ed.), *Research and multicultural education: From the margins to the mainstream* (pp. 107–121). Washington, DC: Falmer Press.

McCalman, C. L. (2007). Being an interculturally competent instructor in the United States: Issues of classroom dynamics and appropriateness, and recommendations for international instructors. *New Directions for Teaching and Learning, 110*, 65–74.

McKenzie, K. B., & Scheurich, J. J. (2004). Equity traps: A useful construct for preparing principals to lead schools that are successful with racially diverse students. *Educational Administration Quarterly, 40*(5), 601–632.

Mezirow, J. (2000). Learning to think like an adult: Core concepts of transformation theory. In J. Mezirow (Ed.), *Learning as transformation* (pp. 3–34). San Francisco, CA: Jossey-Bass.

Nieto, S. (2000). *Affirming diversity: The sociopolitical context of multicultural education* (3rd ed.). New York, NY: Addison Wesley.

Norrington-Sands, K. (2002). *Sister-to-sister: The influences of family socialization messages, internalized oppression, personal self-esteem, and collective self-esteem on social-comparison jealousy among African American women* (Unpublished dissertation). Alliant International University, Los Angeles, CA.

Payne, R. K. (2005). *A framework for understanding poverty* (4th ed.). Highlands, TX: Aha! Process.

Peterson, E. A. (1999). Creating a culturally relevant dialogue for African American adult educators. *New Directions for Adult and Continuing Education, 82*, 79. doi:10.1002/ace.8206

Philip, T. M., Rocha, J., & Olivares-Pasillas, M. C. (2017). Supporting teachers of color as they negotiate classroom pedagogies of race: A study of a teacher's struggle with "friendly-fire" racism. *Teacher Education Quarterly, 44*(1), 59.

Poutiatine, M. I. (2009). What is transformation? Nine principles toward an understanding of the transformational process for transformational leadership. *Journal of Transformative Education, 7*(3), 189–208.

Pyke, K. (2010). What is internalized racial oppression and why don't we study it? Acknowledging racism's hidden injuries. *Sociological Perspectives, 53*(4), 551–572. doi:10.1525/sop.2010.53.4.551

Quezada, R., & Romo, J. J. (2004). Multiculturalism, peace education and social justice in teacher education. *Multicultural Education, 11*(3), 2–11.

Richards, H. V., Brown, A. E., & Forde, T. B. (2007). Addressing diversity in schools: Culturally responsive pedagogy. *Teaching Exceptional Children, 39*(3), 64–68. doi:10.1177/004005990703900310

Schwalbe, M., Godwin, S., Holden, D., Schrock, D., Thompson, S., & Wolkomir, M. (2000). Generic processes in the reproduction of inequality: An interactionist analysis. *Social Forces, 79*(2), 419–452. doi:10.2307/2675505

Shields, C. M., Bishop, R., & Mazawi, A. E. (2005). *Pathologizing practices*. New York, NY: Peter Lang.

Sleeter, C. E. (2017). Critical race theory and the Whiteness of teacher education. *Urban Education, 52*(2), 155–169.

Smolen, L. A., Colville-Hall, S., Liang, X., & MacDonald, S. (2006). An empirical study of college of education faculty's perceptions, beliefs, and commitment to the teaching of diversity in teacher education programs at four urban universities. *Urban Review, 38*(1), 45–61. doi:10.1007/s11256-005-0022-2

Solomon, R. P., Portelli, J. P., Daniel, B., & Campbell, A. (2005). The discourse of denial: How White teacher candidates construct race, racism and 'White privilege.' *Race Ethnicity and Education, 8*(2), 147–169.

Speight, S. L. (2007). Internalized racism. *The Counseling Psychologist, 35*(1), 126–134. doi:10.1177/0011000006295119

Tolliver, D. E., & Tisdell, E. J. (2006). Engaging spirituality in the transformative higher education classroom. *New Directions for Adult and Continuing Education, 109*, 37–47.

Vescio, V., Bondy, E., & Poekert, P. E. (2009). Preparing multicultural teacher educators: Toward a pedagogy of transformation. *Teacher Education Quarterly, 36*(2), 5–24. doi:1868335031

Villegas, A. M., & Lucas, T. (2002a). *Educating culturally responsive teachers: A coherent approach.* Albany, NY: SUNY Press.

Villegas, A. M., & Lucas, T. (2002b). Preparing culturally responsive teachers. *Journal of Teacher Education, 53*(1), 20–32. doi:10.1177/0022487102053001003

Intersections of Race and Class in Preservice Teacher Education: Advancing Educational Equity

Kamala V. Williams and Quinita Ogletree

> Race interlocks with socioeconomic status, sexuality, gender, and other identifying categories to give shape and contour to a complex system of power and privilege.
>
> GARRETT AND SEGALL (2013, P. 294)

America is more racially and ethnically diverse than any other time in U.S. history. This demographic shift has similarly impacted student populations. As the classroom of students continues to grow more diverse, White middle class females dominate the teaching force. Students of color make up the majority of the school population in the 15 southern states (Southern Education Foundation, 2010). White females make up 82% of America's teaching population (National Center for Education Statistics, 2015). This trend is expected to continue as multiracial, multiethnic, Latino and Asian populations are expected to grow. By 2050, children of immigrants will account for the majority of children less than 5 years of age and 42% will live with parents who are not U.S. citizens (Annie E. Casey Foundation, 2014).

According to the U.S. Census Bureau (2012), the U.S. will not have a single racial or ethnic majority under the age of 18. These racially and economically diverse students are being met by teachers who often do not feel prepared to teach them. Teacher preparation programs are making efforts to address this concern. The complexities of race, gender and socioeconomic status are often addressed independently. The study we conducted and report in this chapter uses intersectionality as a theoretical framework to move past individual approaches that studies typically employ. By applying an intersectional lens, research on race, gender, and socioeconomic status is used to reveal the impact these statuses have on teacher education classrooms, clinical and novice teaching experiences. Crenshaw (1989, 1991) describes this collision of sorts as intersectionality. It is the multiple ways oppression can be experienced. She further describes intersectionality as a lens to examine how various biological, social and cultural categories such as gender, race, class, ability, and other axes of identity interact on multiple and often simultaneous levels. This interaction contributes to systematic injustice and social inequality (Crenshaw, 1991). The theory suggests that societal conceptualizations of oppressions, including racism, sexism and classism, do not act independently of each other, but interrelate creating a system of oppression that reflects the "intersection" of multiple forms of discrimination. Thus, intersectionality is used to understand complex systems of oppression including political, structural and representational oppression (Crenshaw, 1991).

1   Preservice Teachers

There is much discussion on what is needed to create highly qualified teachers. Often the discussion focuses on how much course work and clinical experiences are needed and where should these experiences occur. The question teacher educators and researchers have been trying to answer is "Should preparation programs concentrate on preparing teachers for all settings and all students, or should they prepare candidates for specific types of contexts and the students within them?" (Matsko & Hammerness, 2014, p. 128). We argue, as did Haberman (1996), that generic teacher education is not effective, especially as the student population continues to grow more diverse. When it comes to urban schools, new teachers are not fully prepared to handle the complexities of the context (Helfeldt, Capraro, Capraro, Foster, & Carter, 2009). Teacher education programs are in a position that requires preparation for content and context.

Teacher education should help preservice teachers "develop the capacity to analyze the particular setting of any school in which they will eventually teach with an in-depth and nuanced understanding" (Matsko & Hammerness, 2014, p. 129). Teachers should have construct and context knowledge in addition to the ability to engage in critical pedagogy. This begins with reflections and discussions of their coursework and clinical experiences. Some teacher education programs utilize these techniques but clinical experiences have to be deconstructed or stereotypes might be reinforced (Mills & Ballantyne, 2016). These experiences include reflections on how their field experience impacts their beliefs (Tinkler, Hannah, Tinkler, & Miller, 2014). Students in effective teacher education programs should leave with the ability to analyze and deconstruct their context.

Teachers enter the profession with their own belief systems and background knowledge. If they are lacking exposure to diverse environments, their belief systems may be informed by an American culture that reinforces stereotypes and prejudices (Garcia & Guerra, 2004). Often preservice teachers of color enter their educational programs aware of societal and school inequalities

(Brown, 2014) while White preservice teachers may be unaware. This understanding allows teachers of color to make connections faster. However, even when teachers and students are matched by race, social class can create disconnects (Coffey & Farinde-Wu, 2016). This disconnect can be a result of one identity status being more influential at any given time.

White teachers often lack substantial personal or professional experiences with people of color (Henfield & Washington, 2012). When people have a limited exposure to diverse people, "they don't have opportunities to challenge stereotypes and prejudices, develop cross-cultural understanding and communication skills and learn about multicultural perspectives" (Tyler, 2016, p. 291). For White preservice teachers to discuss race or racism the topics had to be provided in their coursework (Ligget & Finley, 2009). White preservice teachers who had diversity coursework and clinical teaching in a racially diverse school were able to discuss race and racism (Walker-Dahlhouse & Dahlhouse, 2006). Mazzei (2008) found in his study that White preservice teachers who only had diversity coursework were unable to apply it in the classroom and when challenged became silent. Teachers are often unable to examine structural inequities and cultural differences because of their beliefs in meritocracy, color-blindness, and individualism (Tyler, 2016). These beliefs can limit expectations and reinforce stereotypes and prejudices.

While in teacher education programs, preservice teachers of color often experience alienating and unsupportive environments that make them feel marginalized, isolated, and not culturally affirmed (Brown, 2014). This is especially true in an environment where most teacher educators are White (Matias & Zembylas, 2014). In a review of research on teachers of color Brown (2014) found two primary themes:

1 Teachers of color often work in classrooms that are predominantly low income and diverse and tend to make professional decisions in order to improve educational and life outcomes of the students.
2 Teachers of color often see themselves as role models, transformative change agents, committed teachers, or giving back to their community.

Teachers of color, nevertheless, can be ill equipped to face the experiences that occur in their classroom. All teachers, including teachers of color benefit, from on-going professional development on culturally relevant and responsive teaching (Cheruvu, Souto-Manning, Lencl, & Calubaquib, 2014; Clark, Zugmunt, & Howard, 2016; Milner & Laughter, 2015). This type of professional development could address feelings of isolation and affirm the cultural backgrounds of all teachers.

2   Race and Poverty in Education

Milner and Laughter (2015) discussed race and poverty in teacher education. Race is thought to be biological when it is a social construct. This means race can change depending on the society in which you live. Race is often viewed as insignificant or simply ignored by teachers (Milner & Laughter, 2015). There are many approaches to understanding race in education. They include critical pedagogy, antiracist pedagogy, multicultural education, culturally relevant teaching, and culturally responsive teaching. Each of these approaches examine race in the context of education and issues of power (Garrett & Segall, 2013).

Race is a topic people struggle to discuss or avoid altogether (Evans-Winters & Hoff, 2011; Milner & Laughter, 2015). According to Banks and Banks (2007), race is a taboo topic and has played a key role in the colorblind perspective which is wide-spread and a promoter of discrimination:

> [E]vidence suggests that this [colorblind] perspective is widespread in schools both within the United States and elsewhere, either as part of official policy or as an informal but nonetheless powerful social norm that applies in many situations...the colorblind approach is also frequently espoused as a goal to be sought in many other realms, including employment practices and judicial proceedings...this research led [him] to conclude...it easily leads to a misrepresentation of reality in ways that allow and sometimes even encourage discrimination against minority group members. (p. 273)

Often, people find it easier to discuss poverty and devalue the importance of race in the discussion or the intersection of race and poverty (Milner & Laughter, 2015). The focus is often on ethnicity, social class, dis/ability, culture, nation, and/or neighborhood but not race when discussing inequities in education (Ferri & Conner, 2014). One reason for this is because racially segregated schools tend to be in areas where the residents are very poor (Darling-Hammond, 2012). When race is devalued and poverty is overvalued there are social disconnects and dysfunctions.

In the U.S., poverty is a major social problem that greatly impacts a student's experience in school (Milner, 2013). Currently, the majority of U.S. public school students are poor (Suitts, 2015). Yet teachers feel underprepared and report concerns, reservations, apprehensions, and anxiety about working with students living in poverty (Milner & Laughter, 2015). Teachers can benefit from knowing about access to quality healthcare, schools, and foods (food deserts) when school communities are located in a low-income area. When poor students attend schools that have high numbers of children living in poverty, they tend to achieve less (Darling-Hammond, 2012). This often leads to teachers equating poverty to a learning or cultural deficit.

Preservice teachers enter the profession with their own beliefs about race and class that is based on their individual backgrounds. Coursework and clinical experiences can modify or change their beliefs and make them more open to work with culturally, ethnically, and economically different students. Often race and class are the differences that are needed to be bridged, understood, and acknowledged in a classroom.

Milner and Laughter (2015) in their study on race and poverty provide three policy and practice recommendations. First, all teachers should have a robust knowledge about race. Teachers are often not required to analyze historical and deep contextual readings about race and if they learn about race it tends to be superficial. Race should be taught from an historical, contemporary, and critical perspective (Milner & Laughter, 2015). Second, teachers' must have an expansive knowledge base about poverty. Teachers need to understand poverty is a fluid construct, and they should not stereotype students or their families based on socioeconomic indicators. There is tremendous amount of knowledge on poverty and education; however, unexamined synthesis of the knowledge can lead to inequity and the status quo and do more harm than good (Milner & Laughter, 2015). Finally, teacher education programs need to focus on the intersectionality of race and poverty. Educators can benefit from a deeper understanding of the race and poverty as independent variables and for intersectionality.

3   Methodology

In our qualitative study the subjects were a sample of convenience and participated in a clinical urban program at a predominantly White institute in the southwestern part of the United States. In lieu of the traditional clinical experience, the subjects accepted their clinical experience in an urban school. They also had an urban specialist who met with them bimonthly and hosted guest speakers. Lastly, they were assigned readings in urban education. The subjects were given pseudonyms. Their interviews were analyzed using content analysis. Intersectionality was used for this content analysis because we sought to understand how race and class impacted teacher education classrooms, including clinical and novice teaching experiences.

Five novice teachers participated in a clinical urban program that was designed to examine a curriculum and its effects on race, class and their intersections in a culturally diverse school settings. Narratives provide insight into novice teachers' personal perspectives and provide context to their responses to questions regarding race and class. The preliminary findings on questions related to race and class are included.

Isabella. Isabella is from a large urban area. She identifies as a middle class, Hispanic female. She describes herself as being from a lower socioeconomic family where her father worked in construction and her mother worked at home. She recounts that although her family struggled economically, her parents sheltered her from their struggle. Her parents wanted her to focus on her education. As she reflects on her days as a college student at her large predominately White institution, she believes she would have gone unnoticed had she not worked for the IT department and could help teachers with technology in their classrooms. Isabella became visibly emotional when she discussed reviewing the free lunch applications for her students and stated "this is me." That realization is what helped her to continue teaching in a school that is predominately Hispanic with students of low socioeconomic backgrounds.

Zoe. Zoe is from a small rural town. She identifies herself as a White, middle class and female. She brings with her a unique cultural experience in that her family adopted two African American girls who she considers her sisters. She believes the experience with her sisters helped open her eyes to the differences that exist among races and economic class. After completing the urban preservice program, she decided not to enter K-12 education. She believes her experiences prepared her for her a professional position working with children in a different area. She recalls strategies her mentor teacher helped her develop. She does not believe that an urban clinical experience should be required, but suggested that some sort of cultural experience is necessary to use strategies in racially and socioeconomically challenged environments.

Katy. Katy describes herself as White, female and middle class from a small rural town. She discovered a void during her undergraduate studies that was filled when she changed her major and decided teaching was a profession that would give her fulfillment. She is not originally from a large urban metropolitan area, but was excited about the opportunity to be a part of a program designed to prepare teachers for urban schools. She spent her first year after graduating in the school where she completed her preservice teaching. She has now moved to a private parochial school in the city. Her student population is diverse in terms of race, culture and ethnicity. She describes this experience as having found her niche by teaching students who are very interested in learning. She believes that her preparation in the urban program prepared her to be able to work in any situation.

Haley. Haley describes herself as female, African American and middle class. She grew up in a large metropolitan urban area and attended urban schools.

During her college years, Haley's only African American professor taught multicultural education. She describes it as being her favorite course. She felt she had to prove that although she did not come from the same area or look like her professors, she was capable of being successful. She believes that her clinical teaching experience in the urban program prepared her to be a better teacher and a better person. Haley believes that every teacher should have exposure to teaching in an urban setting because "you never know where life may take you."

Tiana. Tiana is an African American female with contagious energy. She grew up in what her students would describe as "the hood." She is from a single parent home in a large urban city. Tiana admits that as a young African American, initially she was not connecting well with her African American students. She attributes a conversation she shared about her background as the turning point to making better connections with her students. She told them where she went to school and about her single-family household. She shared with them how those circumstances motivated her to work hard in school, graduate at the top of her class, attend a highly acclaimed university, and travel abroad. She was determined to not allow her circumstances to define her future.

4   Preliminary Findings

In the following sections, we address findings related to coursework on race and class, college experience, and building relationships.

4.1   *Coursework on Race and Class*

Despite the research on the importance of in-depth deconstruction of race and class in pre-service teaching programs, these novice teachers acknowledged they had very limited exposure to these topics in their course work. One teacher called it the "elephant in the room." In reference to race and class, another added, "I think that's definitely the elephant in the room. I don't think we were taught any strategies to approach parents differently. Nobody really talks about it."

They each mentioned a single course in multicultural education as the primary source of information regarding race and class. One of the students recalls this course covering topics of diversity, learning styles as well as learning abilities. Very candidly, one teacher admitted,

"I didn't get what I actually needed, because the courses were biased when they came to race or it was surrounded by stereotypes. We read [deficit model] books by Ruby Payne; it didn't help me a lot."

Each participant felt their clinical experience was most resourceful in gaining experience and exposure to students of different races and classes. The sentiments of one of the teachers echoes in this statement:

> I grew up around …Some Hispanics. But, I was definitely a minority in the schools where I was student teaching. Being around that culture and around the parents of the kids and teaching with people of [a different] race opened up my mind and I learned a lot. Experience [in this environment] taught me the most.

One of the teachers attributed her personal home and clinical experience to broadening her awareness of race and socioeconomic differences. She stated, "I didn't take any specific courses. On the job is where I learned …as well as my own home life." After the clinical experiences Cohen, Hoz, and Kaplan (2013) found that preservice teachers had more favorable attitudes towards multiculturalism, teaching in low income schools, and their prejudices about ethnic differences were reduced.

4.2   *College Experience*

Each of these teachers made the decision to attend a predominately White university. Perhaps for the two White students it was a decision that held no eminent consequences regarding race and social class. For the three teachers of color, there was an obvious impact on their college experience. Isabella remembers feeling very much invisible as a student.

> In college a lot of the students were White and a lot of the teachers were White so I felt like I was never really recognized. By my senior year I was working for the IT department I was known as the IT girl. A lot of my teachers would ask for help with the projectors, et, If it was not for that I feel like I would have just slid through till I got my degree.

Haley looks on her experience as one that promoted a type of motivation.

> I think it affected me in a positive way. Because they didn't look like me, I feel like I had to prove myself. And show them that just because I didn't come from the same area or I don't look like you, doesn't mean that I'm not capable of being successful. I wanted to make sure that even though the odds were kind of against me, I used that to motivate me and I did not let that discourage me.

During open discussions with her peers in her classes, Tiana discovered significant differences in her experiences compared to those of her peers. "Most of my peers were White middle class and upper class females, so when we were speaking about our experiences, they were completely different than mine." This realization influenced her decision to teach in an urban school.

"I thought I would better serve an urban school because that is where I [live]."
Zoe's candid reflection speaks to the opposite experience many students from
diverse racial and socioeconomic backgrounds encounter in their classrooms.
Often, students of color become tired of trying to prove themselves and learn
over time that it is their right to be included in the classroom and instructed by
a professor who has high expectations for them.

4.3   *Building Relationships*
These novice teachers discovered that one of the most important things
a teacher could do was learn about their students. This held true regardless
of racial and socioeconomic similarities and differences. Tiana admitted,
"Initially I thought that you needed to come from the place where your
students come from in order to teach them; however, when I started student
teaching, I realized that was not always true." She found that it was more
important to know your students and build relationships with them and
their parents.

> I have a student who is not poor, he doesn't even know what a ramen
> noodle is, he does not like basketball or football, he likes soccer and it is
> completely different than what I am used to...so just because you are a
> certain race does not mean all your students will come from where you
> came from... you need to take the initiative to learn...exactly who you are
> teaching.

Dilworth and Brown (2008) reminds us that while teachers of color may be
successful with students of color, simply pairing a student and teacher who
share the same race, but not the same socio-cultural background, will not
ensure student progress. Isabella extended this point regarding the Hispanic
students who she taught. Her suggestions encompassed actions that reflected
self-denial and communalism verses individualism. Although Isabella now
earned a middle-income salary she kept her wardrobe for school modest. She
resisted wearing her designer clothes and handbags and wore basic t-shirts,
slacks and casual shoes to remain relatable to her students. It was a barrier she
could control and made the effort to do so.

> Drive around the neighborhood of your school to get to know [your
> students]...A lot of my students live in trailer homes...For some kids,
> it is a motivation...don't be too flashy. I learned that right away. There
> were some kids who were impressed with it and some who were thinking,
> my mom doesn't have things like that or my sister can't get things
> like that...

Isabella continues by explaining her responsibility as a role model. She knows she represents something far more than just a teacher for her students.

> Be aware of what you are presenting because they see teachers as role models...they look at you and whatever you have they are gonna try to get one day. So, I am always dressed [nicely, but] casual...I don't want them to think I am trying to be better than them.

Tiana offered a similar response. She made connections with her students and her parents by sharing her story with her students in the classroom and with their parents at school sporting events.

As stated earlier, sharing racial and ethnic backgrounds does not guarantee connections but employing culturally responsive teaching practices as done by Isabella and Tiana aid the success of the students. Coffey and Farinde-Wu (2016) examined the first year teaching practices of an African American female and found that even though they identified with race there were other areas of sociocultural dissonance. Therefore, the teacher created culturally informed relationships by listening to the students' person stories creating connectedness, community, and collaboration. The instructional strategy of culturally informed relationships was used by Isabella, and Tiana in their classrooms.

5   Conclusion

Each of the teachers offered their opinions of what they believed would help new teachers. They overwhelmingly felt more field experience and additional courses with meaningful discussions on race and socioeconomic class in the classroom would be helpful. They all believed their race and socioeconomic background intersected with their experiences as students and new teachers. One of the teachers expressed that an effort should be made to prepare teachers for all students. She stated, "At the end of the day, we become teachers, not to teach one particular type of student, we become teachers to teach all types of students."

It should be noted that the two White, female preservice teachers did not remain in the urban school district to complete their clinical teaching. One moved to a private parochial school with a diverse student population but a higher socioeconomic status. Her move supports the study by Freeman, Scafidi, and Sjoquist (2005) who found that White teachers who move usually go to schools that have fewer African American students, fewer low income students and higher achievement scores.

To become teachers of all students one must believe that students of all races and socioeconomic classes can learn and that we have an obligation to teach all children. Classrooms with students from diverse racial and economic backgrounds need teachers who are culturally responsive and can be cultural mediators that bridge the gap between home and school. Like Milner and Laughter (2015), educators and researchers must ask, does poverty manifest differently based on race and, if so, how are the manifestations similar and different? And finally, what is important to understand about these similarities and contrasts in public schools? The examination of these questions may bring teachers, teacher educators, researchers, and policy makers to a clearer intersectional understanding as to how best to prepare teachers for the next generation of racially and economically diverse students. Efforts to improve teacher preparation programs warrant an investigation into the intersectionality of race and class and how they contribute to the preparation of teachers for diverse learning environments.

References

Annie E. Casey Foundation. (2014). *Data book state trends in child well-being* (25th ed.). Baltimore, MD: Annie E. Casey Foundation. Retrieved from www.aecf.org

Banks, J., & Banks, C. (2010). *Multicultural education: Issues and perspectives* (7th ed.). Hoboken, NJ: Wiley & Sons Publishers.

Brown, K. D. (2014). Teaching in color: A critical race theory in education analysis of the literature on preservice teachers of color and teacher education in the US. *Race Ethnicity and Education, 17*(3), 326–345.

Cheruvu, R., Souto-Manning, M., Lencl, T., & Chin-Calubaquib, M. (2014). Race, isolation, and exclusion: What early childhood teacher educators need to know about the experiences of pre-service teachers of color. *The Urban Review, 47*(2), 237–265.

Clark, P., Zygmunt, E., & Howard, T. (2016). Why race and culture matter in schools, and why we need to get this right: A conversation with Dr. Tyrone Howard. *The Teacher Educator, 51*, 268–276.

Coffey, H., & Farinde-Wu, A. (2016). Navigating the journey to culturally responsive teaching: Lessons from the success and struggles of one first-year, Black female teacher of Black students in an urban school. *Teaching and Teacher Education, 60*, 24–33.

Cohen, E., Hoz, R., & Kaplan, H. (2013). The practicum in preservice teacher education: A review of empirical studies. *Teaching Education, 24*(4), 345–380.

Crenshaw, K. (1989). Demarginalizing the intersection of race and sex: A Black feminist critique of antidiscrimination doctrine, feminist theory and antiracist politics. *University of Chicago Legal Forum,* (1), 139–167. Retrieved from https://chicagounbound.uchicago.edu/cgi/viewcontent.cgi?article=1052&context=uclf

Crenshaw, K. (1991). Mapping the margins: Intersectionality, identity politics, and violence against women of color. *Stanford Law Review, 43*(6), 1241–1299.

Darling-Hammond, L. (2012). *The flat world and education: How America's commitment to equity will determine our future.* New York, NY: Teachers College Press.

Dilworth, M. E., & Brown, A. L. (2008). Teachers of color: Quality and effective teachers one way or another. In M. Cochran-Smith, S. Feiman-Nemser, D. J. McIntyre, & Association of Teacher Educators (Eds.), *Handbook of research on teacher education: Enduring questions in changing contexts* (3rd ed., pp. 424–444). New York, NY: Routledge; Co-published by the Association of Teacher Educators.

Evans, V.-W., & Hoff, P. (2011). The aesthetics of White racism in pre-service teacher education: A critical race theory perspective. *Race, Ethnicity, and Education, 14*(4), 461–479.

Ferri, B. A., & Connor, D. J. (2014). Talking (and not talking) about race, social class and dis/ability: Working margin to margin. *Race Ethnicity and Education, 17*(4), 471–493.

Freeman, C. E., Scafidi, B., & Sjoquist, D. L. (2005). Racial segregation in Georgia public schools, 1994–2001: Trends, causes and impact on teacher quality. In J. C. Boger & G. Orfield (Eds.), *School resegregation: Must the south turn back* (pp. 148–163). Chapel Hill, NC: The University of North Carolina Press.

Garcia, S. B., & Guerra, P. L. (2004). Deconstructing deficit thinking: Working with educators to create more equitable learning environments. *Education and Urban Society, 36*(2), 150–168.

Garrett, H. J., & Segall, A. (2013). (Re)considerations of ignorance and resistance in teacher education. *Journal of Teacher Education, 64*(4), 294–304.

Haberman, M. (1996). Selecting and preparing culturally competent teachers for urban schools. In J. Sikula, T. Buttery, & E. Guyton (Eds.), *Handbook of research on teacher education* (2nd ed., pp. 747–760). New York, NY: MacMillan Reference Books.

Helfeldt, J., Capraro, R. M., Capraro, M. M., Foster, E. S., & Carter, N. (2009). An urban schools-university partnership that prepares and retains quality teachers for "high need" schools. *Teacher Educator, 44*, 1–20.

Henfield, M. S., & Washington, A. R. (2012). "I want to do the right thing but what is it?" White teachers' experiences with African American students. *Journal of Negro Education, 81*(2), 148–161.

Liggett, T., & Finley, S. (2009). "Upsetting the apple cart": Issues of diversity in preservice teacher education. *Multicultural Education, 16*(4), 33–38.

Matias, C. E., & Zembylas, M. (2014) 'When saying you care is not really caring': Emotions of disgust, Whiteness ideology, and teacher education. *Critical Studies in Education, 55*(3), 319–337.

Matsko, K., & Hammerness, K. (2013). Unpacking the "urban" in the urban teacher education: Making a case for context-specific preparation. *Journal of Teacher Education, 65*(2), 128–144.

Mazzei, L. A. (2008). Silence speaks: Whiteness revealed in the absence of voice. *Teaching and Teacher Education, 24*, 1125–1136.

Mills, C. M., & Ballantyne, J. (2016). Social justice and teacher education: A systematic review of empirical work in the field. *Journal of Teacher Education, 67*(4), 263–276.

Milner, H. R. (2013). Analyzing poverty, learning, and teaching through a critical race theory lens. *Review of Research in Education, 37*, 1–53.

Milner, H. R., & Laughter, J. C. (2015). But good intentions are not enough: Preparing teachers to center race and poverty. *Urban Review, 47*, 341–363.

National Center for Education Statistics. (2015). *Number and percentage distribution of teachers in public and private elementary and secondary schools, by selected teacher characteristics: Selected years, 1987–1988 through 2011–2012.* Retrieved from http://nces.ed.gov/programs/digest/d13/tables/dt13_209.10.asp

Pearson, N. (2016). Focus on teacher education: Race and identity: Crafting counter-stories with early childhood educators of color. *Childhood Education, 92*(4), 329–332.

Southern Education Foundation. (2010). *A new diverse majority: Students of color in the South's public schools.* Atlanta, GA: Author. Retrieved from http://www.southerneducation.org/Our-Strategies/Research-and-Publications/ New-Majority-Diverse-Majority-Report-Series/2010-A-New-Diverse-Majority-Students-of-Color-in-t.aspx

Suitts, S. (2015). *A new majority research bulletin: Low income students now a majority in the nation's public schools.* Atlanta, GA: Southern Education Foundation.

Tinkler, B., Hannah, C., Tinkler, A., & Miller, E. (2014). Analyzing a service-learning experience using a social justice lens. *Teaching Education, 25*(1), 82–98.

Tyler, A. C. (2016). "Really just lip service": Talking about diversity in suburban schools. *Peabody Journal of Education, 91*(3), 289–308.

U.S. Census Bureau. (2012). *U.S. Census Bureau projections show a slower growing, older, more diverse nation a half century from now.* Retreived from https://www.census.gov/ newsroom/releases/archives/population/cb12-243.html

Walker-Dalhouse, D., & Dalhouse, A. D. (2006). Investigating White pre-service teachers' beliefs about teaching in culturally diverse classrooms. *Negro Educational Review, 57*(1–2), 69–84.

CHAPTER 5

The Elephant in the Room: Approaches of White Educators to Issues of Race and Racism

Amy J. Samuels

Racialized disparities and tensions are clearly documented in K-12 schools and teacher preparation programs. Nevertheless, race-related dialogue is perceived as *the elephant in the room*. In other words, race and racism are obvious major issues that too many educators avoid as subjects for discussion because those topics feel uncomfortable or irrelevant. Race-related topics are frequently avoided, minimized, or misrepresented as something other than race; however, implications of race are deeply rooted and resulting sociopolitical consequences are indisputable. Consequently, race-related discourse must be engaged and explored in education through purposeful dialogue in an effort to name, expose, and examine the elephant in the room.

There are some who assert people of color, mainly African Americans, are to be held accountable for racialized ideologies and disparities in the United States (Bonilla-Silva, 2006). It is important to be mindful that one of the greatest forms of oppression is continually placing responsibility for oppression on the backs of the oppressed. Given the reality of White privilege and institutionalized structures that advantage Whiteness, it is essential that White people be held accountable and involved in conversations about race and the implications of racial ideology in education. It is imperative White people talk about race and challenge their own world views in an effort to see themselves as racialized and constructively engage with race-related power, privilege, and oppression.

Taking into account an inclusive representation of Whiteness and the resulting impact of intersectionality, the idea of a consistent White narrative is an elusive concept. There is undoubtedly a dominant narrative that continues to support a power structure that advantages those who are already privileged and there are standard assertions of group identity. In relation to Whiteness, it is critical to understand there are also differences between White people that transpire conflict (Bright, Malinsky, & Thompson, 2016). While many White people proclaim America is post-racial and race is no longer relevant, others understand the institutional nature of racism and the sociopolitical and economic implications of race. Although many White people defend

© KONINKLIJKE BRILL NV, LEIDEN, 2018 | DOI 10.1163/9789004365209_005

or deny White privilege, others understand it is a real concept from which they benefit. While many advocate a colorblind ideology and proclaim they do not see color, others acknowledge that to overlook race and the resulting implications is racist within itself; therefore, the colorblind or race neutral agenda must be interrupted. Even though there are shared experiences and privileges that contribute in shaping a social construction of Whiteness, it is imperative to recognize there is not a one-dimensional notion of Whiteness. Since orientations toward one's race and dispositions about other races are complicated by a multi-dimensional notion of identity, experiences, and beliefs, it is also critical to understand there is a counter narrative related to Whiteness to explore.

This chapter examines the effects of race and racism in K-12 education and education preparation programs by investigating perceptions, experiences, and racial discourse of White educators who are committed to educational equity and reducing current disparities. First, I provide an overview of pertinent research of White educators' perceptions of race and racism that contribute to educational inequities. Following this, I discuss a qualitative study of White educators that I conducted. The research study was informed by intersectionality, a concept that explores "the interaction of multiple identities and experiences of exclusion and subordination" (Davis, K., 2008, p. 67). It employed the tenets that Crenshaw (1991) highlights in her foundational research in that intersectionality is (1) centered on the lived experiences of people, particularly people of color; (2) framed around the complexity of identity where both individual identity and within-group differences are considered; (3) examines how systems of power and privilege support inequality; and (4) promotes an overarching goal of supporting social justice and change. It is important to emphasize that while this research does not explore the experiences of people of color, it does serve as a parallel to the concept of a counter narrative since the experiences explored are complex, frequently marginalized, and underrepresented in educational research (Jones, 2015).

Despite participants' desires to challenge the racial status quo, they highlight the complicated and complex nature of advocacy and allyship as well as the deeply entrenched reality of racism. Participants explored institutional systems of power and privilege such as achievement gaps and disproportionality, both of which continue to perpetuate academic inequity by further marginalizing students of color. They also expose genuine implications of cultural capital and how it sustains oppressive patterns by highlighting structures that exclude students of color. Consequently, participants highlight the need to disrupt the current narrative related to conscious and unconscious racism, as well as the often deafening silence of race and racism in educational contexts.

1   **Review of Research**

Research literature emphasizes how race reinforces systems of power, privilege, and oppression in education and education preparation. Although racial disparities are prevalent in schools throughout the United States, race and racism are rarely discussed in education preparation. Therefore, educators are not prepared to consciously engage with race since they have limited knowledge on how to respond to oppression in constructive ways.

1.1   *Racial Disparities in Education*
Modern racialized ideologies encourage practices that normalize Whiteness and promote disparities in access and opportunity that subsequently advantage White students over students of color. Research is robust with the assertion that schools overall are failing to meet the needs of students of color (Anyon, 2014; Kozol, 2006; Ladson-Billings, 2000). For example, sizable and noteworthy discrepancies exist between White students and students of color in academic performance (Darling-Hammond, 2010; Rothstein, 2004; Wiggan, 2007) and perceptions of schooling (Ferguson, 2007). Substantial disparities exist between racial groups in academic, extracurricular, and behavioral progress (Davis, P., 2008; Scheurich & Skrla, 2003). White students achieve overall higher academic success, outscoring their Black and Brown peers on standardized tests and maintaining higher grade point averages (Darling-Hammond, 2010; Rothstein, 2004; Wiggan, 2007). Black and Latino students often attend less desirable schools with poor educational climates and experience less rigorous curriculum than White students (Anyon, 2014; Kozol, 2006; Wiggan, 2007), inopportunely, resulting in higher drop-out rates (Darling-Hammond, 2010) and leaving them under-prepared (Kozol, 2006). Given the structures and conditions, educational climates are positioned to maintain an "unstable equilibrium" (Omi & Winant, 1986, pp. 78–79) that advantages White students and disadvantages students of color.

While most educators acknowledge racial gaps in academic, extracurricular, and behavioral progress, many highlight the influence of socioeconomic status on these disparities and disregard or minimize the impact of race. In an attempt to expose the silenced elephant in the room, it is critical to consider the influence of cultural capital on such disparities. With schools in most of the Western world putting a focus on White middle-class ideals, students of color are generally behind their White peers when they first enter school, leaving them academically lagging from the onset (Kumashiro, 2000; Scheurich & Skrla, 2003). Ladson-Billings (2006) refers to the differentiated progress as an "education debt" to underscore the significance of the disparities and highlight the influence of "historical, economic, sociopolitical, and moral components"

(p. 3). Referred to as the "assimilationist ideology," supporting further the reality of cultural capital, many believe it is the responsibility of students of color to adopt the norms of the dominant culture and model the behavior of the White majority (Kumashiro, 2000, p. 27). Ladson-Billings (2000) further explained, "Schools and teachers treat the language, prior knowledge, and values of African Americans as aberrant and often presume that the teacher's job is to rid African American students of any vestiges of their own culture" (p. 206). In contrast, when White students arrive at school with their "cultural capital" in hand, it positions them at a greater advantage since "both the school and their culture share more or less the same understanding, values, and artifacts" (Ndimande, 2004, p. 201). Consequently, the sociopolitical structure of schools and mindsets of educators are framed to perpetuate racial disparities.

1.2   *Silencing of Race in Preparation Programs*

Discourse on race and racism is missing from education programs which further perpetuates White privilege by positioning White people to continue to see themselves as unracialized and perceive race as something they do not need to engage or discuss. Considering the normalizing of Whiteness (DiAngelo, 2011; Niemonen, 2010; Thompson, 2003) and the pervasive nature of racism in United States (Closson, 2010; Smedley, 2007; Wise, 2005), many educators do not approach issues of racial inequity because they do not recognize them in the real-world context. As such, race and racism are rarely discussed in schools or education training (Darling-Hammond, 2010; Ladson-Billings, 2000).

The majority of educators report their professional preparation left them underprepared to meet the needs of racially diverse learners (Boske, 2010; Hernandez & Marshall, 2009; Ladson-Billings, 2000). Research conducted with pre-service teachers found students' knowledge of diverse cultures is minimal and illustrates a pervasive sense of deficit thinking (Davis, P., 2008; Ladson-Billings, 2000). Research also reveals in-service educators often employ a deficit paradigm and discourse of victimization where they blame students and their families for lower academic achievement and perceived inadequacies rather than considering the implications of oppression and marginalization (Darling-Hammond, 2010; Ladson-Billings, 2000). In addition, there is constant critique of educational leadership programs because they are charged with low-quality instruction, failure to prepare future leaders to foster achievement for diverse learners, and slowness to initiate change regarding racial equity (Boske, 2010; Hernandez & Marshall, 2009). As such, when collectively reflecting on education programs, from pre-service teachers to educational leaders, it is clear educators overall have not been prepared to think complexly about race or employ a worldview that challenges power, privilege, and oppression.

2   A Study of White Educators' Perception of Race and Racism

The purpose of this particular study was to investigate further the silence on race by exploring how White educators understand and address race and racism in their work. The research prompted discussion about personal histories, dispositions, and experiences that influenced participants' desires to oppose racial inequity, promote racial equity, and counter deficit-based notions of race. In addition, the research created a space to discuss how to recognize, confront, and dialogue about race and to engage reflective thinking in those who identify with an advocacy stance for racial equity. The study was an effort to advance beyond the dominant narrative where many White educators are not racially literate (Johnson Lachuk & Mosley, 2011) and struggle to see the need to discuss race by exploring the perceptions and experiences of those who are more vigilant and understand race has deeply-rooted implications. The study served to challenge the dominant narrative of race-based silence by purposefully engaging race in the conversation.

The research investigated the thoughts and perceptions of White educators who are conscious about race and racism in an attempt to deepen and extend conceptualizations of race and racism. In order to reflect multiple perspectives, educators from three distinct groups were represented: (1) in-service teachers, (2) educational leaders, and (3) recently retired educators.

I worked with professors and educational directors who have explored race and racism in their professional work to develop a list of potential participants. Professors and directors were asked to identify educators who they perceived as aligning with the established criteria: (a) self-identify as White, (b) engage in conversations about race and racism, (c) want to explore perspectives on race and racism, (d) work in schools with students of color, (e) believe racism continues to play a role in education, and (f) oppose racial inequity and oppression.

I selected eight participants who represented a continuum of ages from the late-20s to mid-60s. Four were male and four were female. All participants identified as low to upper-middle class socioeconomic status. Four had either earned or were nearing completion of a Master's degree, two had earned a doctorate, and two were pursuing a doctorate. Three participants were teachers, two were principals, one was an acting supervisor, and two were recently retired supervisors.

The study provided an opportunity for participants to (1) explore their histories, experiences, and dispositions that influence their thoughts and actions about race and racism, (2) reflect on the motivation of their interest in racial equity, and (3) consider how anti-racist philosophy will be or has been manifested in their work.

Responsive interviewing was employed (Rubin & Rubin, 2005) and two semi-structured interviews with each of the participants were conducted to explore the following research questions: (1) How do White educators frame the impact of race and racism? and (2) How do White educators describe their perceptions and experiences recognizing, confronting, and dialoguing with others about race and racism? To promote analytical triangulation, I provided participants the opportunity to review their transcripts and offer feedback to check the "accuracy, completeness, fairness, and perceived validity" of what was represented (Patton, 2002, p. 560).

3   Study Findings

It is important to highlight the study was not an effort to necessarily answer the research questions, but rather utilize the questions to guide the research and make audible participants' voices (Rubin & Rubin, 2005).

3.1   *Power of Experience*
Even though all of the participants had professional experiences working with students of color, it quickly became noticeable that personal encounters and interactions with people of color outside the professional realm were extremely influential in the development of a race-based critical consciousness. Each of the participants had personal encounters and interactions that destabilized their previous understanding of Whiteness and influenced their conceptualizations of race and racism. Whether it was a college roommate, living in a country where White people did not represent the dominant culture, or developing friendships with people of different races, these experiences were seemingly critical incidences because thoughts related to the experience influenced participants' frame of reference and a paradigm shift regarding race and racism. Given the nature of their relationships, once they had developed a personal connection, race consciousness was no longer optional, but rather something they had to become more aware and understand. They were no longer in an "insulated environment of racial protection" (DiAngelo, 2011, p. 54), but rather positioned with a developed awareness of their Whiteness. While most of the participants had previously been able to ignore the notion of race, deny the existence of racism, and stay silent on the topic, once they had a personal connection to people who were deeply impacted by both individual and institutional racism, White ignorance was interrupted and complicity was exposed.

Additionally, since participants developed personal stories, they appeared to see value in exploring the topics of race, racism, and privilege and were willing to talk about their thoughts, beliefs, and actions. All participants agreed their experiences (roommates, close colleagues, living abroad) grew to be something more than an experience and attributed to how they perceived race. Furthermore, many characterized their experiences as transformational in their thoughts, actions, and manifestations of how they positioned themselves in their educational roles. Whereas nearly all participants began with little exposure to people who were racially different, experiences with people of color increased their awareness, interrupted their comfort with a racialized status quo (DiAngelo, 2011), and increased their consciousness about race. Participants' heightened cognizance of race and racism increased their sensitivity to the deep-rooted foundations of racial inequity and oppression. Whether it was by chance or by choice, participants found themselves in circumstances or experiences where they were influenced to see race and racial identity from a positioning other than how they were raised, influenced, or socialized.

3.2 *Danger of Subtle Racism*

Participants agreed that institutionalized and systemic racism is pervasive in both education and society. Most participants named racism as "subtle." Yet, they asserted that racism is troublesome, not only because of its existence but because it continues to perpetuate oppressive invisible structures and inequities for students of color. Additionally, the subtleness, ambiguity, and failure to explicitly name racism made recognition complex because race-related dynamics are often not clearly characterized as such. Consequently, since implications are indirect, perhaps unintentional, many people may not recognize such thoughts and comments as racist. Nevertheless, even though it may be difficult to identify in certain contexts, participants argued that racism is pervasive in schools and can be recognized in the form of biases, prejudice, lack of objectivity, lower expectations, microaggressions, inequitable access and resources, and systemic exclusion.

3.3 *Unsilencing Racism*

Commonalties in participants' perceptions about how they confronted racism were also explored. They consistently shared ideas of how racism can be confronted through one's own thinking and reflection. The most widely referenced idea was the simple process of drawing attention, clearly naming, and exposing what is being said or done. When something is racist or has racist undertones, it was critical to expose this reality through probing or clarifying questions. Participants also agreed on the importance of highlighting inconsistencies, counterexamples, and contradictions. For example, when a teacher frequently reprimands African American students for being too loud in the hallway or cafeteria but says nothing to equally vocal White students, one might ask probing questions to highlight this inconsistency. Or, if a school is comprised of a racially diverse population but racial diversity is not represented in Advanced Placement (AP) or honors courses, one might initiate a conversation about this underrepresentation and the implications on future educational trajectories. Conversely, when students of color comprise less than 25% of a school's population but represent 75% of behavioral referrals, one can deliberately draw attention to this harsh inconsistency and encourage related dialogue.

Participants explained that confronting racism can also take the form of engaging conversations with colleagues to heighten awareness. They frequently reflected on the value of discourse and explained dialogue was not only an opportunity to express their personal thoughts and ideas but an attempt to increase race consciousness of others. Despite the value in such conversation, participants were in agreement that the subjects of race, racism, and racialized disparities are frequently avoided, redirected, or altogether silenced. Participants agreed that conversations about race and racism are rarely held in schools. While related ideas might be referenced in cultural competency training or when a negative, race-related scenario occurs, discussions about race and racism were generally uncommon and perceived as socially inappropriate.

Participants' narratives emphasized that social positionality influences what people are able to see, but also highlighted that experiences and dialogue can heighten awareness, increase consciousness, interrupt sociocultural influences, and destabilize White identity. Even though White people may not regularly consider the impact of race and implications of racism (Applebaum, 2007; DiAngelo, 2011), the data suggests an awareness and increased critical consciousness can be fostered through interactions and reflective thought. While the dominant narrative on Whiteness submits that White people are in a state of crisis where they frequently ignore and remain silent about issues related to race (Applebaum, 2007; Wise, 2005), this particular study shows that with purposeful relationships, meaningful interactions, and exposure, one's inclination to stay silent can be interrupted and unlearned. When race consciousness is heightened, the ability to see Whiteness and deconstruct its implications is enhanced.

4   Implications

This study further problematizes the silence on race and racism and encourages interrogation of structures that authorize power, privilege, and oppression. It offers implications for further exploring intersectionality related to the lived experiences of White people who encourage the advancement of traditional conceptualizations of Whiteness and want to reconsider strategies for advocacy and enhancing race-based consciousness.

4.1   *Intersection of Advocacy and Whiteness*

Participants considered themselves opponents of racial inequity and most considered themselves advocates of racial equity. Nevertheless, many struggled to align themselves with anti-racism as they did not always feel they were in a position to take action in alignment with their beliefs and values. Participants alluded to the concept of thoughtful inaction (Samuels, 2017): Even when they were aware that something was unfair or inequitable, they purposefully decided not to act or speak. Even if the inaction resulted in guilt, there were times when they could not inspire self-action. Given the controversial connotations associated with racism and the historical implications of race, participants underscored sociopolitical influences and repercussions to be considered, systems to navigate, and tensions to negotiate. Although there were times when they wanted to act or speak, their conflicting identities prevented this. For example, participants highlighted expectations of their professional roles and the need to adhere to policy, protocol, and positively promote the educational institution. They also spoke of the fear of being "labeled" and potential repercussions on their career trajectory once they are categorized as someone who asks too many questions or causes friction. For example, if someone always voices concern regarding situations that are unfair or socially unjust, they will likely be characterized as such and it is challenging not to wonder about the potential implications. If someone consistently advocates for underrepresented populations and brings attention to themselves in that regard, will that advocacy limit future professional opportunities? Although speaking against inequity is a socially just action, White educators in this study apparently worked to internally balance what was right for others and what was right for themselves. As a result it may be helpful to reflect on what places a person in a position where they feel they have the authority to act. What factors enable (or limit) and empower (or disempower) such advocacy?

4.2   *Negotiating the Consciousness of Whiteness*

Participants' narratives also uncovered implications of race-based advocacy and White privilege. Since White privilege is an elusive concept, many people are completely unaware they benefit from the privilege. As such, it is difficult to transition to a place where the privilege is recognized and acknowledged. It can be challenging to step outside the insulated, protected environment of

Whiteness and experience racial stress (DiAngelo, 2011), particularly when the White worldview typically is endorsed as truth and goes unchallenged.

This research suggests there is discomfort in the process of increased White race consciousness and questioning or unlearning the norms and values the dominant culture serves to reinforce. Related to Festinger's (1957) theory of cognitive dissonance, it is not surprising participants faced discomfort when their experiences with people of color resulted in information that conflicted with what they had been taught or socially normed to believe. It became problematic when their worldviews were confronted with alternate worldviews. When their values and ideas were challenged, they had to determine whether to uphold their existing beliefs or embrace new understandings.

Although people generally see and hear what they are looking to find, what happens when what people see and hear contradicts their "truth"? What happens when one learns it was not a lack of motivation or work ethic on the part of African American students that limited access to AP courses, but rather the deficit paradigm employed by educators that established a systemic barrier excluding many students of color? What happens when one realizes there is nothing "wrong" or flawed with the person of color, but rather the system is damaged and reproduces structures of underrepresentation in some areas and overrepresentation in others?

Even when individuals were positioned in circumstances where they felt they should be a voice for equity, they sometimes avoided confronting situations for fear of potential conflict. Given individuals' tendency to strive for internal consistency (Festinger, 1957), data from this study suggest opportunities must be provided for people to purposefully explore and learn their dispositions related to race and racism so they are better prepared to negotiate information that contradicts with their "truth" rather than automatically ignore, deny, avoid, or minimize conflicting information in an attempt to maintain equilibrium.

5   Conclusion

It is clear denying or silencing racialized ideologies will not eradicate racism or the deep-rooted consequences. Therefore, it is critical to consider ways to encourage educators to think and talk about race, power, and privilege. Racism is not a disappearing factor but rather profoundly embedded in sociopolitical and economic structures. School systems and preparation programs must commit to finding approaches to unsilence racialized disparities and implications of racism in schools. Research suggests there is value in dialogue and exposure. Thus, it is essential to embrace these conversations in the work and professional development of educators regardless of any resulting educator dissonance, distress, or discomfort. Racial disparities, White privilege, racially coded language, and corresponding systems of oppression and privilege must be exposed, explicitly named, and examined in order to give students and educators the tools to develop a critical consciousness and become racially literate (Johnson Lachuk & Mosley, 2011). No longer should White educators categorize sociocultural and educational disparities as corollaries of socioeconomic status alone or race as something that is no longer relevant; White educators must foster a culture and climate that encourages honesty and is responsive to the existing biases, discrimination, tension, and racism. Along with exposing and exploring power, privilege, and oppression, it is critical to give educators the opportunity to explore their own worldviews, as well as how they can challenge the fundamental problems of domination, group struggle, marginality, and structural inequality. Since this work is an attempt to shift the paradigm and position educators in a place they have not, yet, been, it is essential to imagine new possibilities and new spaces. Educators, particularly White educators, must consider how they can collaborate and work together to transform equity-based dispositions into advocacy, action, and change. They must be empowered by preparation and training so they are positioned and equipped to speak and take action. Considering the invisible structures, exclusionary practices, and levels of racial intolerance, educational systems must build capacity in approaching White race consciousness as well as a multi-dimensional understanding of Whiteness. Taking into account the complexity of the matter, opportunities must be provided so people, particularly White educators, can recognize how Whiteness and advocacy can intersect and how White privilege can be negotiated in various contexts.

Reflecting on how to situate Whiteness, it is reckless to maintain that White people are unracialized and do not benefit from racism. Furthermore, it is both irresponsible and negligent to assert that the Western world is colorblind and post-racial. Racist ideology is a theme embedded into Western mainstream histories with significant consequences for both White people and people of color. Although participants assert that modern racism could be perceived as subtle, perhaps more aligned with microaggressions, it is important to note that even subtle components result in exclusionary consequences that can restrict educational access and opportunity. Therefore, it is critical for White educators to constructively engage with matters of race and racism to advance beyond their "truth" and work to see, hear, and understand other "truths." To be authentically inclusive and embrace diversity, White educators should view the process as a journey and be vigilant and willing to advocate for what is socially just. Educators must believe fear cannot be the deciding factor for (in) action. If White educators allow fear to guide their positions, they will likely continue to silence the racialized elephant in the room. Self-examination must be fostered to reflect on the source of one's socially constructed reality and interpretation of the truth. Working to unsilence, disrupt, and take action can empower White educators to better recognize, name, and examine the elephant. Consequently, it can be advantageous for White educators to apply this wisdom on their journey to recognize the importance of critical reflection, fostering change within oneself, understanding racialized disparities, and disrupting oppressive structures to inspire increased race consciousness and advocacy for educational equity.

References

Anyon, J. (2014). *Radical possibilities: Public policy, urban education, and a new social movement.* New York, NY: Taylor & Francis.

Applebaum, B. (2007). White complicity and social justice education: Can one be culpable without being liable? *Educational Theory, 57*(4), 453–467.

Bonilla-Silva, E. (2006). *Racism without racists: Color-blind racism and the persistence of racist inequality in the United States.* Lanham, MD: Rowman & Littlefield.

Boske, C. A. (2010). "I wonder if they had ever seen a Black man before?" Grappling with issues of race and racism in our own backyard. *Journal of Research on Leadership Education, 5*(7), 248–275.

Bright, L. K., Malinsky, D., & Thompson, M. (2016). Causally interpreting intersectionality theory. *Philosophy of Science, 83*, 60–81.

Closson, R. (2010). Critical race theory and adult education. *Adult Education Quarterly, 60*(3), 261–283.

Crenshaw, K. (1991). Mapping the margins: Intersectionality, identity, politics, and violence against women of color. *Stanford Law Review, 43*(6), 1241–1299.

Darling-Hammond, L. (2010). *The flat world and education: How America's commitment to equity will determine our future.* New York, NY: Teacher's College Press.

Davis, K. (2008). Intersectionality as buzzword: A sociology of science perspective on what makes a feminist theory successful. *Feminist Theory, 9*(1), 67–85.

Davis, P. (2008). Something every teacher and counselor needs to know about African-American children. *Multicultural Education, 15*(3), 30–34.

DiAngelo, R. (2011). White fragility. *International Journal of Critical Pedagogy, 3*(3), 54–70.

Ferguson, R. (2007). Become more sophisticated about diversity. *National Staff Development Council, 28*(3), 33–34.

Festinger, L. (1957). *A theory of cognitive dissonance.* Palo Alto, CA: Stanford University Press.

Gay, G. (2010). *Culturally responsive teaching: Theory, research, and practice* (2nd ed.). New York, NY: Teachers College Press.

Hernandez, F., & Marshall, J. M. (2009). "Where I came from, where I am now, and where I'd like to be": Aspiring administrators reflect on issues related to equity, diversity, and social justice. *Journal of School Leadership, 19*(3), 299–333.

Johnson Lachuk, A. S., & Mosley, M. (2011). Us & them? Entering a three-dimensional narrative inquiry space with White preservice teachers to explore race, racism, and anti-racism. *Race, Ethnicity, and Education, 15*(3), 311–330.

Jones, S. (2015). Forward. In D. J. Davis, R. J. Brunn-Bevel, & J. L. Olive (Eds.), *Intersectionality in educational research (Engaged research and practice for social justice in education)* (pp. xi–xii). Sterling, VA: Stylus Publishing.

Kozol, J. (2006). *The shame of the nation: The restoration of Apartheid schooling in America.* New York, NY: Random House.

Kumashiro, K. (2000). Toward a theory of anti-oppressive education. *Review of Educational Research, 70*(1), 25–53.

Ladson-Billings, G. (2000). Fighting for our lives preparing teachers to teach African American students. *Journal of Teacher Education, 51*(3) 206–214.

Ladson-Billings, G. (2006). From the achievement gap to the education debt: Understanding achievement in U.S. schools. *Educational Researcher, 35*(3), 3–12.

Ndimande, B. S. (2004). [Re]Anglicizing the kids: Contradictions of classroom discourse in post-Apartheid South Africa. In K. Mutua & B. Swadener (Eds.), *Decolonizing research in cross-cultural contexts* (pp. 197–214). Albany, NY: SUNY Press.

Niemonen, J. (2010). Public sociology or partisan sociology? The curious case of Whiteness studies. *American Sociology, 41*(1), 48–81.

Omi, M., & Winant, H. (1986). *Racial formation in the United States.* New York, NY: Routledge.

Patton, M. (2002). *Qualitative research & evaluation methods.* Thousand Oaks, CA: Sage.

Rothstein, R. (2004). A wider lens on the Black-White achievement gap. *The Phi Delta Kappan, 86*(2), 104–110.

Rubin, H., & Rubin, I. (2005). *Qualitative interviewing: The art of hearing data* (2nd ed.). Thousand Oaks, CA: Sage.

Samuels, A. (2017). The dialogue of denial: Perpetuating racism through thoughtful inaction. *Understanding and Dismantling Privilege, 7*(1), 66–82.

Scheurich, J. J., & Skrla, L. (2003). *Leadership for equity and excellence creating high-achievement classrooms, schools, and districts.* Thousand Oaks, CA: Corwin.

Smedley, A. (2007). *Race in North America: Origin and evolution of a worldview.* Boulder, CO: Westview Press.

Thompson, A. (2003). Tiffany, friend of people of color: White investments in antiracism. *Qualitative Studies in Education, 16*(1), 7–29.

Wiggan, G. (2007). Race, school achievement, and educational inequity: Toward a student-based inquiry perspective. *Review of Educational Research, 77*(3), 310–333.

Wise, T. (2005). *White like me: Reflections on race from a privileged son.* Brooklyn, NY: Soft Skull Press.

CHAPTER 6

Teaching African American and Latinx Learners: Moving beyond a Status Quo Punitive Disciplinary Context to Considerations for Equitable Pedagogy in Teacher Education

Gwendolyn C. Webb-Hasan, Victoria L. Carter Jones and Chi Yun Moon

Ayinde – Man, This is Messed Up!

I'm in ninth grade…I get into trouble a lot at school. But I can tell you it is not usually my fault. They don't like the way I walk. They don't like the way I talk. They don't even like the way I wear my hair! The other day I got in trouble for combing my hair. Can you believe that, I don't even use a comb! I got this sponge thing and I just rubbed it through my hair as I was walking to my desk. I look good, don't I? Most of my teachers don't listen to me. They end up sending me to the office or getting me suspended…The teacher actually "encouraged," that's the word the teacher used, my parents to have me tested for an Attention Deficit Disorder, with Hypersomething. When I protested her disregard for the fact that I had my hand up again and was being ignored, she insisted that I be respectful. My teacher said I have an attitude. I got three detentions, and now I gotta go to inschool suspension. Three days!! How do they expect me to get that Algebra stuff if I am there for three days? Man this is messed up! They never send any work to in school suspension. I should know because I am in there enough.

Amira – So What Do You Expect Me to Do?

I am in ninth grade…I had never been suspended from school. Yes, I have had a few office referrals because I like to talk when the teacher is talking, especially when she is not saying anything new or I have finished my work… "I'm A Pretty Little Black Girl!" I am not little anymore, I am a young lady, but I do like that book, cause I am a pretty little Black girl…I like to look good. My hair, my clothes, they are all important to me. I like school, but my teachers spend more time talking about what they think is wrong with students than they do talking about what they should be teaching. I get to high school and I was really enjoying myself. Not because of what is going on in the classroom. I am in the hall one day and this girl comes up to me with some "he said, she said" stuff. She pushed me; I pushed her back. She hit me; I hit her back. I got in trouble. I could not believe it. They would not listen to my side of the story. They would not listen to my mother. What did they expect me to do, just let her hit me and get away with it? I had to go to the alternative school for 45 days.

Angeles – Do You Know My "Real Life?"
    I am in the fifth grade. I just got a in-school suspension for the first time. I am in the bilingual program at my school and thinking in both English and Spanish has been hard for me. This school year has been hard for me. I feel good doing my work in Spanish. I get so nervous when I have a test in English. My teacher is pushing me and she might think she is doing a good thing, but her loud voice makes me so nervous. I am trying my best. But it has been hard for me to concentrate on school. My mother has cancer and she has been going through treatments all this school year. No one at school except for my teacher from 3rd grade ever asks about my family. I wonder do they care. So when a student at the playground said "your mama is stupid," I lost it. What do any of them know about my mother? I sat in that room all day long and the work my teachers were suppose to send never made it and I couldn't talk to no one. I am going to be a principal one day. These teachers need some help and I am so upset.

1   Punitive Discipline

Ayinde, Amira, and Angeles are recipients of punitive discipline. The word punitive comes from the Latin root, punire, which means to "inflict a penalty on." As learners of color, they offer examples of some of the penalties inflicted on students of color at disproportionate rates. Teachers play a central role in applying broad state and national discipline policies in classrooms. As policy actors, they interpret and implement the practice of a policy. They determine when a student warrants dismissal from class or when their behavior warrants discipline beyond the classroom context (i.e. in school suspension, out of school suspension, alternative school placement, expulsion). School discipline policies grounded in school-to-prison pipeline frameworks have yielded racially disproportionate outcomes that result in the exclusion of high numbers of students of color, from classroom and academic intervention. Simson (2014) asserts,

> Punitive approaches to school discipline such as zero tolerance policies have failed America's youth. They are robbing students of needed educational opportunities and are contributing to a wide variety of social problems...Improper racial stereotypes and implicit bias continue

to distort our perception and evaluation of others' behaviors, and thus negatively affect our decision making regarding how to respond to instances of what the majority considers inappropriate behavior. (p. 562)

Simson's argument is most often ignored, refuted, and/or dismissed from teacher education discussions and practice. However, teacher education programs, as they prepare or help refine the pedagogy of teachers, are responsible for producing teachers who are culturally responsive, respectful and effective. How are teachers equipped to teach students demonstrating a spectrum of culturally informed and stylized behaviors, like those of Ayinde, Amira, and Angeles? Further, in the midst of an increasingly punitive discipline climate in schools, how do developing teachers make sense of race and gender intersections, while also focusing on the "academic" needs of learners of color?

This chapter focuses on how educators can and should resist the school-to-prison pipeline policies established by national and state mandates. We begin a brief overview of Critical Race Theory (CRT) tenets for the purpose of situating teacher education practice in strength-based rather than deficit-based ideologies. Of particular interest in this chapter is how the cultural identity perceptions and cultural consciousness of learners of color intersect with their racial/ethnic identities and how they are understood in the school context, especially when teacher education programs prepare and develop preservice and inservice teachers. Finally, we explore how programs can and should prepare teachers for negotiating their role as policy actors in the classroom.

2   Historical and Conceptual Background of CRT

CRT was developed out of the discipline of law. It provides a critical analysis of race and racism from a legal point of view. According to Delgado (1995), CRT emerged in the 1970s with the early work of Derrick Bell, who was distraught about the slow pace of racial reform in the U.S. During this time period, theories and methodologies in the field of law did not recognize or address the complexity of structural and institutionalized racism that marginalized populations and created disparities among people of color. There were philosophies about race that shaped research, but because investigators were not critical about their relationships to racial and social contexts, they could not write creditably about racism in their work (Ford & Airhihenbuwa, 2010). CRT, however, was not introduced into the field of education until 1995 by a number of scholars (e.g., Closson, 2010; Ford & Airhihenbuwa, 2010; Ladson-Billings, 1998; Ladson-Billings & Tate, 1995). Furthermore, within this historical context, the contributions of people of color, who might have challenged underlying assumptions, were largely excluded.

By 2002, CRT was taught, innovated and adapted in fields such as education, political science, women's studies, ethnic studies and sociology (Ford & Airhihenbuwa, 2010). In terms of significance, CRT scholars believe that Bell's racial typology can be used to deepen understanding of educational barriers, as well as exploring how these barriers are resisted and how to overcome them (Taylor, Gillborn, & Ladson-Billings, 2009). Scholars applied CRT to the educational field by using Bell's theoretical and analytical framework in educational research. Scholars addressed areas such as school achievement, science, intelligence, beauty, and Whiteness. CRT is also referred to as a theoretical and/or interpretive framework as well as a movement.

Scholars who critically analyze the tenets of CRT suggest that CRT (a) situates the experiential knowledge of people of color and their communities as valid and essential to analyzing racial inequalities, racial inequities and other phenomena; (b) challenges the existence and attainability of neutrality, objectivity, colorblindness, and meritocracy, which are central to a liberal racial ideology of equality and equal opportunity; and (c) centers race-consciousness as an intentional consideration of race necessitated by racism. According to CRT, racism is interwoven into the fabric of American life, it is considered ordinary (Parsons, Rhodes, & Brown, 2011). Yet in it being ordinary, it is not to be accepted as status quo. Racism is to be confronted in teacher development and service delivery on a daily basis. As a result, our critique uses counter storytelling and interest convergence to frame a discussion on teaching male and female learners of color beyond a status quo punitive disciplinary context.

3   Intersections for Gender and Students of Color in the Pipeline

The intersections of gender, race and ethnicity are real. For example, male identity is perceived as dominant and privileged vis-a-vis the social construct and hierarchical value of masculinity. Yet, when the identity of males is intersected, or "interlocked," with a race of color or ethnicity, they are a gendered person of color simultaneously and their male identity or masculinity is no longer privileged but instead essentialized as hypercriminal and demonized by institutions such as schools (Andersen, 2010; Ferguson, 2001; Harris, 1995; Rios, 2007).

Male students of color undergo such experiences in schools and are often compounded when they experience criminalization in a variety of institutional settings. Rios (2007) calls this "multispatial and multidimensional" oppression

(p. 18). The severity is that over time, the cumulative experience is internalized, or believed, by students. Further damaging is the impact of essentializing males of color as deviant and hypercriminal (Harris, 1995). As a result, Milner (2010) has called for teacher education programs to prepare teachers who have conceptual repertoires of diversity.

In the opening scenarios, Ayinde, Amira, and Angeles shared experiences that led to discipline challenges because teachers had not taken the time to get to know them as dynamic cultural beings worthy of an effective, meaningful, and useful education. Their presence in the hallway, the classroom, the playground, or a sports field, should be examined from strength perspectives based on the culturally responsive learning environment that nurtures them on a daily basis. These relationships cannot be based on "drive or walk-bys" in those learning communities. Teacher educators must embrace a modified African proverb: "It takes an entire village to educate a child, but we must first reconstruct the village to better serve learners of color."

4   Equitable and Socially Just Contexts in Teacher Education

Educators often carry the unfair burden of educational reform and are frequently scapegoats when these fail (Weingarten, 2012). In the face of mass incarceration that parallels the Jim Crow era of discrimination in a punitive discipline climate in schools that has been fueled by a "war on drugs," youth of color are often perceived as deviants and criminal suspects (Alexander, 2010; Rios, 2007). Rather than placing the onus on educators themselves for educational policies and practices around discipline, we offer a perspective that contextualizes educator roles and situates them within a broader network of variables impacting school discipline and the perceived school-to-prison pipeline.

Equitable and socially just ideologies and practices assist the field in unpacking the role of teacher education programs in preparing emerging educators for the student bodies they will teach and the ways they can interrogate their own biases in teaching students of color. As a result, we offer tools to better understand the role of student identities, and ways to explore the power of the teacher/educator positionality in those processes.

Teacher education programs are a focal point of interrogating ways in which they, as well as schools, are institutions that "have power to create, shape, and regulate social identities" (Ferguson, 2001, p. 2). Given the influence of teacher education programs, they can be used as a foundation for reconsidering the school-to-prison pipeline mania that is contributing to deficit perspectives.

Further, teacher education programs are often to justify punitive discipline practices taught in many teacher education programs and most important reinforced in many public school settings.

5 Teacher Education Beyond Status Quo through Culturally Responsive Teaching

For mainstream teacher education programs to move beyond a racialized status quo, we briefly consider culturally responsive teaching (CRT), an academic achievement gap, and issues of cultural mismatches. Such issues are important in the effective development of pre and inservice teachers.

All preservice and inservice teachers need to know culturally responsive teaching (CRT). There is a substantial body of research that ethnic diversity of the U.S. population and school system is increasing (Apple, 2011). Moreover, through the year 2020, the U.S. Census Bureau (2013) predicted that the student of color population in public schools will continue to increase. In response to this reality, future educators should prepare for teaching to the integrity of such diversity in schools. CRT can help prepare students in teacher education to meet diverse learners' needs, especially in the area of punitive discipline (Gay, 2010; Skiba, Michael, Nardo, & Peterson, 2002).

5.1 Definition of Culturally Responsive Teaching

CRT is an instructional pedagogical ideology that is "the behavioral expressions of knowledge, beliefs, and values that recognize the importance of racial and cultural diversity in learning" (Gay, 2010, p. 31). In other words, CRT is effective in not only learners' cognitive development, but also in their social/emotional development. According to Gay (2010), CRT uses the different cultural characteristics, experiences and perspectives of ethnically diverse students as conduits for teaching them more effectively in classrooms.

CRT is validating, comprehensive, multidimensional, empowering, transformative, and emancipatory. It is based on three propositions for which students must (a) experience academic success, (b) maintain or/and develop cultural competence, and (c) develop a critical consciousness through which they challenge the current social order (Ladson-Billings, 1995; Larke, 2013). To be more specific, academic success among diverse students can be achieved by teaching with the learners' own cultural filters (Larke, 2013). Further, teaching critical consciousness assists students in developing a broader perspective of sociopolitical consciousness to assist them in critically analyzing societal relationships (Gay, 2010; Ladson-Billings, 1995; Larke, 2013) within and through an educational context.

5.2   *The Achievement and Receivement Gap*

Gay's (2010) essential elements of CRT should be a part of all 21st century teacher education programs because teachers are very critical in a learner's development. Teachers need both theoretical knowledge and the ability to manipulate those theories into their pedagogy within unique contexts, with strategic foci on countering the use of punitive discipline. They must know how "typical" learners learn and the cultural patterns of learners of color (Irvine, 2003; Gay, 2010; Howard, 2015). Teachers should know themselves as well as their learners (Carter, Webb-Hasan, & Williams, 2016). As a result, teacher education programs should provide knowledge base and skill development in the (a) content of culturally responsive curriculum, (b) cultural patterns of learners of color, (c) social/emotional development of students of color, and (d) cognitive theories that include effective teaching models in CRT contexts. This posture is necessary because distorted perceptions and knowledge bases in understanding often contribute to why an achievement gap persist.

The achievement gap is constantly discussed in relation to public schools in the U.S. The definition of academic achievement gap is a continuous, pervasive, significant and persistent disparity in educational achievement among groups of students (Larke, Webb-Hasan, Jimarez, & Li, 2014). Academic achievement is usually measured by standardized tests and a preponderance of research studies show there is a consistent disparity that produces negative outcomes depending on race, ethnicity, gender and social class status (Larke, Webb-Hasan, Jimarez, & Li, 2014). Such gaps impact academic achievement, graduation rates, matriculation to college, and later, income levels (Valencia, 2015). Many achievement gap studies focus on the gap between European American and Asian American students on one side, and African American and Latinx students on the other (Chambers, 2009). The publication of *Equality of Education Opportunity* (Coleman, 1966) started the trend to discuss those gaps in academic performance. The report concluded that 12 years after the 1954 *Brown v. Board of Education* students of color disproportionately remained in schools with glaring inequities.

A similar trend is found in other achievement data. For example, gender is also a factor that accounts for an academic achievement gap. Most studies show the results of gender academic achievement and females students do better than male students do in reading, spelling, literacy and writing (Jacobs, 2002). However, in STEM fields, the gender trend of academic results is different. According to NAEP 4th grade mathematics test results, male students' scores were significantly higher than female students in 1990, 2000 and 2015.

The academic achievement gap is generated by disparate socioeconomic circumstances as well. A 2010 analysis of the Coleman data set (Borman & Dowling, 2010), concluded that "both the racial/ethnic and social class composition of a student's school are 1¾ times more important than a student's individual race/ethnicity understanding educational outcomes" (p. 1202). Some studies report that learning opportunities and teacher quality such as teaching experience, teacher qualification and rate of teacher turn over are unevenly distributed by ethnicity and SES in the America's public schools (Barton & Coley, 2009; Goodwin, 2012).

Consequentially, Chambers (2009) suggested a "receivement gap" as a more appropriate concept than "achievement gap." She explained that a receivement gap focuses on teacher input and structures rather than the output of students. Students who have received more educational opportunities show higher achievement than students who have been provided fewer opportunities, and they are regarded as more capable and skilled (Flores, 2007). Furthermore, she asserted that students tend to have a lack of control over their educational settings. Educators should pay attention to input sources such as caring and well-qualified teachers, high quality instruction, advanced classes and policies that encourage students to find their talents (Chambers, 2009).

5.3   Test Bias, Cultural Mismatch, and Cultural School Capital

Researchers have tried to explain score disparities of different social and ethnic groups with various reasons (Kornhaber, 2004). One of the factors which attributes pervasive performance gaps is test bias. There are test score differences across groups and the tests include questions which ask knowledge and experiences that might be more available to European American and middle-income students (Sturm & Guinier, 1996) than to students of color.

A second reason is cultural mismatch and a lack of cultural school capital (Ladson-Billing, 2006; Sturm & Guinier, 1996). Cultural mismatch refers to a pattern of incompatibilities between a learner's home and school. This involves language and narrative style (Bergin & Bergin, 2014). Students of color may speak a different first language from the one used in school or they may use language structure in a different way than their peers, teachers or tests given in school settings. It is difficult for those students to find connections between their home and school settings.

There is also a demonstrated lack of cultural school capital among lower scoring groups. Cultural capital is defined as knowledge and relationships that can be passed on to the next generation (Lareau & Weininger, 2003). In educational settings, cultural capital includes knowledge such as how to study for tests, how to find mentors, and how to request education services. Cultural capital also includes the importance of relationships (Bergin & Bergin, 2014). Middle-income families are likely to have more school-relevant social relationships with teachers, principals, counselors and special educators (Lareau, 1989). When learners have relationships with people who help them access educational opportunities and provide models of success, they tend to score better on academic achievement assessments. In the U.S., cultural capital is related to both social class status and ethnicity. One study found that African American students from lower SES households with fewer resources, tend to visit fewer museums and had less experience with out-of-school music, art and dance classes than European American students (Eitle & Eitle, 2002).

6   School-to-Prison Pipeline

Research documents that there has been a systematic development of policies and legislative measures that have resulted in an institutional connection between school districts and juvenile court systems (Casella, 2003; Valles & Villalpando, 2013). These overarching policies have been reflected in school discipline practices. Increased zero tolerance policies, expulsions, suspensions and the complementary growth in juvenile detention rates for male students of color, combined with prison-like surveillance and policing of students are examples (Kim, Losen, & Hewitt, 2010; Reyes, 2006; Skiba, Michael, Nardo, & Peterson, 2002). Collectively these policies and practices have progressively led to heightened punitive responses to school discipline that has created the climate for a school-to-prison pipeline. Rios (2007) has pointed out that the racial/ethnic demographic of males of color impacted most by the school-to-prison pipeline is tied to geographic region more than anything. While in most urban centers African American male students are the most impacted.

6.1   *Significance of Disproportionate Discipline*
It is a well-known fact that a discipline gap exists, especially as it relates to learners of color in PreK-12 settings (Losen, Hodson, Keith, Morison, & Belway, 2015). Differential treatment, e.g., office referrals, in and out-of-school suspension, and expulsion, persists in the public school system's efforts to address this gap, especially in examining the school outcomes among leaners of color. For example, African American boys are more likely to be disciplined when compared to all other learners and African American girls follow close behind. If African American learners experience poor academic and social skill experiences in school, problems in the community and with law enforcement often follow. African Americans, for instance, are 2.5 times as likely as white Americans to be shot and killed by police officers (Lowery, 2016). A significant pattern of disproportionally exists in the discipline of African American learners (especially boys) in public schools.

Some teachers demonstrate a disposition for implicit bias (Staats, 2015/2016). African American boys are watched more closely (42%) in comparison to European American boys (34%) (Hathaway, 2016). Okonofua and Eberhardt

(2015) posited that student behavior should be viewed as malleable rather than as a reflection of a fixed student disposition that assumes a learner of color is a troublemaker.

Research has failed to support the common perception that racial and ethnic disparities in school discipline stem from issues of poverty and increased misbehavior among students of color (Skiba, 2002; Walker, 2012). Racial disparities in discipline are likely to occur at all socio-demographic levels, and a variety of statistical approaches have failed to find evidence that students of color act out at higher rates that justify differential punishment.

6.2   Impact of Punitive Discipline on Academic Engagement

The disproportionate exclusion of students of color from the academic setting as a result of discipline removal is not unique to school settings. In fact, many of the earlier concerns centered on how school exclusion led to the topic is not new, yet much has not changed over the past 40 years (see Edelman, Beck, & Smith, 1975). Furthermore, a growing body of research (e.g., (Losen & Martinez, 2013; Skiba, 2015) clearly finds

1 Race confounds issues of disproportionality in discipline.
2 The discipline gap cannot be explained by poverty or differential rates of behaviors.
3 Exclusion from school yields increased risk of other negative consequences (i.e., reduced academic engagement, increased drop out potential, increased juvenile justice contact.
4 School suspension is more likely in middle and high school (2.4% in elementary, 11% in middle and high school).
5 Suspension rates for African American learners, rose from 11.8% in 1972 to 24.3% in 2010.
6 African American males have the highest rate of suspension, while African American females have the second highest in comparison to males from all other races.

Researchers have closely connected learners of color to exclusionary discipline in school settings followed by exclusionary discipline in societal or community settings (Skiba, Nardo, & Peterson, 2002).

7   Teachers as Policy Actors in the Pipeline

The role of the teacher in the school-to-prison pipeline has the potential to be central. While constrained by school policies, teachers have opportunities to disrupt this pipeline by using their agency and influence. According to Rios and Galicia (2013),

> [W]hen educators fear young people because of the way they dress, where they come from, or where they live, they have little capacity to educate them, and, instead, have to rely on discipline as the key system for managing their pupils. (p. 62)

Drawing on Lipsky's (1980) concept of street-level bureaucracy, teachers can operate as policy agents when they can interpret discipline policy and implement them in practice. This concept sheds light on the possibility for teachers to exercise the power they have in determining *what* merits punitive punishment and *when* they should invoke elements of the school-to-prison pipeline. In most discipline instances teachers are the touchstone that connects students to punishment and in this way may have more agency or power than generally assumed.

Therefore, we offer the following critical *recommendations for teacher education programs*.

1 Transform content and methods of delivering curriculum to include culturally responsive pedagogy and teaching for all students.
2 Facilitate visits to the homes, playgrounds, community centers, afterschool programs, religious centers or churches, and businesses. Visits should be the consistent norm, facilitated by established relationships across the community and with teacher education programs. This will mean that the leadership of our colleges of education become a part of this process. As a result, preservice and inservice teachers will develop continuous examples of how school communities interact to support learning and behavioral patterns.
3 Provide internship hours in rural, suburban, and urban environments to support prospective teachers learning how to listen and see patterns of differences in the way students of color and their families interact at school, at home and the community.
4 Provide opportunities for preservice teachers to engage in service learning projects in the communities of the schools where they teach. Service learning experiences will provide hours of engagement where reciprocal relationships can be built in mentoring, coaching and teaching contexts. Provide such experiences so that preservice teachers may reflect on the intersections of race and equity as it relates to discipline practice (Brown-Jeffy & Cooper, 2011).
5 Provide intentional and purposeful time for exploration of discipline practices used in learner of color homes across a variety of generational and social economic contexts.

6 Restructure coursework to explicitly teach the differences between classroom management and classroom discipline in culturally responsive contexts (Weinstein, Curran, & Tomlinson-Clarke, 2003).

8   Conclusion

A clear understanding of why a receivement gap (Chambers, 2009), and discipline disproportionality (Skiba, 2015; Lose et al., 2016), exists and persists is lacking from a critical race perspective in the literature and the research in teacher development and teacher education. Further, although the field knows well *what* is occurring with students, the *why* remains perplexing. What stakeholders believe, know, and most importantly use from research-based perspectives is questionable and sometimes negligible at the school level. Yet, extreme consequences for punitive discipline infractions among learners of color are consistent. Students of color are removed from academic environments at pervasive rates.

Addressing the issues of disproportionate discipline among learners of color is a teacher education and leadership issue on a variety of levels. Leadership matters (Edmonds, 1979). If schools are going to affect meaningful change in disproportionate discipline practices, school leadership will have to address their own, as well as teacher knowledge bases and understandings about learners of color. Teachers cannot follow leaders unless they grow in their understanding of culturally responsive teaching and learner integrity. Many stakeholders believe that learners of color are deserving of the excessive discipline that removes them from learning environments. Skiba (2015) views the challenge as more systemic:

> The single most important finding from this analysis may well be that systemic, school-level variables contribute to disproportionality in out-of-school suspension far more than either student behavior or individual characteristics. Such a finding strongly suggests that those wishing to have an effect on racial disparities in discipline would be well advised to seek interventions that focus on the school rather than the characteristics of students or their behaviors. (p. 108)

Teacher education programs are an important entity to understand how teachers should be equipped to enter today's classrooms to eradicate punitive disciplinary contexts when they face a student body with significant populations of learners of color. Ferguson (2001) made a compelling observation in light of the school-to-prison pipeline that powerfully conveys the importance of teacher education programs and the preservice and inservice teachers they target for development. "Punishment is a fruitful site for a close-up look at routine institutional practices, individual acts, and cultural sanctions that give life and power to racism in a school setting that not only produces massive despair and failure among...students, but that increasingly demonizes them" (p. 19). In other words, there is tremendous potential power facilitated by teacher education institutions when their pedagogical foci includes a culturally responsive knowledge and action base as it relates to discipline practices, for every teacher who walks into a classroom. He or she has the power to shape students of color experiences in life-altering ways. Most important, students like Ayinde, Amira, and Angeles are depending on such teachers to teach to their integrity and honor the cultural capital they bring to a classroom because they are known, and respected by teachers who know how to effectively "teach."

References

Alexander, M. (2010). *The new Jim Crow: Mass incarceration in the age of colorblindness.* New York, NY: The New Press.

Andersen, M. L. (2010). The nexus of race and gender: Parallels, linkages, and divergences in race and gender studies. In P. H. Collins & J. Solomos (Eds.), *The handbook of race and ethnic studies* (pp. 166–187). London: Sage Publications.

Apple, M. W. (2011). Global crises, social justice, and teacher education. *Journal of Teacher Education, 62*(2), 222–234.

Ashley, D. M. (2016). It's about relationships: Creating positive school climates. *American Educator, 39*(4), 13–16.

Barton, P. E., & Coley, R. J. (2009). *Parsing the achievement gap.* Princeton, NJ: Educational Testing Service.

Bergin, C. C., & Bergin, D. A. (2014). *Child and adolescent development in your classroom.* Stamford, CT: Cengage Learning.

Borman, G., & Dowling, M. (2010). Schools and inequality: A multilevel analysis of Coleman's equality of education opportunity data. *Teachers College Record, 112*(5), 1201–1246.

Brown-Jeffy, S., & Cooper, J. E. (2011). Toward a conceptual framework of culturally relevant pedagogy: An overview of the conceptual and theoretical literature. *Teacher Education Quarterly, 38*(1), 65–84.

Carter, N., Webb-Hasan, G. C., & Williams, K. (2016). *Teaching all children* (3rd ed.). San Carlos, CA: Infinity Press.

Casella, R. (2003). Are zero tolerance policies effective in the school? An evidentiary review and recommendations. *American Psychologist, 63*(9), 852–862.

Chambers, T. V. (2009). The "receivement gap": School tracking policies and the fallacy of the "achievement gap." *The Journal of Negro Education, 78*(4), 417–431.

Closson, R. B. (2010). Critical race theory and adult education. *Adult Education Quarterly, 60*(3), 261–283.

Coleman, J. S. (1966). *Equality of educational opportunity.* Washington, DC: National Center for the Educational Statistics.

Delgado, R. (Ed.). (1995). *Critical race theory: The cutting edge.* Philadelphia, PA: Temple University Press.

Dubin, J. (2016). Learning to switch gears: In New Haven, a restorative approach to school discipline. *American Educator, 39*(4), 17–21.

Edelman, M., Beck, R., & Smith, P. (1975). *School suspensions: Are they helping children?* Cambridge, MA: Children's Defense Fund.

Edmonds, R. (1979). Effective schools for the urban poor. *Educational Leadership, 37*(1), 15–24.

Eitle, T. M., & Eitle, D. J. (2002). Race, cultural capital and the educational effects of participation in sports. *Sociology of Education, 75*, 123–146.

Ferguson, A. A. (2001). *Bad boys: Public schools in the making of masculinities.* Ann Arbor, MI: University of Michigan Press.

Flores, A. (2007). Examining disparities in mathematics education: Achievement gap or opportunity gap? *The High School Journal, 91*(1), 29–42.

Ford, C. L., & Airhihenbuwa, C. O. (2010). The public health critical race methodology: Praxis for antiracism research. *Social Science & Medicine, 71*(8), 1390–1398.

Gay, G. (2010). *Culturally responsive teaching: Theory, research, and practice* (2nd ed.). New York, NY: Teachers College Press.

Goodwin, B. (2012). Research says: New teachers face three common challenges. *Educational leadership, 69*, 84–85.

Hathaway, B. (2016). Implicit bias may help explain high preschool expulsion rates for Black children. *Yale News.* Retrieved from http://news.yale.edu/2016/09/27/implicit-bias-may-help-explain-high-preschool-expulsion-rates-black-children

Howard, T. C. (2015). *Why race and culture matter in schools: Closing the achievement gap in America's classrooms.* New York, NY: Teachers College Press.

Irvine, J. J. (2003). *Educating teachers for diversity: Seeing with a cultural eye.* New York, NY: Teachers College Press.

Jacobs, B. A. (2002). Where the boys aren't: Non-cognitive skills, returns to school and the gender gap in higher education. *Economics of Education Review, 21*, 589–598.

Kim, C., Losen, D., & Hewitt, D. (2010). *The school to prison pipeline: Structuring legal reform.* New York, NY: New York University Press.

Kornhaber, M. L. (2004). Assessment, standards, and equity. In J. S. Banks & C. C. McGee Banks (Eds.), *Handbook of research on multicultural education* (pp. 91–109). San Francisco, CA: Jossey-Bass.

Ladson-Billings, G. (1995). But that's just good teaching! The case for culturally relevant pedagogy. *Theory into Practice, 34*(3), 159–165.

Ladson-Billings, G. (2010). Just what is critical race theory and what's it doing in a nice field like education? *International Journal of Qualitative Studies in Education, 11*(1), 7–24.

Ladson-Billings, G., & Tate, W. F. (1995). Toward a critical race theory in education. *Teachers College Record, 97*(1), 47–68.

Lareau, A. (1989). *Home advantage: Social class and parental intervention in elementary education.* London: Falmer Press.

Lareau, A., & Weininger, E. B. (2003). Cultural capital in educational research: A critical assessment. *Theory and Society, 32*, 567–606.

Larke, P. (2013). Culturally responsive teaching in higher education: What professors need to know. *Counterpoints, 391*, 38–50.

Larke, P. J., Webb-Hasan, G. C., Jimarez, T., & Li, Y. (2014, September). Analysis of Texas achievement data for elementary African American and Latino females. *Journal of Case Studies in Education, 6*, 1–6. Retrieved from http://www.aabri.com/jcse.html

Lipsky, M. (1980). *Street-level bureaucracy: Dilemmas of the individual in public services.* New York, NY: Russell Sage Foundation.

Losen, D., Hodson, C., Keith, M. A., Morrison, K., & Belway, S. (2015). *Are we closing the school discipline gap?* (The Center for Civil Rights Remedies). Los Angeles, CA: UCLA Civil Rights Project.

Losen, D. J., & Martinez, T. E. (2013). *Out of school and off track: The overuse of suspensions in American middle and high schools* (Civil Rights Project). Retrieved from https://www.civilrightsproject.ucla.edu/resources/projects/center-for-civil-rights-remedies/school-to-prison-folder/federal-reports/out-of-school-and-off-track-the-overuse-of-suspensions-in-american-middle-and-high-schools

Lowery, W. (2016, July 11). Aren't more White people than Black people killed by police? Yes, but no. *The Washington Post.* Retrieved from https://www.washingtonpost.com/news/post-nation/wp/2016/07/11/arent-more-white-people-than-black-people-killed-by-police-yes-but-no/

Milner, H. R. (2010). What does teacher education have to do with teaching? Implications for diversity studies. *Journal of Teacher Education, 61*(1–2), 118–131.

Okonofua, J. A., & Eberhardt, J. L. (2015). Two strikes: Race and the disciplining of young students. *Psychological Science, 26*(5), 617–624.

Parsons, E. R. C., Rhodes, B., & Brown, C. (2011). Unpacking the CRT in negotiating White science. *Cultural Studies of Science Education, 6*(4), 95.

Reyes, A. (2006). *Discipline, achievement & race: Is zero tolerance the answer?* New York, NY: Rowman & Littlefield.

Rios, V. M. (2007). The hypercriminalization of Black and Latino male youth in the era of mass incarceration. In M. Marble, I. Steinberg, & K. Middlemass (Eds.), *Racializing justice, disenfranchising lives* (pp. 17–34). New York, NY: Palgrave Macmillan.

Rios, V. M., & Galicia, M. G. (2013). Smoking guns or smoke & mirrors? Schools and the policing of Latino boys. *Association of Mexican-American Educators, 7*(3), 54–66.

Rumberger, R. W., & Losen, D. J. (2016). *The high cost of harsh discipline and its disparate impact.* Los Angeles, CA: Center for Civil Rights Remedies at the Civil Rights Project at UCLA.

Simson, D. (2014). Exclusion, punishment, racism and our schools: A critical race theory perspective on school discipline. *UCLA Law Review, 61*(2), 506–563. Retrieved from https://www.uclalawreview.org/pdf/61-2-5.pdf

Skiba, R. J. (2015). Interventions to address racial/ethnic disparities in school discipline: Can systems reform be race-neutral? In R. Bangs & L. Davis (Eds.), *Race and social problems* (pp. 107–124). New York, NY: Springer.

Skiba, R. J., Michael, R. S., Nardo, A.C., & Peterson, R. (2002). The color of discipline: Sources of racial and gender disproportionality in school punishment. *The Urban Review, 34,* 317–342.

Staats, C. (2015/2016). Understanding implicit bias: What educators should know. *American Educator, 39*(4), 29–33.

Sturm, S., & Guinier, L. (1996). The future of affirmative action: Reclaiming the innovative ideals. *California Law Review, 84*(4), 953–1036.

Taylor, E., Gillborn, D., & Ladson-Billings, G. (2009). *Foundations of critical race theory in education.* New York, NY: Routledge.

United States Census Bureau. (2013). *Census 2000 gateway.* Retrieved from https://www.census.gov/main/www/cen2000.html

Valencia, R. R. (2015). *Students of color and the achievement gap: Systemic challenges, systemic transformations.* New York, NY: Routledge.

Valles, B., & Villalpando, O. (2013). A critical race policy analysis of the school-to-prison pipeline for Chicanos. In M. Lynn & A. D. Dixson (Eds.), *Handbook of critical race theory in education* (pp. 260–269). New York, NY: Routledge.

Webb-Johnson, G. C., & Carter, N. (2007). Culturally responsive urban school leadership: Partnering to improve outcomes for African American learners. *The National Journal of Urban Education and Practice, 1*(1), 77–99.

Weingarten, R. (2012). The role of teachers in school improvement: Lessons from the field. *Harvard Law & Policy Review, 6,* 9–38.

Weinstein, C., Curran, M., & Tomlinson-Clarke, S. (2003). Culturally responsive classroom management: Awareness into action. *Theory into Practice, 42*(4), 269–276.

CHAPTER 7

Intersectionality of Ethnicity, Gender, and Disability with Disciplinary Practices Used with Indigenous Students: Implications for Teacher Preparation and Development

Denise K. Whitford

Intersectionality is an identifier for the intersection, or overlap, of identities that compose the unique characteristics of all individuals (Crenshaw, 2012). Intersectionality is not an additive process where all components of an identity are separate in the experiences and interactions of the individual, but they are interactive (Landry, 2007). Individual identities that interact to create the experiences lived by every person, include but are not limited to socioeconomic class, race and ethnicity, gender, and disability status (Crenshaw, 2012). To analyze a person or group of people through the lens of only one of these identities does not necessarily capture the complex social matrices in which individuals and groups live.

Intersectionality is not a new phenomenon, but it is a relatively new field of research, particularly as it relates to applications within education. Furthermore, there are several populations who are underrepresented in both educational and intersectionality research. The purpose of this chapter is to introduce the reader to the intersectionality of ethnicity, gender, and disability with the disciplinary practices that have been used with Indigenous students, particularly those in the continental United States. The chapter explores research findings relevant to the intersection of gender and ethnicity for Native American student discipline. The chapter further delves into implications for teacher preparation and professional development to improve academic, social, and emotional outcomes of Indigenous students.

1 Indigenous People

Native Americans comprise roughly 1.2% of the U.S. population (United States Census Bureau, 2015) with nearly 600 federally recognized Native American tribes across the United States (USDI, 2017). Indigenous students, each with

© KONINKLIJKE BRILL NV, LEIDEN, 2018 | DOI 10.1163/9789004365209_007

unique languages and cultures, as well as varying access to resources, are diverse in socioeconomic and socio-cultural upbringing. Additionally, not all Native American students are members of a federally recognized tribe or have knowledge and access to a tribe and tribal resources. Colonization brought with it disparities and inequities that have had significant impacts on many Indigenous people. Little attention has been given to the education disparities and inequities faced by Native Americans, possibly due to their relatively low population size and isolation from the American mainstream consciousness, especially as they often lack significant or appropriate representation in politics, entertainment, and other areas of high exposure to mainstream America.

2   Indigenous Students in Public Education Settings

The following are historical data related to Indigenous students in U.S. public schools; areas include academics, disability, and student behavior and disciplinary actions.

Academically, Native American students have demonstrated the same low rate of improvement as many other student populations nationally. Native American students have collectively increased performance on the National Assessment of Educational Progress (NAEP) (IES, 2016) from 2009 to 2015 in 8th and 12th grade mathematics and literacy, as well as 4th grade science, but have yet to reach levels of proficiency in these areas. Additionally, aggregated NAEP scores in 8th and 12th grade science, as well as 4th grade reading have decreased from 2009 to 2015 (IES, 2016).

In regard to disability and special education placement, Native American students are placed in special education programs at twice the rate of students in other racial/ethnic categories (National Education Association, 2008, 2010/2011). In a report for the National Research Council, Donovan and Cross (2002) analyzed the disability placement data of students by race and ethnicity from the Office of Special Education Programs (OSEP). The authors found that 13% of all Native American students were enrolled in special education programs and were most often placed within the learning disability category (55.8%), followed by speech and language impairment (18.4%), intellectual disability (9.1%), emotional disturbance (7.6%), other health impairment (3.2%), multiple disabilities (2.1%), hearing impairment (1.4%), orthopedic impairment (0.8%), visual impairment (0.6%), autism (0.5%), traumatic brain injury (0.3%), developmental delay (0.1%), and deaf/blindness (0.04%).

Student behavior in U.S. schools is often documented and analyzed based on information provided in office discipline referrals (ODR) (Sugai, Sprague,

Horner, & Walker, 2000), which are the printed or electronic forms used by teachers, administrators, and staff to record student behavior infractions. McIntosh, Campbell, Russell Carter, and Zumbo (2009) provide a thorough description of the disciplinary referral process and Scott and Barrett (2004) estimate that the average ODR causes a 20–40 minute student removal from academic instruction.

Behaviorally, studies indicate that just like other students of color, Native American students predominantly receive ODRs for subjective reasons, like defiance, disrespect, and noncompliance (Whitford & Levine-Donnerstein, 2014). Furthermore, Native American students have been significantly overrepresented in the number of ODRs received, relative to their proportion in the public school population and are the largest overrepresented group, second only to Black students (Whitford & Levine-Donnerstein, 2014). The volume of ODRs do not necessarily equate to suspension and expulsion volume but often share a positive relationship.

Behavioral infractions in U.S. schools often result in administrative disciplinary action, which are essentially the immediate consequences of an ODR. They range across common levels of severity that include minor and moderate actions. These actions vary from verbal and written warnings, parent conferences or notices, community service during nonacademic times, to exclusionary discipline, such as in-school suspensions, out-of-school suspensions, and expulsions, all of which exclude students from academic instruction.

Native American students have been significantly overrepresented in the number and severity of disciplinary exclusions received, relative to their proportion in the public school population; the largest overrepresentation, second only to Black students (Whitford, Katisyannis, & Counts, 2016; Whitford & Levine-Donnerstein, 2014). Representing just over 1% of the public school population for the 2013–2014 school year, Native American students represented just over 2% of documented suspensions, expulsions, and implementation of corporal punishment (U.S. Department of Education, 2016). At first glance, 2% may not seem to be a significant portion of the population. However, this 2% represents nearly 47,000 students in an already small subset of public education. Disciplinary exclusion can have a significant impact on student learning and achievement (Sugai, O'Keeffe, & Fallon, 2012). Sprague, Vincent, Tobin, and Pavel (2013) found Native American and Alaska Native students lost 4.5 times as many instructional days as White students due to disciplinary exclusion.

Whitford and Levine-Donnerstein (2014) examined the ODRs, suspensions, and expulsions of two public school districts in the Southwestern U.S. that had a combined population of 23.5% Native American students. The study indicated that Native American students contributed to 32.7% of the ODRs for the school year and were two times more likely to receive a referral than White and Hispanic/Latino students, but were half as likely to receive an ODR as Black students. Most astounding were the disparities at the elementary schools. In elementary school settings Native American students were four times more likely to receive ODRs than White students and nearly three times more likely than Hispanic/Latino students. Lastly, Whitford, and Levine-Donnerstein (2014) determined that Native American students were significantly more likely to receive suspensions and expulsions for the same behavior documented by both White and Hispanic/Latino students.

In analyses of ODRs and disciplinary exclusions for Native American students in special education in which Native American students represented 29.2% of the sample, they were obtaining ODRs at rates proportional to their representation in the population (Whitford, 2017). However, Native American students in special education were more likely to receive exclusionary discipline, specifically out-of-school suspensions and expulsions than both Hispanic/Latino and White students in special education for the same or similar behaviors (Whitford, 2017).

3   Intersectionality Research

In an effort to expand on the work of Whitford (2017) and Whitford and Levine-Donnerstein (2014), this chapter includes previously unpublished results that elaborate on the previous findings and incorporate the gender component of intersectionality for the Native American population previously examined. Although results from the previous study indicated a higher probability of Native American boys receiving ODRs than Native American girls, visual inspection of the data provided preliminary indications to support the analysis of ODR patterns of girls, unaccompanied by those of boys. Although there were more boys than girls with at least one ODR, and boys demonstrated larger interquartile ranges overall, the largest medians were found primarily in the data for Native American and Black girls. This indicated that the number of boys obtaining ODRs was greater than the number of girls obtaining ODRs, but also suggested Native American and Black girls who obtained ODRs may have, on average, accumulated them in larger quantities than boys and other girls who also obtained ODRs.

Studies have indicated boys obtain significantly more ODRs than girls; upwards of 76% of disciplinary referrals were reported for boys (Whitford, 2017), 75% from Kaufman et al. (2010), 72% from Brown and DiTillio (2013), and 66% from Whitford and Levine-Donnerstein (2014). With such a large proportion of referrals given to boys over girls, it would be easy to determine that school discipline is a male problem and interventions should be created accordingly. This assumption may have led to the disregard of girls, who nonetheless have also been receiving large numbers of ODRs as demonstrated by current data.

Data from the Arizona Department of Education for the 2010–2011 school years were gathered and analyzed in 2013. School districts were located in the U.S. Southwest and roughly one quarter of the students identified as Native American. Detailed methodological considerations, including school characteristics, measures, and data analysis techniques can be found in the original study at Whitford and Levine-Donnerstein (2014).

The subsample was composed of 4,395 girls from pre-kindergarten through twelfth grade. The girls in the sample were 42.5% White, 27.6% Hispanic/Latina, 23.7% Native American, 1.3% Asian, 1.3% Black, and 3.6% multiracial. From the subsample, 40.82% of the girls were on free or reduced priced lunches. Elementary school lunch program enrollment ranged from 11.5% to 99.3% ($M = 60.1\%$) at individual school sites, middle school lunch program enrollment ranged from 28.8% to 74.1% ($M = 58.2\%$) at individual school sites, and high school lunch program enrollment ranged from 20.8% to 65.7% ($M = 37.1\%$) at individual school sites.

Twelve percent of the girls obtained one or more office discipline referrals of which 37% were White, 34% Native American, 26% Hispanic/Latina, and 3% Black. During the school year 1,239 ODRs were reported for an average of 0.28 referrals per girl and an average of 2.40 referrals per girl with one or more ODRs. Detailed data tables and statistical analyses are available upon request.

When all school types were combined, data indicated that relative to their proportion within the sample, Native American girls were overrepresented in disciplinary referrals. Although Native American girls comprised 23.7% of the sample, 34% of them obtained one or more ODRs and contributed to 39% of the total number of ODRs distributed during the school year. Black girls were also overrepresented, while White and Hispanic/Latina girls appear to have been underrepresented in ODRs.

At elementary schools, Native American girls were seven times more likely to obtain an ODR than White girls and three times more likely to obtain an ODR than Hispanic/Latina girls. At middle schools, Native American girls were two times more likely to obtain an ODR than White girls and nearly two times more likely to obtain an ODR than Hispanic/Latina girls. At high schools, Native American girls were slightly less likely to obtain an ODR than Black girls. When data for elementary, middle, and high school girls were combined, Native American girls were 1.7 times more likely to obtain an ODR than White girls, 1.4 times more likely to obtain an ODR than Hispanic/Latina girls, but 0.36 times less likely to obtain an ODR than Black girls.

The girls in the sample obtained ODRs in 36 different behavioral categories. More than 85% of ODRs were documented for defiance, disrespect, and noncompliance, aggression, attendance, and disruption. For Native American girls, 32% for defiance, disrespect, and noncompliance, 21% for attendance, 18% for aggression, 16% for disruption, and 13% for all other behaviors.

When compared to White girls, analysis of the top four ODR categories indicated that Native American girls were almost 23 times more likely to obtain a referral for defiance, disrespect, and noncompliance, nine times more likely to obtain a referral for aggression, 23 times more likely to obtain a referral for attendance, and 18 times more likely to obtain a referral for disruption. When compared to Hispanic/Latina girls, Native American girls were seven times more likely to obtain a referral for defiance, disrespect, and noncompliance, four times more likely to obtain a referral for aggression, eight times more likely to obtain a referral for attendance, and four times more likely to obtain a referral for disruption.

Girls obtained administrative consequences in five categories: minor consequences, moderate consequences, in-school suspensions (ISS), out-of-school suspensions and expulsions (OSS), and unknown consequences. Girls generally had a higher probability of receiving minor consequences for their behavior, followed by moderate consequences, OSS, and then ISS. Research models indicated the strong influence behavior had on administrative consequences, independent of girls' races/ethnicities. Nevertheless, Native American girls were more likely to have obtained ISS than girls who were Black (2.7 times), Hispanic/Latina (1.6 times), and White (1.4 times). Indigenous girls were slightly less likely to have obtained ISS than Asian American girls and less likely to have obtained OSS than Black girls.

Findings indicate Native American girls have had higher probability of obtaining ODRs than White and Hispanic/Latina girls, but lower odds of obtaining ODRs than Black girls. The majority of referrals that were given to Native American girls were for defiance, disrespect, and noncompliance, followed by attendance, aggression, and then disruption. Native American girls had excessively higher chances of receiving ODRs in all four main classifications of behavior than either White or Hispanic/Latina girls. Additionally, Native American girls have had a higher probability of receiving in-school suspension than Black, White, and Hispanic/Latina girls, but a slightly lower likelihood of receiving an in-school suspension than Asian girls, and an out-of-school suspension than Black girls.

The findings are comparable to those of DeVoe and Darling-Churchill (2008) and Brown and DiTillio (2013), who each concluded Native American students have been disproportionately represented in school suspensions and expulsions. DeVoe and Darling-Churchill (2008) found that a combination of Native American and Alaska Native girls had higher percentages of suspension than girls from other races/ethnicities, except Black girls. However, data were not disaggregated to determine if Native American girls or Alaska Native girls had more weight in the final results. Additionally, the results were for suspensions, and did not include behaviors or frequency of ODRs that eventually led to those suspensions. In a sample with 4.8% Native American students, Brown and DiTillio (2013) found similar results, not accounting for gender. Their findings indicated Native American students were nearly three times more likely to obtain an ODR than White students, more than twice as likely to obtain an ODR as Hispanic/Latino students, and had equally likely prospects of obtaining an ODR as Black students (Brown & DiTillio, 2013).

Although Black girls represented just slightly more than 1% of the sample, they had a higher probability of obtaining ODRs than Native American girls at the high school level and overall. Although the sample of Black girls was considerably small, the data indicate these girls continue to be disproportionately referred for behavioral infractions. This supports the findings of Blake, Butler, Lewis, and Darensbourg (2011), who determined Black girls were more likely to receive ODRs than girls of other races/ethnicities.

4   Intersectionality and Critical Race Theory

These findings, as well as those from previous studies, are not evidence that Native Americans receive high rates of ODRs or administrative consequences based solely on the intersection of their ethnicity, gender and disability status. The results only indicate that relationships exist. However, there is clearly a large problem with behavior reporting and administrative outcomes at all levels of public education for this population.

Exclusionary consequences can place students at a great disadvantage in comparison to their peers, often leading to poor academic performance, dropouts, and incarceration (Aud, Fox, & KewalRamani, 2010). Scholars have theorized that inequalities faced by culturally and linguistically diverse students, including Native Americans, can be traced back to systemic bias and power structures. These systems of bias have been examined under the frameworks of Critical Race Theory (CRT) (Ladson-Billings, 2009) and TribalCrit (Brayboy, 2005). In CRT, race and racism are the focus of analysis and discussion, however, emphasis is also placed on their interaction with gender and socio-economic status. Critical race theorists maintain race plays a major contribution to interactions between individuals and groups, while the addition of gender differences and socio-economic differences add to the complexities of those interactions (Delgado & Stefancic, 2012).

TribalCrit is a sub-discipline of CRT (Brayboy, 2005), which posits that there has been a racial hierarchy embedded in American beliefs and attitudes, often through institutional racism and implicit bias (Delgado & Stefancic, 2012). In addition to the principle tenets of CRT, TribalCrit presupposes that policies and practices geared toward Native Americans have been enacted for the purpose of further colonization (Brayboy, 2005). Furthermore, TribalCrit leads to the theorization that education-based practices that have affected Native American students have been linked with the "problematic goal of assimilation" (Brayboy, 2005, p. 429). Scholars who support the principles of TribalCrit have encouraged the establishment of a greater emphasis on Native American cultural acceptance, as opposed to assimilation, as part of an effort to improve the lives of Native Americans (see Brayboy, 2005).

5   Teacher Preparation and Professional Development

In regard to student behavior and school discipline, researchers and school personnel frequently target student behavior to improve discipline outcomes. In some situations this is appropriate. In fact, it is estimated that roughly 1–5% of students require individualized behavior supports (PBIS, 2016). However, less attention is given to the behaviors and backgrounds that teachers bring to the classroom and their impact on student behavioral and academic outcomes, although this can have a strong impact on the remaining 95–99% of students. In a series of meta-analyses, Hattie (2009) found that combined teacher factors (e.g., participation in professional development, expectations on student ability, and relationships with their students) had a greater impact on student achievement, than combined student factors (e.g., personality, attitude about content, creativity, and gender) or combined home factors (e.g., family structure, maternal employment, use of public assistance, and television usage).

As such, it is essential that teacher preparation programs and long-term professional development opportunities take into account teacher behavior within the classroom. Although the average public school classroom is comprised of students from varying races, ethnicities, socioeconomic backgrounds, etc., there are no nationwide mandates that require teachers and school personnel be trained to work with students from culturally and linguistically diverse backgrounds. However, when teachers participated in professional development that required them to constructively confront their misconceptions about diverse student learning needs and abilities, students identified as low achievers and those in special education experienced positive academic effects (Hattie, 2009). The infusion of cultural issues in preparation programs cannot guarantee changes in deeply engrained teacher beliefs and attitudes that may have an impact on disciplinary policies, actions, and outcomes as well as referral to special education. Nevertheless, researchers in the field have provided promising practices that include culturally responsive/ sustaining pedagogy and culturally revitalizing pedagogy.

When communication, teaching, and learning styles of students do not mirror those of their teachers, students are more likely to breach classroom rules and procedures. Implementing policies and practices that favor one culture over another may inevitably lead to increasing behavioral challenges within the classroom and increased behavioral referrals and administrative consequences, as well as referrals to special education. Research suggests Native American students have thrived in classrooms where teachers have developed a working knowledge and understanding of various student cultures (Morgan, 2010; Pewewardy, 2002).

Higher education faculty must focus on preparing pre-service teachers to provide culturally responsive/sustaining pedagogy (Ladson-Billings, 1995, 2014; Paris, 2012; Paris & Alim, 2014). These pedagogies involve developing and sustaining concepts of self and others, maintaining social relationships, and concept in knowledge (see Ladson-Billings, 2014; Paris & Alim, 2014).

The complexities of the diversity among Native American students with respect to language, culture, sacred histories and land, in addition to the intersectionality of class, ethnicity, academics, and discipline, is often generalized as a monolithic culture in educational practice. This has created circumstances that falsely legitimatize a past that is overwhelmingly negative and includes a history of Native Americans who were forced into boarding schools where Indigenous culture, language, and identity were violently suppressed. Recognizing the role of past and present experiences of Native Americans within the formal education environment is essential. An opportunity exists for policy makers and those responsible for teacher preparation programs to facilitate the development of a critical consciousness among educators about their positionality and how to question whether their position can continue to perpetuate or reduce the challenging circumstances of Native American students' experiences in the American education system.

Culturally revitalizing pedagogy follows the same tenets of culturally responsive/sustaining pedagogy, but primarily emphasizes the revitalization of disappearing cultures and languages that have endured systematic extinction throughout the colonization and assimilation processes (McCarty & Lee, 2014). Culturally revitalizing pedagogy draws attention and advocacy for the recognition of Indigenous educational sovereignty, for an acknowledgement of asymmetrical power relations, and for efforts to reverse the effects of colonization (see McCarty & Lee, 2014).

6   Conclusion

Native American students are an underreported group in educational research that has been greatly impacted by the outcomes associated with inadequate formal education. The purpose of this chapter was to introduce the reader to the intersectionality of ethnicity, gender, and disability with the disciplinary practices that have been used with Indigenous students in the United States. An overview of results that included outcomes relevant to the intersection of gender and ethnicity for Native American student discipline was provided. With the exception of Black students, Native American students have had higher suspension and expulsion rates than all other students, (DeVoe & Darling-Churchill, 2008). They have also had higher dropout rates than all other students, with the exception of Hispanic/Latino students (DeVoe & Darling-Churchill, 2008) and higher incarceration rates than White students (Sprague et al., 2013).

There has been an ever increasing need for a greater emphasis on student culture and culturally relevant strategies for improving access to high quality academic instruction and classroom settings. As evidenced by the studies discussed in this chapter, this is particularly true for Native American students. Teacher preparation programs and long-term professional development opportunities must be designed and organized to educate pre-service and in-service teachers on identifying their own cultural norms, values and biases, in addition to expanding their repertoire of cultural knowledge and using relevant information to advocate for and advance student learning in their classrooms and across school sites.

References

Aud, S., Fox, M. A., & KewalRamani, A. (2010). *Status and trends in the education of racial and ethnic groups* (NCES 2010–015). Washington, DC: U.S. Government Printing Office.

Blake, J. J., Butler, B. R., Lewis, C. W., & Darensbourg, A. (2011). Unmasking the inequitable discipline experiences of urban Black girls: Implications for urban educational stakeholders. *Urban Review, 43*(1), 90–106. doi:10.1007/s11256-009-0148-8

Brayboy, B. M. J. (2005). Toward a tribal critical race theory in education. *The Urban Review, 37*(5), 425–446. doi:10.1007/s11256-005-0018-y

Brown, C. A., & DiTillio, C. (2013). Discipline disproportionality among Hispanic and American Indian students: Expanding the discourse in U.S. research. *Journal of Education and Learning, 2*(4), 47–59.

Crenshaw, K. (2012). *On intersectionality: The essential writings of Kimberle Crenshaw.* New York, NY: Perseus Distribution.

Delgado, R., & Stefancic, J. (2012). *Critical race theory: An introduction* (2nd ed.). New York, NY: New York University Press.

DeVoe, J. F., & Darling-Churchill, K. E. (2008). *Status and trends in the education of American Indians and Alaska Natives: 2008* (NCES 2008–084). Washington, DC: Center for Education Statistics, Institute of Education Sciences, and U.S. Department of Education.

Donovan, M. S., & Cross, C. T. (Eds.). (2002). *Minority students in special education and gifted education.* Washington, DC: National Academies Press.

Hattie, J. (2009). *Visible learning: A synthesis of over 800 meta-analyses relating to achievement.* New York, NY: Routledge.

Kaufman, J. S., Jaser, S. S., Vaughan, E. L., Reynolds, J. S., DiDonato, J., Bernard, S. N., & Hernandez-Brereton, M. (2010). Patterns in office referral data by grade, race/ethnicity, and gender. *Journal of Positive Behavior Interventions, 12*(1), 44–54. doi:10.1177/1098300708329710

Ladson-Billings, G. (1995). Toward a theory of culturally relevant pedagogy. *American Educational Research Journal, 32*(3), 465–491.

Ladson-Billings, G. (2009). Race still matters: Critical race theory in education. In M. W. Apple, W. Au, & L. A. Gandin (Eds.), *The Routledge international handbook of critical education* (pp. 110–121). New York, NY: Taylor & Francis.

Ladson-Billings, G. (2014). Culturally relevant pedagogy 2.0: a.k.a. the remix. *Harvard Educational Review, 84,* 74–84.

Landry, B. (2007). *Race, gender, and class: Theory and methods of analysis.* Upper Saddle River, NJ: Prentice Hall.

McCarty, T. L., & Lee, T. S. (2014). Critical culturally sustaining/revitalizing pedagogy and Indigenous education sovereignty. *Harvard Education Review, 84,* 101–124.

McIntosh, K., Campbell, A. L., Russell Carter, D., & Zumbo, B. D. (2009). Concurrent validity of office discipline referrals and cut points used in schoolwide positive behavior support. *Behavioral Disorders, 34*(2), 100–113.

Morgan, H. (2010). Improving schooling for cultural minorities: The right teaching styles can make a big difference. *Educational Horizons, 88*(2), 114–120.

National Assessment of Education Progress. (2017). *The nation's report card.* Retrieved from https://www.nationsreportcard.gov/

National Education Association. (2008). *Disproportionality: Inappropriate identification of culturally and linguistically diverse children* (NEA Policy Brief). Retrieved from http://www.nea.org/assets/docs/HE/mf_PB02_Disproportionality.pdf

National Education Association. (2010/2011). *Focus on American Indians and Alaska Natives: Charting a new course for native education.* Retrieved from http://www.nea.org/assets/docs/AIAnfocus2010-2011.pdf

Paris, D. (2012). Culturally sustaining pedagogy: A needed change in stance, terminology, and practice. *Educational Researcher, 41*(3), 93–97.

Paris, D., & Alim, S. (2014). What are we seeking to sustain through culturally sustaining pedagogy? A loving critique forward. *Harvard Educational Review, 84,* 85–100.

Pewewardy, C. (2002). Learning styles of American Indian/Alaska Native students: A review of the literature and implications for practice. *Journal of American Indian Education, 41*(3), 22–56.

Positive Behavioral Interventions and Support [PBIS]. (2016). *Multi-Tiered Systems of Support (MTSS) & PBIS: What is Multi-Tiered Systems of Support (MTSS)?* Retrieved from http://www.pbis.org/school/mtss

Scott, T. B., & Barrett, S. B. (2004). Using staff and student time engaged in disciplinary procedure to evaluate the impact of school-wide PBS. *Journal of Positive Behavior Interventions, 6*(1), 21–27. doi:10.1177/10983007040060010401

Sprague, J. R., Vincent, C. G., Tobin, T. J., & Pavel, M. (2013, March). Preventing disciplinary exclusions of students from American Indian/Alaska Native backgrounds. *Family Court Review, 51*(3), 452–459.

Sugai, G., O'Keeffe, B. V., & Fallon, L. M. (2012). A contextual consideration of culture and school-wide positive behavior support. *Journal of Positive Behavior Interventions, 14*(4), 197–208. doi:10.1177/1098300711426334

Sugai, G., Sprague, J. R., Horner, R. H., & Walker, H. M. (2000). Preventing school violence: The use of office discipline referrals to assess and monitor school-wide discipline interventions. *Journal of Emotional and Behavioral Disorders, 8*(2), 94–101. doi:10.1177/106342660000800205

United Nations. (2016). *Indigenous people, Indigenous voices factsheet.* Retrieved from https://www.un.org/development/desa/Indigneouspeoples/

United States Census Bureau. (2012). *The American Indian and Alaska Native population: 2010 census briefs.* Retrieved from http://www.census.gov/prod/cen2010/briefs/c2010br-10.pdf

United States Department of Education. (2016). *ED data express: Data about elementary and secondary schools in the United States.* Retrieved from http://eddataexpress.ed.gov/index.cfm

United States Department of Education, Institute of Education Sciences [IES]. (2016). *National Assessment of Education Progress (NAEP).* Retrieved from http://www.nationsreportcard.gov/

United States Department of the Interior, Indian Affairs [USDI]. (2017). *Frequently asked questions.* Retrieved from https://www.bia.gov/FAQs/

Whitford, D. K. (2017). School discipline disproportionality: American Indian students in special education. *The Urban Review, 49*(5), 693–706. doi:10.1007/s11256-017-0417-x

Whitford, D. K., Katsiyannis, A., & Counts, J. (2016). Discriminatory discipline: Trends and issues. *NASSP Bulletin, 100*(2), 117–135. doi:10.1177/0192636516677340

Whitford, D. K., & Levine-Donnerstein, D. (2014). Office disciplinary referral patterns of American Indian students from elementary school through high school. *Behavioral Disorders, 39*(2), 78–88.

CHAPTER 8

"That Kind of Affection Ain't Welcome from a Black Man": The Intersections of Race and Gender in the Elementary Classroom

Dawn Tafari

The counterstory is a "provocative format of story" and an exciting "product of experience and imagination" (Bell, 1992, pp. 12–13). It is filled with powerful snippets of actual historical events woven into a fictional storyline that draws the reader in and can empower Black people at the same time. Counterstories provide instances of opposition to a dominant metanarrative. Solorzano and Yosso (2002) explain that "within the histories and lives of people of color, there are numerous unheard counter-stories. Storytelling and counter-storytelling these experiences can help strengthen traditions of social, political, and cultural survival and resistance" (p. 32).

This chapter is a composite counterstory (CCS). I utilized data from my interviews and interactions with 9 Black men who were elementary school teachers to create composite characters as a way to share their counternarratives to majoritarian stories that perpetuate the privileging of Whiteness and heteronormativity in U.S. public schools. The participants in this year-long study were all Black men in White feminized spaces: elementary schools. They were impacted by racist systemic structures designed to create and facilitate the maintenance of a social hierarchy that places poor Black children at the bottom and pushes Black men outside the margins. Thus, in this chapter, I discuss the marginalization of Black men in a White feminized profession, the role of heteronormativity within these spaces, and the importance of eros as a pedagogical process for Black men. The following questions guided the study:

1 How do dominant narratives of Black male sexuality perpetuate heteronormative notions of superiority?
2 How does heteronormativity not only problematize homosexuality but also perpetuate sexist perspectives of women as caregivers?
3 How do majoritarian narratives of Black masculinity impact how Black male teachers navigate eros as a pedagogical process?

© KONINKLIJKE BRILL NV, LEIDEN, 2018 | DOI 10.1163/9789004365209_008

1   **Literature Review**

> Unless we focus on the few alongside the many, we not only lose the
> voices of the few, but we also lose any meaningful understanding of
> the relationship between the few and the many, particularly in terms of
> power, privilege, disempowerment, and empowerment. (Estelle Disch as
> cited in Sargent, 2001, p. 16)

The epigraph above is from Sargent's *Real Men or Real Teachers? Contradictions
in the Lives of Men Elementary School Teachers* (2001), a book with a title that
is telling of the problems existing in the teaching profession today. These
"problems" stem in large part from an 1880s movement to feminize teaching
that created and cultivated an ideology that teaching was "women's work"
(Villaverde, 2008). Men were not considered "real men" if they taught,
especially if they taught young children. Hence, the act of teaching is generally
constructed as contrary to the U.S. masculine ideal because it does not match
heteronormative notions of superiority impacting the intersections of race
and gender (McCready, 2010; Mutua, 2006). Consequently, Black men looking
to enter the teaching profession often encounter negative stereotypes that
paint distorted images of them, especially if there is any semblance of eros
present in their pedagogy (hooks, 2004). Therefore, I write for "the few": Black
male teachers of young children who wade their way through the treacherous
waters of a profession dominated by middle-class White women. Because
there are so few Black male teachers, their voices are often not heard, and they
can go about their work misunderstood, disempowered, and alienated.

The CCS includes a verse of "I Need Love" by LL Cool J (Ladies Love Cool
James). Rap's first ballad, James' song had a tremendous impact on the young,
growing hip-hop community. Though rap was still very young, it had already
begun to take on very heteronormative and hypermasculine qualities. However,
this song set the tone for young Black men of the hip-hop generation to reveal
the vulnerable sides of themselves. The CCS presented in this chapter serves
that role as well: to counter the narrative that Black men are apathetic (Gibson,
2009), that they do not want or need love, or that eros is not an important
aspect of their pedagogy.

2   **Methodology**

The intersections of race and gender are central components in this study
for which I used a critical race methodology (Howard, 2008; Lapayese, 2007;
Solórzano & Yosso, 2002). Composite counterstorytelling is "a critical race

methodological tool [that] exposes the ways in which race and racism affect the lives of racial minorities in education" (Cook, 2013, p. 182).

The 9 research participants self-identified as Black male elementary school teachers and preferred, as a group to be referred to as "gentlemen" in this study. They teach pre-kindergarten, second, fourth, and fifth grades in 4 different states along the eastern U.S. coast. Their classroom teaching experiences range from 2 months to 17 years. I interviewed each gentleman individually, either face-to-face, or via telephone for 45 to 90 minutes. The gentlemen also participated in a Facebook focus group (FBFG). I created the FBFG as a closed, private group and, then, added each participant (see Facebook, 2016). A series of questions, song lyrics, and graphics were posted in the group over the course of three weeks. The gentlemen's comments on the posts were maintained as data. FBFG data and one-on-one interview transcripts were transcribed and coded – first to identify overarching themes and then to narrow down the themes to major purposes for teaching. Once the purposes for teaching were identified, the specific purposes were separated to help create different composite counterstories.

After I identified the overarching theme of this CCS (passion/eros), I selected a real setting for the fictional interaction, carefully designed the characters to embody qualities of each of the 9 gentlemen in the study, and then crafted the dialogue. The dialogue, like the characters, is a composite of the data garnered from the interviews and FBFG transcripts (Cook, 2013). In this CCS, we meet Kamau Miller, a third grade teacher from New York City, who lives and teaches at Derrick Bell Elementary School in the Hill District in Philadelphia, Pennsylvania. We also meet Kamau's long-time friends, Adam and Terence, and their new friend, Eric, who helps to facilitate our understanding of the contradictions that arose during the interviews. Kamau and his friends take us on a journey through the souls and minds of 9 Black male teachers who love what they do.

3   I Can't Hug the Kids

Kamau Miller loved being back home. His boys were there. His family was there. Don't get me wrong; he loved the Hill, where he has lived for the past five years and teaches third grade at Derrick Bell Elementary School. He loves teaching there, and he loves his students: he calls them his "Little homies." But New York City was HOME. It was where he could spread his wings and be himself. It's where his family and his oldest friends were. Most importantly, it's where Rucker Park was! Yep, The Rucker was where legends were made and legends-in the-making played. Rucker Park is a historic and world-renown basketball court in Harlem, and it was only a few blocks from Kamau's sister's apartment (where he stayed whenever he was in town). Kamau loved catching up with his boys at the Rucker. They would joke with one another and share their latest adventures while playing ball or sitting and watching a game.

The three friends could hear the deejay playing Black Rob's "Star in Da Hood" from three blocks away, and Black Rob music led the way as the three friends walked to the park. The park was not as full as it normally was, so Kamau sat next to his longtime friends, Adam and Terence, on the first row of the bleachers. Eric, a young brother Kamau had never met before, walked up to them and asked, "Yo, mind if I run with you guys?"

Kamau replied, "Sure. You make four. What's your name? I'm Kamau." Kamau looked at his friends and nodded. "These my boys, Adam and Terence."

Adam and Terence stood up and gave Eric a pound,[1] "Sup man?"

Eric was 17 years old and a senior at Dewitt Clinton High School in the Bronx, a bit younger than Kamau and his friends. He responded, "Nice to meet you guys," and then tossed his basketball back and forth in his hands, looking back and forth between the guys and the court,

"You bruhs play here on the reg[2]?"

"Here and there," Terence said, "especially when my man is in town."

Eric looked at Kamau, and Kamau added, "Yeah. I'm from Frederick Douglass Projects, but I live out in the Hill now – That's the Hill District in Pittsburgh. I teach out there."

"The Hill?" Eric nodded, "I got family out there. I used to go out there all the time when I was little. It's tough out there. How you like it?" He sat down next to Kamau.

"You're right; it's tough, but I do my best to take care of my lil homies." Kamau smiled.

"Your lil homies?" Eric laughed.

Laughing, Adam pinched the shoulder of Kamau's shirt and said, "Yeah. He's talking about his students. They gave him this cute lil shirt." Kamau was wearing a yellow t-shirt with "Derrick Bell Elementary" printed in large font on the front. The 26 third graders in Kamau's class had signed their names in varying forms of script, filling in much of the blank yellow space on the front and back of the shirt. Terence started laughing with Adam.

"Stop hatin'!" Kamau laughed. "My kids love me, and I love them."

Eric stopped laughing and focused his gaze on the court but was intrigued by Kamau's last statement, "What made a brother from Frederick Douglass become a teacher?"

Kamau explained, "My mom was a teacher, and when I was younger, whenever I was out of school, I would spend a lot of time tutoring and volunteering in her classroom, ya know, to stay out of trouble myself. This kinda built a strong passion to work with children; it also brought to my attention that a lot of young men don't have positive role models, so I decided that I would become one. Ya feel me? Some people spend their whole lives searching for that thing that makes sense…that makes their heart beat. *But I knew right off the bat this was the right thing for me."*

"Hmm" Eric began. "So you went to school for that?" Eric handed Kamau the basketball as if he were handing him a talking stick. Kamau dribbled the ball between his feet and thought for a second. He loved talking about what he did – his job and his kids, but he knew that he could get passionate about the topic and didn't want to get clowned by this new cat. He palmed the ball in both hands, shrugged his shoulders, then went for it: "Yeah. I went to Cheyney University in PA, and when I did my student teaching, *I fell in love with the little kids.*… Every day of it was great – even the bad days…it's different in Cheyney than in Pittsburgh, but up near Cheyney, with those kids, it was a lot of love. Like, they'd see me in the morning, their faces light up, come give me a hug, and made me feel good. I'd hug them back, and we'd have a good day. Now, in Pittsburgh, the kids are a little different – the culture's different. I can't hug the kids just because it would be taken the wrong way."

Adam shook his head. "It always bugs me out when you talk like that about your students. You my man and all, but you gotta be careful when you talk about how much you *love* your kids and be hugging on them and stuff like that." Terence jumped in: "But why? Now you've known this man since y'all was in the 8th grade. You know he ain't no pedophile, and yo' mama knows he ain't gay!"

Adam pushed Terence, and the four guys all laughed. Adam asserted, "Of course I know my bruh ain't gay or no pedophile, but everybody else don't know that, and unfortunately, that's what some people think about Black men who teach little kids."

"Yeah, I know what they think," Kamau started, "and that's probably one of the hardest parts of my job – not the ever-changing curriculum, not the important responsibility that comes with mentoring children, not the low pay – but dealing with the stereotypes from people who believe that I'm doing White women's work. They're waiting for White women to come in and save the day – be the Great White Hope, like in *Freedom Writers* or *Dangerous Minds*. It definitely sucks that more males of color aren't elementary teachers because these kids need it. They need to see figures like me and other brothers who are passionate about learning, passionate about education, and are going to be there to help them."

"But instead, we gotta watch how we talk and every little thing we do instead of focusing on showing these children, especially Black boys, the door of opportunity. I mean, it's always shut in front of them." Kamau tossed the ball between his hands and stared into space. His mind was back in The Hill. He continued, "One particular Black boy, I tutored when I first started at my school.... His teacher had nothing good to say about him – nothing good at all. I would just sit there like, 'What you mean you don't have nothing good to say about this kid? This boy was bright. You know?'"

"And she said that he was the worst of the worst. I got the same boy in my class that next year. He scored at the Proficient level on the PSSA[3] in language arts and math, the first time around. I was like, he was never (laughs) – 'the worst,' you know what I'm saying? But from her perspective, that's what he was. And that's how she treated him, to the point where he couldn't succeed, but with the right opportunity, he succeeded."

Kamau dribbled the ball with one hand. He passed the ball to Terence just as the deejay mixed in LL Cool J's "I Need Love." Terence laughed, and rapped along as the song played: When I'm alone in my room, sometimes I stare at the wall, and in the back of my mind I hear my conscience call. Telling me I need a girl who's as sweet as a dove. For the first time in my life, I see I need love (Smith, 1987).

"Maaaaaaaaaaaan! LL changed the game when he dropped this one! Nobody was talking about love and stuff like that before L. He made it okay for brothers to be all vulnerable and stuff."

Adam laughed at himself, "But you don't know nothing about that, Youngin'. You young cats are too hard for that, right?" Adam teased Eric.

Eric laughed with Adam, shook his head, and said, "Nah, we not all like that." Then, he looked back at Kamau, who had truly piqued his interest. "So you like helping the kids?" Kamau smiled and replied, "Oh man. I love it, and *I need love*. As soon as I started, my mentoring and tutoring experience kicked in, and I was a natural. From day one, I hit the ground running, and I've been educating kids, pushing kids ever since. Real talk: teaching isn't just being in the classroom; it's impacting the lives of people who will impact the future. I mean, when you teach, you're investing in a kid's life – not just book lessons. I take my job very seriously because when I'm in front of a kid, I'm literally molding him. I am chipping away at that kid, and that can mean life or death for a young Black male, you feel me? So I take great honor in having the opportunity to teach kids that are not my own because I know that I'm going to go in there and treat them like my own."

"You talk a lot about all the good stuff – how much you love your job and the kids, but it can't be all that hot, right? I'm saying...what do you hate about it?"

Kamau stood up, facing the court, and stretched his arms above his heads, sighed, and put his hands on hips. Then, he turned to Eric with a serious, almost sad, look on his face and responded, "When I first came to the Hill, the school principal told me that I must..." Kamau changed his voice to mock his principal's tone, "*refrain from showing the children any hands-on affection.*"

He finished, "She said that only a high five or fist bump were appropriate forms of touch for me. When I met the district superintendent, a Brother, he told me that as a Black man, I needed to be extra careful and that I needed to make sure I didn't touch the kids because it would be misconstrued. When I was working in Cheyney, the parents encouraged hugs and affection, you know? They were happy to know that their kids came to a teacher that gave them love and was able to give them a hug and calm them down. But in the Hill, that kind of affection ain't welcome from a Black man. I really hate that. I don't like paying taxes either, but I just have to deal with that." Kamau shrugged his shoulders and looked back at the guys playing ball on the court.

After their game was over, Kamau gave Eric his number and told him to hit him up the next time he was in Pittsburgh or if he wanted someone to talk to about college. The guys exchanged dap[4] and went their separate ways: Adam, Terence, and Kamau went back to Frederick Douglass, and Eric crossed the street and entered his apartment building. As he waited for the elevator, Eric hummed the rhythm to "Star in Da Hood." The elevator arrived, and as Eric attempted to open the door, Trent pulled the door closed and said, "Yo, take the stairs." The building elevator was often used for illegal business transactions, and Eric understood Trent's command to mean that either drug dealing or pimping was happening on the elevator, so he heeded the warning and took the stairs. Trent was a well-known drug dealer who Eric did not want to cross because he knew that would mean some form of retaliation. Besides, this was nothing new for him, and he was feeling energized after the time he spent with Kamau, Adam, and Terence anyway.

When Eric left his 10th floor apartment earlier that afternoon, he had no idea he would meet such cool "old dudes." As he returned to his apartment, he was thoughtful. He walked over to the kitchen table and picked up the pile of college applications. He looked at the one on the top, picked up a pencil off the table, found the "Major" section, and erased the checkmark he had placed in the "Undecided" box. He sat down in the chair, placed the applications down in front of him, and looked out the window overlooking Rucker Park. After a few minutes, he looked down at the application, and then checked the box next to "Elementary Education."

4   **Black Masculinity, Heteronormativity, & Eros: Oh My!**

I used a critical race theory lens to critique heteronormative notions of Black masculinity and eros in the classroom. In the CCS, we hear Kamau and

Adam talk about the struggle Kamau faces because of the intersection of his Blackness with his maleness. Heteronormative ideologies would pit him as not interested in working with young children, as these "rules" dictate that teaching is women's work, and the classroom is not a safe place for Black masculinity. The concept of homosexuality enters the conversation because one of the stigmas associated with men who teach is that since they are doing "women's work," they must be effeminate or gay.

Though the friends joke about this topic ("yo mama knows he ain't gay"), this was a point of indignation for the gentlemen in the study. In fact, during the interviews, several of them made a point to declare their heterosexuality ("I have a girlfriend" or "I'm not gay"). Kamau expresses the sadness and frustration the study participants feel as they bear the weight of constantly pushing back against these oppressive structures that reify and perpetuate heteronormativity in P-12 schools.

As I talked with the Black male teachers who participated in this study, I admired the level of passion that they shared with me. Perhaps, I was particularly open to this purpose because I see the world through the eyes of a hip-hop feminist who thoroughly relates to feminist critical pedagogy's "insistence of *not* engaging the mind/body split" (hooks, 1994, p. 193).

However, many of them spoke at some point during their one-on-one interviews or during the FBFG about "passion" as it relates to them as teachers and as it relates to their reasons for teaching. This was particularly intriguing because the construction of masculinity in America has done such a disservice that it is typically not safe to be a Black man who cares – especially if one considers himself "hip-hop."

However, the gentlemen in this study have unlearned this distinction, and Kamau embodies that notion. Through him, we see how much the participants believe that passion and love are necessary emotions to have as fuel for the purpose for teaching. Kamau was first introduced to the concept of teaching through volunteer work. His experience as a tutor and volunteer gave him the opportunity to interact directly with children who did not have significant Black male figures in their lives. For Kamau, his empathy compelled his desire to work with young children.

For Kamau, eros was present, and his body and soul were parts of his overall teaching experience. He stated that he "fell in love" with the students. He spoke openly of how much he "loved" student teaching, how much he "loves" the kids, and of how much "love" filled the school. He was unapologetic as he talked about his experience working with his fourth graders. However, being splashed in the face with the harsh reality of gendered racism – a reality in which it is unacceptable for a Black man to express any kind of physical emotion toward his students "because it *can and will* be seen as something more" was painful for Kamau. He was hurt that his passion for teaching and his love for his students could be "misconstrued" as sexual misconduct.

Thus, Kamau represented the battles the 9 gentlemen had with the stigma attached to showing "too much" love for their students. Because of the stigma of Black men doing White women's work and the stereotypes associated with Black masculinity, they were bound to "highfive" and "fist bump" their students instead of giving hugs that more effectively would have demonstrated the 9 gentlemen's love and compassion for their students.

5   Conclusion

As I wrote this chapter, I recalled images of the first Black U.S. president, Barack Obama (2008–2016). Truly embraced by the hip-hop generation, he made himself vulnerable on many occasions. A perfect example of this is much of the shock regarding Obama's public displays of care and concern, and even tears, in the wake of his re-election in 2011 and the aftermath of the Sandy Hook Elementary School shootings in 2012. As president, he openly displayed passion for his wife and two daughters as well as for the people of the United States – especially those who were experiencing extreme pain and/or misfortune. Obama can be seen wiping away tears as he sorrowfully addressed the public regarding the shootings of 26 children and adults at Sandy Hook in Newtown, Connecticut. In an America that does not make it easy for Black men to display passion without vilification, Obama proved himself to be a leader who transgresses – as were the men in this study. They may have not been leaders of the U.S. government, but in their classrooms, they were leaders who led with compassion and love.

The 9 gentlemen who shared their life stories with me cared for "other people's children" (Delpit, 1988) as if they were their own. They yearned to embrace their students. They hurt when their students were hurt. They cared about their students' cognitive, social, and emotional well-being. They brought fruit to school to share with their students and attended their basketball games. They visited their homes and built partnerships with their families and communities. They created authentic learning experiences in their classrooms by integrating science and technology with music. They built their students' self-esteem by teaching them that the music they loved and the dialect they spoke were a beautiful part of their overall being, and they were welcome in the academic space they shared. These Black men led by example. And Kamau Miller represented their spirit, their passion for service, and commitment to changing young people's lives.

This composite counterstory focused on Black men who teach elementary school and love what they do. They are "the few," and unless teachers and teacher educators begin to focus more on "the few," educators will continue to perpetuate a tradition in an educational system that unjustly marginalizes specific groups of people. When we shift our focus to "the few," Black male teachers, educators and the general public will no longer ask "real men *or* real teachers?" because they will understand that real men *are* real teachers.

Notes

1 A "pound" is an "urban" term used to describe a clasp of hands similar to a handshake.
2 Translation: "Do you play ball here regularly?"
3 PSSA refers to the Pennsylvania System School Assessment, Pennsylvania's statewide standardized test for children in grades 3–8. A Proficient score indicates that the child is considered on grade level.
4 Another form of acknowledgement and/or form of affection, similar to a pound. "Dap" could be when one person taps the side of one fist on top of the side of the recipient's fist and vice versa; dap could be the same as a "pound."

References

Bell, D. (1992). *Faces at the bottom of the well: The permanence of racism.* New York, NY: Basic Books.

Cook, D. A. (2013). Blurring the boundaries: The mechanics of creating composite characters. In M. Lynn & A. D. Dixson (Eds.), *Handbook of critical race theory in education* (pp. 181–193). New York, NY: Routledge.

Delpit, L. D. (1988). The silenced dialogue: Power and pedagogy in educating other people's children. *Harvard Educational Review, 58*(3), 280–298.

Facebook. (2016, October 20). *What are the privacy settings for groups?* Retrieved from https://www.facebook.com/help/220336891328465?helpref=popular_topics

Gibson, J. R. (2009). *Why Black men don't teach and why we should: Understanding the existing African-American male teacher shortage.* New York, NY: KITABU Publishing.

hooks, b. (1994). *Teaching to transgress: Education as a practice of freedom.* New York, NY: Routledge.

hooks, b. (2004). *We real cool: Black men and masculinity.* New York, NY: Routledge.

Howard, T. C. (2008). Who really cares? The disenfranchisement of African American males in pre-k-12 schools: A critical race theory perspective. *Teachers College Record, 110*(5), 954–985.

Lapayese, Y. V. (2007, September). Understanding and undermining the racio-economic agenda of no child left behind: Using critical race methodology to investigate the labor of bilingual teachers. *Race, Ethnicity, and Education, 10*(3), 309–321.

McCready, L. T. (2010). *Making space for diverse masculinities.* New York, NY: Peter Lang.

Mutua, A. D. (2006). Theorizing progressive Black masculinities. In A. D. Mutua (Ed.), *Progressive Black masculinities* (pp. 3–41). New York, NY: Routledge.

Sargent, P. P. (2001). *Real men or real teachers? Contradictions in the lives of men elementary school teachers.* Harriman, TN: Men's Studies Press.

Smith, J. T. (1987). I need love [Recorded by J. T. Smith a. k. a. L L Cool J]. *On bigger and deffer* [CD]. New York, NY: Def Jam & Columbia Records.

Solorzano, D. G., & Yosso, T. J. (2002). Critical race methodology: Counter-storytelling as an analytical framework for education research. *Qualitative Inquiry, 8*(1), 23–44.

Villaverde, L. E. (2008). *Feminist theories and education.* New York, NY: Peter Lang Publishing.

CHAPTER 9

We're Not Misbehaving: Cultivating the Spirit of Defiance in Black Male Students

Marlon C. James, Kelly Ferguson, Willie C. Harmon Jr. and Kevin L. Jones

The overrepresentation of children of color, particularly African Americans, in a variety of school disciplinary outcomes has been documented for over the past 25 years (Skiba, Michael, Nardo, & Peterson, 2002). Additionally, Skiba, Horner, Chung, Karega Rausch, May, and Tobin (2011) reported, "Students of color have been found to be suspended at rates two to three times that of other students, and similarly overrepresented in office referrals, corporal punishment, and school expulsion" (p. 86). The federal Office for Civil Rights (2014) analysis revealed that while Black students represent only 16% of the student population nationally, they are 32% of suspensions and 42% of students expelled from U.S. public schools. In comparison, White students are 51% of US public school students, but are underrepresented in suspensions (31%) and expulsions (40%) relative to their proportion of the student population. These disparities are magnified when considering the intersections of race, gender and school disciplinary patterns. Research confirms that boys of color are over 4 times as likely as girls to receive school discipline (Monroe, 2006; Skiba et al., 2002; Skiba et al., 2011). A national survey of schools concluded that among males, Blacks were 3 times more likely than Whites to receive out-of-school suspensions (Office for Civil Rights, 2014). Intersectionality research has further concluded that Black male students are most often disciplined for subjective infractions such as "defiance," "disrespect," and "insubordination," (Skiba et al., 2011; Fenning & Rose, 2007; Gregory & Weinstein, 2008; Losen & Martinez, 2013).

Moreover, several theories have been offered in an attempt to explain why these disparities persist. Cultural mismatch theories are forwarded as one possible explanation for Black males' disproportionality in subjective areas of discipline. Accordingly, cultural mismatch theories posit that conflict arises when teachers' cultural backgrounds differ from their students (Milner, 2010). African American pupils tend to have a distinct cultural orientation based on their African heritage (Monroe, 2006), which are often marginalized in Eurocentric classrooms. Without culturally sensitivity and responsiveness among educators, too often Black male students' attitudes, speech, behaviors, referents, and impassioned or emotive interactional patterns are misconstrued as combative or argumentative (Monroe, 2006; Skiba et al., 2011).

Another line of research takes a more sociological or systems approach to understanding the persistent nature of Black male overrepresentation in school discipline. Mincy (2006) and the National Urban League (2007) assert that a school-to-prison pipeline is animated by the misapplication of "zero tolerance" policies, which were designed to eradicate drugs and weapons from schools through harsh punishments. This approach was designed to make schools safer, but was expanded, creating harsher penalties for all student misbehavior. The result has been disproportionate numbers of Black males being pushed out of schools into the prison industrial complex and economic disenfranchisement (Mincy, 2006). This "school to prison pipeline" is most concentrated in urban schools among low income, African American male learners. These two competing lines of inquiry (cultural and structural) converge in classrooms as teachers and Black male students interact.

1   Critical Race Theory

Guiding our orientation toward Black males' educational, social, and professional development is Critical Race Theory (CRT). CRT has five key tenets to guide research: (1) the centrality of race and racism, (2) challenge given to the dominant perspective, (3) commitment to social justice, (4) value placed on experiential knowledge, and (5) the value of interdisciplinary knowledge and multiple perspectives (Kohli & Solorzano, 2012). In our research on Black males, we found tenets 1 (centrality of race/racism) and 4 (experiential knowledge, voice or courterstorytelling) were most germane.

2   Asset-Based Frameworks for Black Male Development

Asset-based frameworks, counter deficit thinking and problem-centered research on Black males and can provide positive and practical insights to support Black male development. Milner (2010) addressed cultural conflict as that which occurs when teachers' cultural background and expectations of classroom behavior differ from students' cultural orientations. Milner forwards the idea that many times teachers are quick to discipline students for behaviors they see as socially unacceptable before teaching the child the expectations. Because behavior norms can differ greatly from one culture to another, it is vital that teachers take this into account when educating and disciplining students. Rather than trying to "fix" students and remediate them to catch up with their "normal" peers, it is important to recognize the cultural knowledge that students bring to the classroom and build upon it through means that allow creativity and critical thinking to occur (Milner, 2010).

Another asset-based framework to consider is *Blackmaleness*, which focuses on how highly educated African American males develop amidst multiple forms of oppression (James & Lewis, 2014). Despite the educational consequences of limited social, political and economic opportunity, Black males can navigate systems of oppression to obtain a measure of academic and career success (James & Lewis, 2014). Blackmaleness is a multidimensional, shifting, and oftentimes contradictory reality of Black males that consists of two extremes and a void that must be traversed through contemplation, choice and chance to solidify a truer Black male identity. Blackmaleness is "theorized as a transgenerational collective force, organized to contest, defy, resist, and persist despite the presence of social barriers particularly constructed to make war with the potential of Black males in American society and education" (James & Lewis, 2014, p. 7). Knowledge of this construct can help teachers develop and embrace approaches informed by the lived experiences of successful Black males (James & Lewis, 2014; Lewis, James, Hancock, & Hill-Jackson, 2008). Blackmaleness conceptually provides a perspective that departs from dysfunctional ideologies that tether Black male learners to expected mediocrity (James & Lewis, 2014).

3   A Spirit of Defiance

For the remainder of this chapter, we explore Black male students' "misbehaving" or defiance as an early indicator of leadership potential rather than a marker of social deviance. For the purposes of this study, we assert that defiance is a personal and collective set of resistance strategies that evolved to counter the economic, racial and social constraints unique to Black male life in U.S. society and schools. Our intentional focus on the lived experiences of successful Black men yields a clearer understanding of the developmental pathways, processes and educational supports needed to promote maturation among Black male youth. Defiance for these participants began as "misbehaving" in the classroom, but evolved into a set of essential personal, social and cultural traits which they employ in their personal and professional lives. In this light, defiance as a framework can inform new approaches for teachers, schools and communities to support the development of Black male youth through the cultivation of a *spirit of defiance*.

When defiance is channeled constructively, Black males use it to foster productive academic, social and professional lives while countering negative stereotypes. Defiance often begins as "misbehaving" in classrooms but evolves into a set of essential personal, social and cultural leadership traits among college educated Black males.

One guiding research question was addressed in our study: How do successful Black men develop socially, academically and professionally? The researchers' analysis of 8 college educated Black males' lived experiences provides important insights into why teachers usually struggle to understand and relate to Black male students. Intersectionality research as a mode of inquiry has encouraged researchers to integrate the impact of interlocking systems of oppressions related to race, class and gender (Simien, 2007). Increasingly, educational researchers have turned to intersectionality research to offer fresh perspectives on persistent and unresolved issues of social justice in education (Davis, Brunn-Bevel, & Olive, 2015). Here we examine how the intersection of race and gender impacts educational and professional development of African American males in concert with the goal of remediating their overrepresentation in school disciplinary actions. This led to the development of an inductive framework entitled a spirit of defiance.

Participants were selected using purposive sampling to ensure that participants had experience with the phenomenon being studied. Accordingly, participants needed to be Black males 25 or older who demonstrated success as defined by their (a) *educational attainment* (a minimum of an associate's degree or professional certification), (b) *employment* (current working professionals), and (c) *leadership* (those who provide service in the community as mentors to Black male youth for a minimum of three years. The average participant was 34 years old, and all had earned either a bachelor's or advanced degree).

4   Acts of Academic Defiance

Data revealed acts of academic defiance as an emergent theme which described how participants held a positive academic identity of themselves contrary to the negative imaging of Black males. Acts of academic defiance allowed Black males exposed to images of Black male intellectual inferiority to develop positive academic identities, primarily through culturally responsive educational experiences. Participants reported experiencing firsthand, through stories from other Black males and various forms of social media, a daily assault of negative images and stories about Black men. In their lives, this occurred throughout their schooling experiences to varying degrees and included insults by everyone from teachers to peers. They recalled terms like "incompetent," "unintelligent," "stupid," and "lazy" being used about themselves and other Black males. Despite these challenges, participants demonstrated positive scholar identities and high intellectual capacity through their high grade point averages in college, leadership roles within school organizations, their athletic achievements connected to school-based sports, and their ability to balance all of these responsibilities. While these acts of academic defiance were individually unique, they evolved within the context of culturally responsive classrooms.

Participants in this study also identified elements of culturally responsive pedagogy (CRP) in their interviews and discussed how these experiences were important throughout their elementary and post-secondary schooling experiences. CRP is teaching that uses the cultural knowledge, prior experiences, frames of reference, and performance styles of ethnically diverse students to make learning encounters more relevant and effective for students (Gay, 2013). Participants articulated how they valued their cultural backgrounds being affirmed through the use of textbooks that addressed "real issues," "local problems," and "the Black Experience."

Simply being exposed to relevant texts was not enough. Rather, *how* teachers used curriculum materials during class-time proved critical for Black males. The participants described how their teachers who they learned the most from seemed to focus more on how abstract ideas could be used to solve real-world problems. This practical application of knowledge heightened both their interest and engagement during lessons. In turn, they were able to recall abstract facts because "the teachers used examples that I could relate to." These higher levels of motivation allowed them to persist when concepts were initially difficult to understand.

Teacher discourse inside and outside of the classroom about relevant issues tied to the curriculum promoted the development of academic defiance because they modeled such defiance for their students in how they refused to teach in a manner that disengaged students. Perhaps the key separator between the effective teachers described by participants and those deemed less effective was the ability of the teacher to tailor corrective guidance, content and instruction to the unique need of Black males. This was only possible when a teacher had deeper insights to Black males through their relations with the community, parents and students themselves. While CRP was found to enrich the learning experiences of the Black male participants, it was found to be an irregular occurrence throughout their schooling. Yet, these teachers were pillars of defiance precisely because they were able to include relevant learning experiences amidst years of absent voices and positive images.

5   Acts of Social Defiance

Acts of social defiance are individual and collective strategies designed to productively respond to negative images and social experiences common among Black males. One participant, Joe, an educator, noted that "I constantly reminded myself that we [Black men] are more than what we see on TV or the news." Joe continued by recalling that

> as a kid growing up in the city between the gangs, the drugs, the guns, the music, the poverty and family issues, I had to decide what kind of man I wanted to be. And that's without really understanding what that meant, what questions to ask or a quality example of manhood, until I was fourteen.

This dilemma was particularly pronounced for participants who did not have a father figure during their elementary years. They reported often examining models of manhood found in television and movies (e.g., "Cosby Show," "A Different World," "Boys in the Hood"), music, and "the streets" to find their ways.

For these men, mentorship found in their communities provided answers and guidance as they tried to figure a path forward. Joe goes on to describe two pressing matters that Black young men faced in his community:

> ...well you had to make some choices. Moms didn't have a lot of money, so how are you going to help out? How I am going to get the clothes and shoes I need to go to school and not be made fun of? I had to hustle, but my mom didn't want us involved with drugs. So, me and older brother, we took peoples' groceries to their cars, cleaned yards, collected cans and bottles, then gave the money to our mother to help out. My mom was so strong that she forced us on the right path until high school. I don't think these young brothers are bad even now days, they just don't know which direction to go in, then they make a wrong choice.

A general theme among participants was access to a network of supports that assisted them in successfully navigating the social uncertainty associated with coming of age as a Black male. For some participants, it was the mentorship received from trusted individuals, older Black males usually, who provided guidance about traversing these local community obstacles and how to navigate well in a predominantly White society. These mentors typically emerged during the middle school years, lived in the community, worked outside of the school, and helped to clarify the type of character that defied negative social images of Black males.

Also, the role of Black fraternities for 4 of the participants were particularly instrumental to their success beginning in college. Participants expressed a sense of belonging through this brotherhood of men who shared experiences unique to Black men. This group consisted of individuals who, as participant Byron described, were

> like-minded…they are really spiritual, they're in the church, they love God, like I love God. They're passionate about the community. They are successful, African Americans who are trying to progress, maybe entrepreneurs, whether it's through the ranks of moving up through their jobs but they all are like-minded like me.

Organizations like Black fraternities promoted acts of social defiance that countered negative social stigmas because the focus was on collegiate education, responsible citizenship, and community service.

Another site of defiance as described by 5 participants was the African American church. Joe described the impact of his mentor on his development:

> When I turned fourteen I met my mentor; he lived in the community and owned a small business. He was a Christian; I mean he lived it. He gave me a job, which I worked after school and on the weekend. He introduced me to Godly wisdom. He wanted to help me know how to treat other people, love other people, how to work hard in school and on my job, how to treat women, and how to honor my mother. He became what it meant to be a Godly Black man to me, and he changed my life.

Other participants articulated similar impacts about their involvement in local churches, which provided them social skills, life lessons, character development, moral character, opportunities to serve others, and a network of resources to resolve almost any challenge. Overall, while acts of social defiance are individual actions, they were born from a network of community support structures that enriched the lives of successful Black males.

6   **Acts of Professional Defiance**

Acts of professional defiance manifested as deliberate practices that participants engaged in to contest or defy the daily challenges associated with being a Black male professional. Like in their academic and social spheres, participants described continuously evolving professionally to meet the daily challenges associated with their professional lives. Participants shared a plethora of epithets used throughout media and on their jobs to describe Black men generally in the U.S. and elsewhere. Unfortunately, these images were also projected upon these college educated professionals. Joe lamented, "You have to overcome all these stereotypes starting day one of your job if you hope to be successful; even still you can be great at your job but it won't stop the stereotyping." A shared sentiment among participants as expressed by Henry was that these images are "controlled by individuals or decision makers that do not look like us and/or do not have the best intent [for us] even though they may not vocalize it." This sample of college educated men in fact believed themselves to be "productive," "hard working," "civic-minded," "intelligent," "caring," "moral," and "ambitious" men who added value to the companies they worked for. But, due to direct patterns of interactions and microaggressions in their workplaces, they felt "unappreciated," "unwanted," "devalued," and "overlooked."

One aspect of participants' success as professional Black men was attributed to an awareness of the stereotypes concerning Black males. This awareness equipped participants with an understanding of how they needed to present themselves to others and how to respond to perceived mistreatment. Participants also employed advice from mentors concerning challenges faced by Black male professionals as well as suggestions for navigating these barriers. Although participants expressed a positive professional concept of themselves, they felt the need to take additional steps to ensure their success. Being positive even in the face of mistreatment, working early and late, and putting in extra effort and energy were all perceived as necessary strategies to demonstrate their intellectual and professional capacities to others and to avoid being stereotyped.

Overall, defiance or determination to define one's own character and potential academically, socially, and professionally was a central experience among successful Black males. Participants articulated strong, positive conceptions of self and their various capacities to weather difficult and unsupportive environments. Although their experiences academically, socially, and professionally didn't always reflect their self-image and affirm their worth, participants' internal drive to succeed and access to support networks allowed them to defy society's expectations of Black men. This success, however, could not have been achieved without participants' network of supports found in their families, mentors, culturally responsive classrooms, fraternities, churches, and the wider community.

7   A Developmental Continuum

As noted earlier, we began with this question: How do successful Black men develop academically, social and professionally? We assert that defiance is set of resistance strategies developed to counter economic, racial and social constraints unique to Black male life in American society and schools.

Yet, *how* speaks to a process of development. Among the participants, defiance began as "misbehaving" in classrooms. By incorporating strategies and insights from support structures, however, defiance evolved into a set of essential personal, social and cultural leadership traits. It is important to note that defiance is ever evolving to counter new obstacles, but it generally manifests in three unique types of defiance at different iterations of development. Table 9.1 outlines developmental markers of defiance of *agitation, assimilation,* and *amelioration* that successful Black males utilized throughout their lives. Table 9.1 also provides strategies for educators to constructively respond to a spirit of defiance as a developmental goal throughout P-12 schooling.

Schools play a critical role in either cultivating or diminishing the spirit of defiance in Black male youth. Among the participants in this study, few teachers impacted their long-term development, but those who did were described as practicing what is commonly termed culturally responsive teaching (Gay, 2013). Unfortunately, most P-12 schools are informed by developmental theories that discourage cultivating defiance in students, particularly among Black males (James & Lewis, 2014). Defiance is criminalized and penalized, leaving far too many students without an essential tool that could promote their success. A spirit of defiance in pre-K-12 classrooms can become an essential leadership trait among Black males and should be cultivated rather than penalized and criminalized in schools.

So, what can schools and teachers do? First, realize that any form of suppressed defiance in pre-K-12 classrooms can hinder the development of Black male students (see Table 9.1).

Suppressing a spirit of defiance can lead to unchecked misbehaving (agitation), strategic conformity given threat level in the classroom environment (assimilation), or disengagement and disinterest (amelioration) all constitute a form of under-investment in these students by teachers and schools, which will ultimately add to preexisting patterns of underdevelopment and underperformance. Table 9.1 provides detailed descriptions of the three expressions of defiance, and how they appear in classrooms, and collegiate and professional settings.

In short, regardless of how they express defiance, Black males need structured attention, awareness and advocacy. Structures within schools (teachers, staff, administrators, policy, instruction and procedures) must become more attentive and responsive to student needs. If several points of school data converge negatively around attendance, suspensions, and test scores for the majority of Black male students, systemic action is necessary.

Noguera (2003), though, reported on the unfortunate tendency of ignoring documented needs of Black male learners. Attending to all of the developmental needs of any group of students is well beyond the capacity of

TABLE 9.1   *The spirit of defiance developmental continuum*

Defiance spirit	Suppressed (PK-12 classrooms)	Evolving (College)	Dynamic (Career)	Cultivation goal *P-12 Strategy*
1. Defiance as agitation	Appears as misbehaving in the classroom, but should be considered a sign of disengagement and resistance to unjust educational experiences and environments.	Appears as a challenge to authority and order, but is actually an inability to make peace with inequality.	Appears as head-strong and uncompromising, but is creative, divergent and socially-just leadership.	The will to agitate or defy the norm is the primary sign of leadership potential among Black male youth. *Provide classroom, school and community leadership opportunities with mentoring.*
2. Defiance as assimilation	Appears as behaving in socially acceptable ways, but may be in need of academic, social or emotional support.	Appears as an outgoing, highly social person with varying groups, but may be overcompensating to avoid negative stereotyping.	Appears harmless and unassuming, but is determined to leverage access, credentials, influence, and their network to effect positive change from within "the system."	The skill and discernment to blend in or to be brazen is an essential method for overcoming social and professional oppression. *Foster relationships with quiet well-behaved boys, so that you can gain a clearer understanding of their academic, social and emotional needs.*

TABLE 9.1   *The spirit of defiance developmental continuum (cont.)*

Defiance spirit	Suppressed (PK-12 classrooms)	Evolving (College)	Dynamic (Career)	Cultivation goal *P-12 Strategy*
3. Defiance as amelioration	Appears as disengagement and disinterest in class, but may be an expression of unrecognized "giftedness."	Appears as confused about pursuing one's professional goals or moral-social responsibilities.	Appears as a multi-talented virtuoso, but he is maximizing his creative capacities to balance professional goals and moral-social calling.	The desire to make a difference, while achieving professional success often drives Black males into leadership roles as creative problem solvers. *Increasingly expose students to curriculum and educational experiences that apply content knowledge to real-world issues featuring the perspectives and contributions of Black male authors.*

any teacher. Hence, school-wide systems are required that provide classroom and community supports.

Yet, before action can be taken, schools should seek greater understanding of the "why" and "how" of defiance among Black male students. The following three questions make reference to more detailed descriptions found in Table 9.1, and can guide teachers or a school to greater awareness of their Black male students.

1 If agitated males disengage and resist unjust educational experiences and environments, how might classroom climates, interactions with staff, and common instructional approaches contribute to their agitation?
2 If Black males students passively conform and are not given the same attention as those demonstrating behavioral problems, how could we learn about their unmet academic, social or emotional needs?
3 If "giftedness" is equally distributed across racial and gender groups, how can we more accurately identify and serve "gifted" Black male students?

Lastly, advocacy is required by both teachers and administrators. This effort must begin by understanding how success evolves among men of color. The mistake is to study the problem and only then begin enacting solutions based on that problem. For example, knowing that Black males are overrepresented in discipline outcomes is not the starting point for solutions. Programmatic solutions must be informed by the lived experiences of successful mature Black males (James & Lewis, 2014). Developmental research (James & Lewis, 2014) provides clear roadmaps for the types of educational and community support structures that promote academic and professional success among Black males. Teachers and schools can also start with men in their schools and communities for a more contextualized plan although mature men of color should be the center piece of any action plan.

8   Conclusion

Critical Race Theory (CRT) was the theoretical framework employed for this study. Focusing on the schooling, social and professional experiences of Black males acknowledged CRT's prioritization of the experiences and realities of those typically dispossessed and marginalized (Ladson-Billings, 2010; Kohli & Solorzano, 2012). Ledesma and Calderon (2015) offered a review of CRT research over the past twenty years and recommend that CRT researchers make direct application of research findings to PreK-12 schools, and explore intersectionality research for new insights into pressing educational challenges. In this light, we offered a continuum of how defiance develops and manifest in P-12 schools, college and career life spans. This approach complicates traditional identity-centric approaches to intersectionality research by considering how defiance evolves among Black males at different developmental intersections (P-12 classrooms, college and career). This equity research practice specifically humanizes Black males by considering how they evolve through a life span approach. This chapter also detailed specific recommendations for systemic changes in schools that would promote the positive cultivation of the spirit of defiance among Black male youth. The fact is that Black males will be defiant as youth and later as men. The spirit of defiance is required to effectively transverse the limited opportunity structures in a society determined to relegate African American males to the status of a second-class citizen. In this context, Black males must be defiant and persistently misbehave until the day their humanity is fully affirmed in American society and nurtured in US educational institutions.

References

Davis, D. J., Brunn-Bevel, R. J., & Olive, J. L. (Eds.). (2015). *Intersectionality in educational research.* Sterling VA: Stylus.

Duncan, G. A. (2002). Beyond love: A critical race ethnography of the schooling of adolescent Black males. *Equity & Excellence in Education, 35*(2), 131–143.

Fenning, P., & Rose, J. (2007). Overrepresentation of African American students in exclusionary discipline the role of school policy. *Urban Education, 42*(6), 536–559.

Ferguson, A. A. (2000). *Bad boys: Public school and the making of Black masculinity.* Ann Arbor, MI: University of Michigan Press.

Garibaldi, A. M. (2007). The educational status of African American males in the 21st century. *Journal of Negro Education, 76*(3), 324–333.

Gay, G. (2013). Teaching to and through cultural diversity. *Curriculum Inquiry, 43*(1), 48–70.

Gregory, A., & Weinstein, R. S. (2008). The discipline gap and African Americans: Defiance or co-operation in the high school classroom. *Journal of School Psychology, 46*(4), 455–475.

James, M. C., & Lewis, C. (2014). Kindling the spark of Black male genius through education. *Journal of African American Males in Education, 5*(2), 267–282.

Kohli, R., & Solorzano, D. (2012). Teachers, please learn our names! Racial microaggressions and the K-12 classroom. *Race Ethnicity and Education, 15*(4), 441–462.

Ladson-Billings, G. (2010). Just what is critical race theory and what's it doing in a nice field like education? *International Journal of Qualitative Studies in Education, 11*(1), 7–24.

Ledesma, M., & Calderon, D. (2015). Critical race theory in education: A review of past literature and a look to the future. *Qualitative Inquiry, 21*(3), 206–222.

Lewis, C., James, M., Hancock, S., & Hill-Jackson, V. (2008). Framing African American students' success and failure in urban settings. *Urban Education, 43*(2), 127–153.

Losen, D. J., & Martinez, T. E. (2013). *Out of school and off track: The overuse of suspensions in American middle and high schools.* Retrieved from http://files.eric.ed.gov/fulltext/ED541735.pdf

Love, B. J. (2004). Brown plus 50 counter-storytelling: A critical race theory analysis of the "majoritarian achievement gap" story. *Equity & Excellence in Education, 37*(3), 227–246.

Merriam, S. (2009). *Qualitative research.* San Francisco, CA: Jossey-Bass.

Milner IV, H. R. (2010). *Start where you are, but don't stay there: Understanding diversity, opportunity gaps, and teaching in today's classrooms.* Cambridge, MA: Harvard Education Press.

Mincy, R. (Ed.). (2006). *Black males left behind.* Washington, DC: The Urban Institute Press.

Monroe, C. R. (2006). African American boys and the discipline gap: Balancing educators' uneven hand. *Educational Horizons, 84*(2), 102–111.

National Urban League. (2007). *The state of Black America 2007: Portrait of the Black male.* Silver Spring, MD: Beckham Publications Group.

Noguera, P. (2003). The trouble with Black boys: The role and influence of environmental and cultural factors on the academic performance of African American males. *Urban Education, 38*(4), 431–459.

Office for Civil Rights. (2014). *Data snapshot: School discipline.* Retrieved from https://www2.ed.gov/about/offices/list/ocr/docs/crdc-discipline-snapshot.pdf

Seidman, I. (2006). *Interviewing as qualitative research.* New York, NY: Teachers College Press.

Simien, E. (2007). Doing intersectionality research: From conceptual issues to practical examples. *Politics & Gender, 3*(2), 264–271. doi:10.1017/S1743923X07000086

Skiba, R. J., Horner, R. H., Chung, C. G., Karega Rausch, M., May, S. L., & Tobin, T. (2011). Race is not neutral: A national investigation of African American and Latino disproportionality in school discipline. *School Psychology Review, 40*(1), 85–107.

Skiba, R. J., Michael, R. S., Nardo, A. C., & Peterson, R. L. (2002). The color of discipline: Sources of racial and gender disproportionality in school punishment. *The Urban Review, 34*(4), 317–342.

Whiting, G. (2014). The scholar identity model: Black male success in the K-12 context. In F. A. Bonner II (Ed.), *Building on resilience: Models and frameworks of Black male success across the P-20 pipeline* (pp. 88–106). Sterling, VA: Stylus.

Willis, P. (1999). Looking for what it's really like: Phenomenology in reflective practice. *Studies in Continuing Education, 21*(1), 91–112.

Woodson, C. G. (2011). *The mis-education of the Negro.* New York, NY: Tribek. [Originally published 1933.]

CHAPTER 10

Black Girls Matter: An Intersectional Analysis of Young Black Women's Experiences and Resistance to Dominating Forces in School

Julia Daniel and Terrenda White

The overuse of harsh discipline for Black and Latino students in the United States has received increased attention as the racial disparity in discipline rates is connected to negative outcomes for impacted students (Gregory, Skiba, & Noguera, 2010; Losen, 2011). This attention, however, has often focused on the outcomes of Black male students, who are disproportionately represented through the *schoolhouse to jailhouse pipeline* (Morris, 2012), but largely ignores experiences of Black female students (Morris, 2016; Wun, 2014).

Young Black female students experience multiple and intersecting forms of oppression in schools – such as racism, sexism, classism, and homophobia – that can impede their academic success. For example, a recent report by Crenshaw, Ocen, and Nanda (2015) found that while Black male students are more frequently suspended than Black female students, Black female students were disproportionally suspended when compared to their White counterparts. While Black boys were suspended more than 3 times as often as White boys, whereas Black girls were suspended 6 times as often as White girls. Young women are also exposed to sexual harassment and violence, and more than 1 in 5 reported being sexually assaulted, with higher rates for LGBTQ populations. Women of color also face racial discrimination that includes being called racial slurs at much higher rates than White women (Chaudhry & Tucker, 2017).

As educational researchers with social justice orientations, we believe that centering experiences of Black girls in schools is a meaningful approach to understanding interlocking forms of oppression faced by students of color and facilitates interventions in schools that are comprehensive and inclusive (Davis, Brunn-Bevel, & Olive, 2015). As such, this chapter contributes to a growing body of research that attempts to understand how young Black women experience and resist measures of discrimination in both school and society. Open-ended interviews conducted with 6 Black women in South Florida helped to understand (a) intersectional challenges to educational attainment related to anti-Black racism, sexism, and classism and (b) repertoires of resistance to survive and persist in spite of challenging conditions.

1   Theoretical Framework

Intersectionality structures the main theoretical framework of this chapter, which is also infused with Black feminist theory to understand how the oppressive structures and cultures of anti-Black racism, class-based discrimination (classism) and sexism work as interlocking systems of domination in schools (Collins, 2000; Crenshaw, 2011; Evans-Winters, 2005; Evans-Winters & Esposito, 2010; Morris, 2016; Wun, 2014). An intersectional analysis implores us to understand interlocking systems of domination as mutually reinforcing in order to avoid overly simplistic solutions that seek to address one symptom of the underlying issue rather than understand and undermine the root causes of the dominating systems themselves.

   In the construction of Black gender ideology, low-income Black women are popularly portrayed and viewed as too strong, promiscuous, or aggressive (Collins, 2000). Attempts to surveil and regulate Black women's bodies and expressions of femininity appear as part of a political project to reinforce systems of domination (Ocen, 2012). In schools, similar forms of regulation have been observed as Black female students are subjected to a variety of punitive disciplining practices.

   Anti-Black racism has remained central to racial formation throughout U.S. history as myths of the lazy and criminal Black person persist and legitimize racist beliefs and policies (Collins, 2000; Dumas, 2016; Wun, 2014). Black people are currently the "paradigmatic objects of racialized state repression" (Wun, 2014, p. 4). Building on research that seeks to understand discriminatory structures through experiences of Black women (Crenshaw, 2011; Evans-Winters & Esposito, 2010; Wun, 2014), this research helps inform our understanding of intersecting forms of oppression through the experiences of young Black women and their strategies for resistance.

2   Disparate Treatment of Black Girls

Black female students are often treated in punitive ways in schools by adults who do not know or understand the kinds of challenges and circumstances facing women of color (Evans-Winters & Esposito, 2010). Stereotypes about low-income Black women inform how they are treated by adults in schools, including those who expect girls to be docile and who view Black girls' behaviors negatively as acts of defiance to dominant norms (Evans-Winters, 2005). Jones (2010) found that Black girls in Philadelphia navigated challenging and sometimes violent settings through a variety of strategies, while having to confront gendered and racialized stereotypes that positioned them as either "good" or "ghetto."

Morris (2016) found that Black women who deviate from dominant norms of White femininity are frequently subjected to criminalizing responses by adults. Disparate treatment is informed by "stereotypes of perceived moral deficit that manifests itself in the form of Black girls' perceived promiscuity or 'bad attitude,' typically associated with her being 'loud,' using profanity, wearing revealing clothing, and confronting people in positions of authority" (Blake et al. as cited in Morris, 2012, p. 9). However, this kind of behavior can be viewed as resilience to the combined effects of racism, sexism and classism, or as assertiveness that is found to be related to academic success (Morris, 2007, 2012). Hence, while the actions of Black girls often demonstrate important leadership and critical thinking skills, they are nonetheless regularly punished or disadvantaged by teachers who interpret their dress, language practices, and behaviors as disruptive, profane, and defiant (Campbell, 2012; Francis, 2012; Morris, 2007, 2016; Wun, 2016). Consequently, girls of color, and Black girls in particular, are not only likely subject to harsher forms of discipline for perceived misbehaviors rooted in implicit racial bias or explicit anti-Black racism, but also are inadvertently encouraged to be less assertive and active learners, reducing their potential as leaders in their schools and communities (Morris, 2007).

Wun (2016) found that school discipline policies and practices often decontextualized and depoliticized Black and Latina girls' behaviors by framing their challenges as individual problems and thus ignoring the ways that their struggles were related to structural inequality. Despite the fact that females in Wun's study experienced both interpersonal and structural forms of violence, she argued, "by defining the girls as problems, structural forms of violence, including violence from school authorities, are obscured in favor of disciplining and punishing the girls" (p. 6). Similarly, this chapter draws from previous research to examine how Black girls attending public schools in Florida experience and resist discriminatory discipline practices including structural forms of violence.

3   Research Approach[1]

By attempting to center this research in the standpoint of young Black women, we try to understand their experiences as illustrative of broader patterns of inequality that uphold bourgeois, white supremacist, heteronormative patriarchal culture (Harding, 2004). The research question guiding our study was: What can we learn about intersecting forms of oppression in schools and communities through the experiences and strategies for resistance of Black women? We used a combination of standpoint epistemology (Harding, 2004) and Black feminist theory (Collins, 2000) to develop our ethnographic case study design and interview protocols.

Dialogic interviews (Naples, 2003) were conducted with 6 Black women 18–21 years old who had attended school in the past 3 years in a large district in South Florida. One of the women was transgender and 2 of them identified as part of the LGBTQ community. They were all from low-income backgrounds and at least 2 were homeless. Their complex and multiplicative identities are shared here because they shaped their experiences in various ways that deepen our understanding of how to respond to their needs. We created pseudonyms for subjects to protect their identities.

4   Findings

Interviews demonstrated that subjects were negotiating complicated situations in schools and communities, conditions which were often challenging, dangerous, and sometimes supportive. Dominant ideas about them and their behaviors were prevalent such that they were simultaneously sexualized, stigmatized, controlled, and punished, all of which created vastly disparate educational opportunities for them.

4.1   *Discouraging Relationships with Teachers*

While some of the women had supportive teachers, the predominant experience was discouraging relationships. When Juicy would ask for more instruction from her teachers, she would get responses such as "I just explained it to you; you don't know how to do this?" This left her feeling mentally slow and embarrassed in front of her classmates. Many of interview subjects heard messages such as what one teacher told Jasmine: "At the end of the day it don't matter because I get my paycheck and I'm smarter than you." Such discouraging messages were common in what the subjects shared. For example, a teacher at an alternative school stated to Juicy, "You're here because you're a dropout and you didn't want no future." Negative messaging from teachers, often in front of other students, was humiliating.

Teachers' perceptions of the women's neighborhoods and parents' economic class also influenced how educators talked with and treated them as students. While many teachers are middle class, when working with low-income students, they "subject Black girls to a particular form of discipline, largely directed at their comportment" (Morris, 2007, p. 501). Brittany experienced her teachers talking badly to her about her mother's parenting skills and treating her differently because they negatively perceived her class background. She reported that teachers would talk about the neighborhood that she was from, which was among the poorest in the county, stating that kids from there were bad, had no one to watch over them, and might as well stay home.

Tiffany, who is transgender, had a particularly challenged relationship with her teachers who spoke unfavorably to her about her parents and her future prospects. Tiffany explained that her principal and teachers criticized her for the way in which she presented herself, alleging that her mother did not look after her or provide water for bathing. Her teachers told her that she would not amount to anything, and it would be hard for her to get a job anywhere except a fast-food restaurant. Tiffany reflected that it "makes you not want to go to school because I felt like everyone was against me and no one was with me." This is consistent with research about young women perceived as "ghetto," deemed as non-conforming, and subjected to criminalizing responses (Morris, 2012, 2016)

4.2   *Regulating Sexuality*

Many of the subjects also experienced or overheard teachers talking negatively about them for being perceived as overly sexual or for getting pregnant. They were told to act more "ladylike," wear less revealing clothing, keep their "legs closed," and not socialize with boys. Black women are regularly stigmatized for being sexually active and dependent financially on welfare programs (Roberts, 1998). Luker (1991) argued that when young women lack aspirations because of their disadvantaged place in life or their academic difficulties, they are more likely to drift into pregnancy, as it won't appear to threaten their options. This points to structural causes for disparities that are largely ignored in the current discourse that blames adolescent girls as too impulsive and ignorant to not become pregnant (Luker, 1991).

In schools, teachers would talk negatively about the girls who were pregnant in front of other students. One teacher told Brittany about another pregnant student: "If that was my daughter, I would have beat her." This type of shaming of females who were seen as sexually active or pregnant was common across the interviewees, but Juicy's experience stands out as particularly egregious. Pregnant at age 14, her mom told her teachers that she was pregnant.

> She told the whole world. I guess my teachers "cared" you know with quotations, they "cared" because they went half on me getting an abortion pill with my mom. My mom paid $400 and they paid $400 on a pill. But my mom did it sneaky – she crushed the pill up and put the pill in my food.

While the teachers' and mother's actions were likely well intended, denying her the choice over what to do with her body didn't respect her autonomy.

The messages they received in school around their sexuality functioned as attempts to control their bodies in a context where U.S. schooling generally does not encourage young people to explore and understand their sexuality and desires (Fine & McClelland, 2006). The discourse on young, low-income Black women's sexuality implies that being "good" is associated with sexual restraint and being sexually assertive risks reinforcing stereotypes of themselves as "hypersexual, unfeminine and immoral" (Froyum, 2010, p. 61).

4.3   Racialized Messages

Anti-Black racism in the schools was prevalent as many of the interview subjects heard negative messages about being Black or having dark skin. Juicy shared, "I got picked on a lot because of how dark I was...the teachers don't care, they picked on me too." Jasmine talked about a time at her high school in which the principal came into the class because the students were being too loud and said, "Your Black asses are in the class here making noise like animals."

Brittney often heard teachers talking about students from her neighborhood, which is very low-income, and teachers would suggest that their parents weren't taking care of them. "They'd talk about the other kid's shoes, picking on them in a way. They'd say that they [the students] were dirty, black, all that." Reinforcing anti-Black messages such as these can have negative consequences on Black students who can internalize ideas about their own inferiority (Morris, 2016). Juicy, for example, used to wish that she were White because she felt like White kids were more intelligent and received more attention.

4.4   Gendered Messaging

Some of the women in the study were reprimanded and disciplined for behaviors that weren't viewed as conforming to traditional gender roles. Polly, who identified as a tomboy, pointed out, "A female teacher said I should be more lady like – I act like a boy because I'll be more with the boys." Tiffany noticed that "a girl using inappropriate language, she'd get in-school suspension, but if a boy did, he'd be told 'don't let me hear you use that word again.'"

Many of the subjects understood that their teachers wanted them to dress in ways that aligned with what was deemed respectable for girls, including the rejection of clothing that was considered too masculine or too revealing for signs of promiscuity. Juicy would wear "boy clothes" to school and had short hair, eliciting "nagging and disrespecting" comments from her teachers about her attire. Juicy was also teased by both teachers and other kids for being "fat, ugly, and too Black, to the point where my self-esteem was very low." Ironically, while prescriptive or cautionary messages about expected norms of dress for the young women may have occurred under the auspices of care and protection for their safety, the messages worked to control and discipline their bodies and ultimately their means of self-expression in ways that reinforced systems of domination.

4.5   *Sexual Harassment*

Lopez (2003) found that "controlling images that are used to justify the exploitation of women who are deemed racially inferior" resulted in their being sexually harassed in the workplace (p. 158). In conversations with the women in our study, it was apparent that they were also being sexually harassed and assaulted at schools by security guards. Jasmine would hear teachers tell other female students that they were "going to be whores" because of how they dressed and simultaneously would see and experience regular sexual harassment from security guards. She shared that there was "one security guard if he saw you by yourself, he'd tap you on your butt. I snatched the broom from him and hit him and I got written up."

While one group of authority figures – teachers – at the school were regulating young women considered dressing promiscuously, another group of authority figures – security guards – were exploiting their power to harass and assault the young women. The combination of these forms of regulation and abuse demonstrated multiple and contradictory ways that Black women's bodies are simultaneously controlled and exploited.

4.6   *Supportive Relationships with Teachers*

In addition to difficult relationships with teachers, many of the women identified teachers who encouraged them to achieve through a combination of support and challenging work. The women often shared that these teachers understood the difficulties they faced outside of schools and did their best to compensate for what the adolescents might need. Jasmine spoke of one of her supportive teachers: "She was a real sweetheart – when you'd come to class she'd give you money if you were hungry, and she'd promise not to let things get back [to other teachers or students] if you wanted to talk to her about something." The teachers' backgrounds sometimes influenced their relationships with the youth. For example, Brittney shared that her Black teachers tended to talk with her and better understand her experiences by giving her equitable opportunities to learn in class.

The women appreciated teachers who were simultaneously supportive and challenging. Jasmine shared that she would do her work when the teachers did challenge her. Juicy recalled one teacher who was strict because she "wanted what's best for me. She always came to me positive. There was never a time when she slipped and didn't tell me about something positive I did." This combination of being both supportive and challenging is an effective way for encouraging Black students to succeed academically and that Black teachers can have important connections with Black students to promote their success (Perry, Steele, & Hilliard, 2003).

5   Resistance

Collins (2000) writes about the importance of Black women practicing self-definition as a means to resist assumptions underlying harmful stereotypes about themselves. By doing so, when they "choose to value those aspects of Afro-American womanhood that are stereotyped, ridiculed, and maligned in academic scholarship and the popular media, they are actually questioning some of the basic ideas used to control dominant groups in general" (Collins, 2000, p. 107). Jones (2010) found that the young women in her study embraced locally held beliefs about the value of female strength:

> This positive embrace and unapologetic expression of female strength, which contrasts with traditional white, middle-class conceptions of femininity, and the gendered expectations embedded in Black respectability, was considered necessary for Black women's survival and for the survival of the Black community. (p. 18)

The young women in our study similarly valued their ways of expressing themselves even when it was discouraged in schools, showing themselves to be agentic critical thinkers, drawing on their own cultural capital as a form of resistance (see Yosso, 2005). Jasmine was able to accomplish this by understanding multiple forms of knowledge and the value of her own intelligence, explaining that "some people have street knowledge and some have book knowledge." Polly was able to take the teacher's doubt and turn it into a positive challenge, sharing that "the fact that they doubt me makes me wanna work harder." This type of resilience represented their determination to succeed academically as well as their understanding of the importance of an education, even when their circumstances weren't always supportive.

Most of the interviewees demonstrated a type of resistance resembling Carter's (2005) description of *noncompliant believers* who view education as important for success but are either unable or unwilling to embrace the norms of the school. Since dominant powers define the social and cultural rules in a school that ultimately translate into success, the noncompliant believers face a predicament in that their rejection of these social and cultural mandates can be seen as self-defeating. "Noncompliant believers," Carter explained, "expose a critical social problem about our measurements of success and achievement. Implicitly they pose the question 'why can't success be multicultural'" (p. 164). Because many educators don't understand Black social capital, students who are marginalized often find power in their voice, but in schools they tend to be punished for it. As Black women are taught at home the importance of self-sufficiency and pushed to do well in school (Carter, 2005), they face a particular set of challenges negotiating school settings that use "discipline, punishment and the juvenile justice system to regulate identity and social status" (Morris, 2016, pp. 224–227). Teachers who could recognize that these women were reacting in understandable ways to their conditions and who can be both supportive and challenging tended to build the best relationships with them.

6   Discussion

This chapter builds on existing scholarship in the field of education that centers the educational experiences and needs of Black girls, who sometimes are overlooked in classed, gendered, and race-based structural analyses (Evans-Winters & Esposito, 2010). The interviewee's stories suggested that academic experiences and opportunities in schools for Black girls are circumscribed by distinct forms of marginalization enacted by authority figures at school. Despite multiple and intersecting forms of oppression Black women can face (Evans-Winter, 2005; Evans-Winter & Esposito, 2010), the women featured in this chapter highlight important forms of resistance and resilience.

In light of the deeply inequitable access to quality education and a gaping *educational debt* owed to Black students (Ladson-Billings, 2013), youth of color see ruptures in ideals of the social contract, which can lead to blatant noncompliance "rooted in an active rejection of middle-class norms" and "deliberately engage in behavior that will ensure their educational failure" (Noguera, 2009, p. 116). While the women who shared their stories here faced verbal stigmatization as and racialized gendered violence at schools, we see their engagement as well as disengagement as strategies for survival.

Similarly, current discourse surrounding issues like teen pregnancy and achievement obfuscates the role of structural forces undergirding leveled aspirations and opportunities for marginalized teens. The interviewed women enacted their agency by both engaging and choosing to disengage and by speaking back to defend themselves. Their experiences and resistance point to multiple ways that public schools are failing to provide adequate support for *all* Black students.

Educational policymakers ideally should want schools in which all young people can pursue "meaningful intellectual, political and social engagement, the possibility of financial independence, sexual and reproductive freedom, protection from racialized and sexualized violence and a way to imagine living in the future tense" (Fine & McClelland, 2006, p. 300). To this end, teachers and school administrators must examine and transform the explicit and implicit messages Black females receive in schools. Meaningful solutions, therefore, must simultaneously critically understand and attempt to dismantle these structural inequalities while acknowledging with Black girls the constraints in their lives and the possibilities available to them. Best positioned are teachers who are supportive in trying to understand the perspectives of Black youth (Milner, 2013; Yosso, 2005).

7   Recommendations and Conclusion

Most clearly from the data from our study and from other research on factors influencing Black girls' positive experiences in schools, it becomes clearer that culturally competent teachers, who affirm the multiple social and cultural identities of their students and simultaneously prepare them to critically analyze and challenge the structural inequities they face in light of those identities, are best able to set them up for success (Milner, 2013; Paris, 2012; Perry, Steele, & Hilliard, 2003). Schools can also create structures to support teachers and other staff in the development of cultural competence. Therefore, we offer the following recommendations:

1 *Increase recruitment, training and support for racially diverse teachers, including those from similar race, class, and gender backgrounds as Black girls and other historically marginalized student groups*
2 *Offer professional development opportunities for teachers and other staff to build deeper cultural competence.*
3 *Train, implement and sustain whole-school restorative justice programs.*
4 *Dismiss school resource officers and security guards who commit sexual harassment or assault on students.*
5 *Offer comprehensive sexuality education in schools.*

We are hopeful that more attention is directed to the developmental needs of Black girls in schools, and that interventions are directly informed by experiences of Black girls themselves. We are encouraged, moreover, by several critical organizations, institutions, and individuals in the field of education, which are leading the way in organizing with Black girls, including Girls for

Gender Equity, and Power U Center for Social Change. These organizations have each brought national attention to recent issues impacting Black girls, such as organizing town hall forums, writing essays to national leaders, and using social media to highlight the voices of Black girls in hopes of shifting the dominant discourse about educational inequality issues in fundamental ways. These organizations also demonstrate the importance of connecting organizing and advocacy work with research on schools. This can create a two-way process to make research accessible to those working in the field with research informed by teachers, students, and community leaders. Indeed, by leveraging research that centers the leadership and knowledge of those often relegated to the margins, including Black girls, it is possible to create schools that value, support, and challenge all students.

Note

1   More information about the methodology of this study is available from the lead author upon request.

References

Campbell, S. (2012). For colored girls? Factors that influence teacher recommendations into advanced courses for Black girls. *The Review of Black Political Economy, 39*(4), 389–402. doi:10.1007/s12114-012-9139-1

Carter, P. L. (2005). *Keepin' it real: School success beyond Black and White.* New York, NY: Oxford University Press.

Chaudhry, N., & Tucker, J. (2017). *Let her learn: Stopping school pushout overview and key findings.* Washington, DC: National Women's Law Center.

Collins, P. (20004). *Black sexual politics.* New York, NY: Routledge.

Crenshaw, K., Ocen, P., & Nanda, J. (2015). *Black girls matter: Pushed out, overpoliced, and underprotected.* Retrieved from https://static1.squarespace.com/static/53f20d90e4b0b80451158d8c/t/54d2d37ce4b024b41443b0ba/1423102844010/BlackGirlsMatter_Report.pdf

Crenshaw, K., Tomlinson, B., Peller, G., Doherty, J., Baskette, S. B., & Morris, M. (2012). Symposium: Overpoliced and underprotected: Women, race, and criminalization. *UCLA Law Review, 59*(6), 1825–1878.

Crenshaw, K. W. (2011). From private violence to mass incarceration: Thinking intersectionally about women, race, and social control. *UCLA Law Review, 59,* 1418–1471.

Davis, D. J., Brunn-Bevel, R. J., & Olive, J. L. (Eds.). (2015). *Intersectionality in educational research.* Sterling, VA: Stylus.

Dumas, M. J. (2016). Against the dark: Antiblackness in education policy and discourse. *Theory into Practice, 55*(1), 11–19.

Evans-Winters, V. (2005). *Teaching Black girls: Resiliency in urban classrooms.* New York, NY: Peter Lang.

Evans-Winters, V. E., & Esposito, J. (2010). Other people's daughters: Critical race feminism and Black girls' education. *Educational Foundations, 24*(1–2), 11–25.

Fine, M., & McClelland, S. (2006). Sexuality education and desire: Still missing after all these years. *Harvard Educational Review, 76*(3), 297–338.

Francis, D. V. (2012). Sugar and spice and everything nice? Teacher perceptions of Black girls in the classroom. *Review of Black Political Economy, 39*(3), 311–320. doi:10.1007/s12114-011-9098-y

Froyum, C. (2010). Making 'good girls': Sexual agency in the sexuality education of low-income Black girls. *Culture, Health & Sexuality: An International Journal for Research, Intervention and Care, 12*(1), 59–72, doi:10.1080/13691050903272583

Gregory, A., Skiba, R. J., & Noguera, P. (2010). The achievement gap and the discipline gap: Two sides of the same coin? *Educational Researcher, 39*(1), 59–68. doi:10.3102/0013189X09357621

Harding, S. G. (2004). *The feminist standpoint theory reader: Intellectual and political controversies.* New York, NY: Psychology Press.

Henry, A. (1998). Complacent and womanish: Girls negotiating their lives in an African centered school in the U.S. *Race, Ethnicity and Education, 1*(2), 151–170.

Jones, N. (2010). *Between good and ghetto: African American girls and inner-city violence.* New Brunswick, NJ: Rutgers University Press.

Ladson-Billings, G. (2013). Lack of achievement or loss of opportunity? In P. Carter & K. Welner (Eds.), *Closing the opportunity gap: What America must do to give every child an even chance* (pp. 11–23). New York, NY: Oxford University Press.

Lopez, N. (2003). *Hopeful girls, troubled boys: Race and gender disparity in urban education.* New York, NY: Routledge

Losen, D. J. (2011). *Discipline policies, successful schools, and racial justice.* Retrieved from http://nepc.colorado.edu/publication/discipline-policies

Luker, K. (1991). Dubious conceptions: The controversy over teen pregnancy. *The American Prospect.* Retrieved from http://publicsociology.berkeley.edu/publications/producing/luker.pdf

Milner, H. R. (2013). Analyzing poverty, learning, and teaching through a critical race theory lens. *Review of Research in Education, 37*(1), 1–53. doi:10.3102/0091732X12459720

Morris, E. W. (2007). "Ladies" or "loudies"? Perceptions and experiences of Black girls in classrooms. *Youth & Society, 38*(4), 490–515.

Morris, M. W. (2012). *Race, gender, and the "school to prison pipeline": Expanding our discussion to include Black girls.* New York, NY: African American Policy Forum. Retrieved from http://www.aapf.org/2013/2013/01/race-gender-and-the-school-to-prison-pipeline-expanding-our-discussion-to-black-girls

Morris, M. W. (2016). *Pushout: The criminalization of Black girls in schools.* New York, NY: The New Press.

Naples, N. A. (2003). *Feminism and method: Ethnography, discourse analysis, and activist research.* New York, NY: Routledge.

Noguera, P. A. (2009). *The trouble with Black boys: ...And other reflections on race, equity, and the future of public education.* San Francisco, CA: Jossey-Bass.

Ocen, P. A. (2011). The new racially restrictive covenant: Race, welfare, and the policing of Black women in subsidized housing [Abstract]. *UCLA Law Review, 59*(6), 1540–1582. Retrieved from https://ssrn.com/abstract=2506866

O'Connor, C. (1997). Dispositions toward (collective) struggle and educational resilience in the inner city: A case analysis of six African American high school students. *American Educational Research Journal, 34,* 593–629.

Paris, D. (2012). Culturally sustaining pedagogy: A needed change in stance, terminology, and practice. *Educational Researcher, 41,* 93–97. doi:10.3102/0013189X12441244

Perry, T., Steele, C. M., & Hillard, A. III. (2003). *Young, gifted, and Black: Promoting high achievement among African-American students.* New York, NY: Beacon.

Roberts, D. (1998). *Killing the Black body: Race, reproduction and the meaning of liberty.* New York, NY: Random House.

Wun, C. (2014). Unaccounted foundations: Black girls, anti-Black racism, and punishment in schools. *Critical Sociology, 42*(4–5), 1–14.

Wun, C. (2016). Angered: Black and non-Black girls of color at the intersections of violence and school discipline in the United States. *Race Ethnicity and Education,* 1–15. doi:10.1080/13613324.2016.1248829

Yosso, T. J. (2005). Whose culture has capital? A critical race theory discussion of community cultural wealth. *Race Ethnicity and Education, 8*(1), 69–91. doi:10.1080/1361332052000341006

CHAPTER 11

Latinx and Education: Shattering Stereotypes

Mónica Vásquez Neshyba

Although much has been written about Latinx academic achievement and graduation rates, few studies have focused specifically on Latina high school students and how they negotiate their identities within school. The data included in this chapter is drawn from a qualitative study conducted by the author, which incorporated methods from ethnography and case study research and relied on a sociocultural perspective of identity (Holland & Lachicotte, 2005; Holland, Lachicotte, Skinner, & Cain, 1998; Vygotsky, 1978) and Chicana feminist theory (Bernal, 1998) to illuminate Latina students' voices and their experiences of *mestizaje*, the mixture of races, ideologies, cultures and/or biologies (Anzaldúa, 1987). Therefore, this chapter focuses on the intersections of race, ethnicity and gender among Latina students who participated in a high school mariachi class. Rather than use the binary term Latina/o to distinguish between males and females, I will use the more inclusive, gender-neutral term Latinx when referring to the group. I use the term Latina specifically in this chapter when referring to research participants and to student data obtained from the school. The term Chicana/Chicano is also used by some to refer to students who are of Mexican descent.

1   Background on Latina/o Student Achievement

The low academic achievement of Latinx students in the U.S. has been cited as a function of deficit thinking, discrimination, and low academic expectations for these students (Diaz & Flores, 2001; Menken & Klein, 2010). Students often disengage from the learning process because they are exposed to isolated, superficial knowledge and culturally irrelevant curriculum (Cummins, 1986). By including a class such as mariachi as a course elective for all students, the school administration conveys a clear message that cultural expression is valued and encouraged.

In *Subtractive Schooling*, Valenzuela (1999) revealed the following problems leading to the dropout rate in her study of a high school in Houston: teachers held low expectations for youth, youth felt that teachers did not care whether they stayed or left, and scheduling problems left as many as 40% of students

© KONINKLIJKE BRILL NV, LEIDEN, 2018 | DOI 10.1163/9789004365209_011

without the correct number of classes or with incorrect classes. Students, parents, and community members inevitably returned to the language of *caring* when they sought to explain the persistence of underachievement and high school dropout at the high school. For them, according to Valenzuela, caring connotes concerns over inequitable school resources, overcrowded and decaying school buildings, and a lack of sensitivity toward Spanish speakers, Mexican culture, and things Mexican.

When considering solutions to the dropout crisis, it is important to understand the chronic failure of the educational system for Chicana/o students, for which Solorzano and Yosso (2000) suggest the following criteria:

1 We must understand the ideologies that have led to this failure by focusing on the intersections of race, gender, and class in the context of Chicana/o education;
2 We need to challenge the ideology that underlies educational inequality and look upon a student's culture as an asset rather than a deficiency and an obstacle;
3 Utilize the Freirean model to incorporate social justice into education;
4 Teachers must make extra efforts to incorporate the histories of all of their students in the classroom until the textbooks no longer ignore or distort the histories of People of Color; and
5 In our research, as we examine both the beneficiaries and the victims of the current system, we must listen to the voices of the people most affected by the failures of the schools by using such methods as individual, family and community histories (pp. 56–59).

What these items have in common is that they support culture and language, which are important aspects of students' identity development, especially in how students' identify themselves and to which groups they feel a sense of belonging. Perhaps, if these criteria were met within all classrooms and Latina/o students' identities were nurtured, more students would be less likely to drop out (Nieto, 2000). The need for schools to value students' culture and identity is exemplified by Valenzuela (1999), who states that "in a world that does not value bilingualism or biculturalism, youth may fall prey to the subtle yet unrelenting message of the worthlessness of their communities" (p. 264).

2   Fieldwork at a Predominately Latinx High School

The fieldwork was conducted at Star of Texas High School (a pseudonym and will subsequently referred to as STHS) and at various performance locations within the school community and central Texas. At this school, in the 2007–2008 school year, the student population consisted of 79% Hispanic students, 14% African-American students, 6% White students and less than 1% Asian students. Eighty percent of the students participated in the free/reduced lunch program (Texas Education Agency, 2009). As of the 2015–2016 school year, 83% of the students were low-income. Within 9 years enrollment percentages increased to 86% Hispanic, decreased to 9% African-American and 4% White, with 1% Asian students (Texas Education Agency, 2017). Regarding the class of 2015, 93% of all students obtained a high school diploma, compared to 55% in 2008 and 61% in 2009 (Texas Education Agency, 2010).

As I began conducting observations of the mariachi in December of 2007, there were 21 students enrolled in the STHS mariachi class. Of the 11 students who participated in this study, 8 were female. The mariachi group as a whole was predominantly female, which was in contrast to the traditional all-male mariachi. What I found most interesting were the dynamic personas I encountered within each Latina interviewed. In this chapter I present a brief profile of two Latina students to demonstrate their unique personalities, identities, goals and experiences and how their identities reflected intersections of race, ethnicity and gender.

I observed and/or conducted interviews during the mariachi class at STHS for two hours, twice a week for 10 months. During the observations, field notes were taken of the student-to-student interactions as well as student-teacher interactions. Semi-structured interviews, as well as follow-up interviews, were recorded and transcribed, and later coded, along with the field notes. Other information was obtained from classroom photos, performance programs, and school newsletters. Demographic data and the information from the school report card were obtained from the school report card available from the Texas Education Agency.

2.1   *Stefany*

Stefany, a very vibrant and engaging personality, volunteered to be the first student interviewed and was very eager to participate and tell her story. Her family was originally from Zacatecas, Mexico. She was born and raised in central Texas and was proud to be bilingual in English and Spanish. Until fifth grade Stefany was in bilingual education classrooms and in sixth grade she was in classroom for learners of English-as-second-language. She indicated that she felt more dominant in Spanish and preferred to speak in Spanish. During our interviews, she interchanged between Spanish and English, particularly using Spanish when describing or using idioms.

Stefany played the violin in the STHS mariachi and shared that "mariachi music is what we grew up with" and that she was very familiar with it. She learned to play the violin in sixth grade in school orchestra and learned to play the flute in eighth grade when she decided to join the school band. She joined mariachi after attending a performance at STHS and was recruited with the other violin players from the STHS orchestra during her sophomore year. Shortly thereafter, most of those recruited decided to quit the orchestra and remain in mariachi, including Stefany.

In mariachi class, Stefany considered herself to be "the spirited one, the motivator of the group." She liked to dance for fun, "like at quinceañeras with my parents." She was the second youngest of 6 daughters and very close to her family and extended family who lived nearby and joined them every Sunday for mass at a nearby Catholic church. Her parents were very supportive of her participation in the STHS mariachi, so much so that her father was the booster club president. Stefany also was a class officer and served as the parliamentarian.

Stefany did very well in school in the past. For example, she scored so well on her state-mandated assessments the previous year that she was recommended for advanced placement classes, which she took during her junior year. Despite her high test scores and the fact that Stefany's parents impressed upon her the importance of school, she had a difficult time maintaining consistent attendance in all of her classes.

> I don't know, like when I was younger, I was a straight A student. But when I got to middle school a lot of things started changing, things started happening, I started thinking differently, and somehow…I messed up with school so much and that made it hard to catch up. All my sisters, [are] nerds. Basically I guess you can say I'm the different one, the one with the attitude, the loud one, the one that's running around all over the house that has the music booming out the speaker.

She admitted that mariachi class was the only class she was motivated to attend; she preferred not to attend any of her other classes due to her dislike of the teachers.

In the beginning of Stefany's senior year, there was a class-scheduling error and she and 4 other mariachi students from the previous year were placed in classes that they had not registered for. Instead of mariachi class, Stefany was placed in an art class. Regardless, she would visit the class when possible. However, without her being in the mariachi classroom, it became very difficult to schedule further interviews as I was only allowed (via an agreement with the principal) to interview the students during their mariachi class time. After school was not an option because Stefany had a night job at a local restaurant, which she secured to assist her parents, who were struggling financially.

Shortly afterwards, Stefany became pregnant, yet managed to keep up with her classes by participating in a credit recovery program. Stefany graduated in May, 2009, and gave birth to a baby boy two months later.

2.2   *Claudia*

A senior like Stefany, Claudia was the most introspective of all the mariachi students interviewed. She played violin and held it closely, strumming it occasionally throughout our first interview. Upon meeting her, she seemed to be fun and engaging, but also very reflective and critical in her thinking. Claudia and Stefany were good friends and, like Stefany, she was eager to be interviewed. They often listened in while the other was being interviewed and would occasionally chime in with a comment. She described herself as "crazy and smart, and funny, I guess." She also shared that her teachers would describe her as "loud, because I'll correct them!" Claudia went on to describe a situation in her U.S. history class. She was asked by the teacher to translate the lecture – which included anti-immigrant sentiment from the teacher – for a new Spanish-speaking immigrant student. After realizing what she was having to translate, Claudia decided to define the term aliens as "green, big-eyed, extra-terrestrials." She then explained her decision to be an advocate for the student and not simply a messenger of the narrative shared by the teacher:

> I'll correct them, you know like in history class or whatever, when they're talking about immigration and illegal aliens this and illegal aliens that – I'll be like "No person is illegal," and [teachers will] argue with me, calling them criminals and quien sabe que [who knows what] – they are human beings.

Claudia grew up in south Texas and, although she spoke Spanish with her family, she lived in a predominantly African-American neighborhood and only spoke English outside of the home. She credited going to Mexico twice a year to visit family as the reason why she was able to maintain her Spanish. After her parents' imprisonment and deportation, she and her siblings moved in with her older sister, who was attending college in a nearby city at the time.

Although her mother returned months later to collect her younger siblings, Claudia chose to stay with her sister so that she could finish her schooling and not return to her "old ways of hanging in the streets and stuff and I didn't wanna go...my sister didn't let me go anyway." By this time her sister had graduated with a bachelor's degree in history and was working for a local grassroots leadership organization.

To help her sister out financially, Claudia worked at a local grocery store 38 hours a week, working after school and 10-hour shifts on the weekends.

Mrs. Reyna, the mariachi director, shared that "if it comes between work and performing, she's going to work because they (Claudia and her sister) need that." At times when her work schedule conflicted with mariachi performances, Mrs. Reyna told her,

> Ok, ask for time off from work, but as the date gets closer, it's like she feels pressure from both me and her sister, because I want her here ... she's a really good player, and then the sister wants her to work because she needs her to help pay, so it's like what's more important? I think, her family, so...but she's been pretty even on that and she's taken a lot from her sister to come with us...whatever we need to go.... (Personal communication, February 24, 2008)

Being the only student in the STHS mariachi who worked close to a full-time, forty-hour work week, Claudia had to address issues outside of school that the other students did not have. At times, Mrs. Reyna contacted the manager of the store to request a work schedule change for Claudia after being initially rejected by the manager.

Claudia was also involved in soccer and basketball at STHS, stating that "anything I can do to keep from going home." Even though she was enrolled in Advanced Placement and dual-credit classes where she could earn college credit, she was not optimistic about attending college: "I don't think I'm even going to go to college. College is whack, right Stefany?" Stefany replied by repeating the phrase in the affirmative from across the room. She worried that since she was working to help her sister and sending money to her mother in south Texas and father in Mexico, she wouldn't be able to afford college. She also admitted, "I just do the work, turn in stuff and get a grade, but I don't get it, I don't get it." When her friends ask her for help after seeing that she received a high grade on an assignment, Claudia says, "I don't know, I just do the work and blank out." Her ultimate goal is to go "back to San Antonio when I'm older and help out, because it's crazy down there." After some deliberations, Claudia decided to move back to San Antonio and live with her mother during her senior year and graduated in May, 2009.

3   A Sociocultural Perspective on Identity

For most high school students, high school is a time to begin to identify themselves in a variety of ways, whether it is in the friends they choose, the classes they enroll in, the activities and clubs they belong to, or simply in how the students elect to spend their time both within and outside of school.

For Latinx students at the secondary level, the desire to assimilate is often so great that it can lead to rejecting all aspects of their culture, including loss of language. "Too often, minority students believe that they must choose between a positive ethnic identity and a strong academic identity" (Nasir & Saxe, 2003, p. 14). For Latinas specifically, the stereotype of the subservient female can create a misconception of these students among teachers who do not take the time to get to know them as individuals.

For a mariachi, which originated as an all-male musical group (Jáuregui, 2007; Sheehy, 2006), to have more females than males in the group at Star of Texas High School was extraordinary and is one example of how the stereotype of the subservient Latina was shattered, especially by students such as Stefany and Claudia. Much like Lucha Reyes, who was regarded by the late 1930s as the "queen of mariachis," Stefany and Claudia "defied the silent and suffering archetype of Mexican femininity" (Gaytán & de la Mora, 2016, p. 197).

The concept of identity, according to Holland et al. (1998), can be described as a self-understanding to which one is emotionally attached and informs one's behavior and interpretations: "People tell others who they are, but even more important, they tell themselves who they are and then try to act as though they are who they say they are" (p. 3). This is particularly evident in adolescence when teenagers are struggling to discover both who they are and to which group(s) they belong. In reference to groups, Holland and Lachicotte (2005) explain that "communities of practice identify, by correlating the usage of a variety of cultural artifacts or emblems, sets of characters in interaction that participants learn as the organizational means for their own activity" (p. 32).

According to Holland et al. (1998), Vygotsky "construed symbols learned through social interaction, as so many ways in which people free themselves from the tyranny of environmental stimuli" (p. 6). These socially-constructed symbols allow one to transport to the past, or more specifically trigger a specific memory. Like other forms of art, the symbols produced by mariachis can elicit powerful reactions from many people.

For people who are unfamiliar with mariachi music or appreciate it as a form of cultural expression may be quick to dismiss it as novelty background music that a distinctly uniformed class plays on Friday nights at the local Mexican restaurant or a customary Cinco de Mayo celebration. What school administrators, teachers, and/or the society in general may fail to realize is that it is much more than a musical style or aesthetic that it represents; for many people it provides a connection to their family and/or community.

Holland et al.'s (1998) definition of identity is relevant here. Each student may display multiple identities throughout the school day depending on the situation (e.g., in an academic class, in the cafeteria, during extra-curricular activities, etc.), including within the mariachi group. The students not only share a common identity as members of the mariachi but also as members of a cultural group that represents their language, home countries and/or communities.

4   Chicana Feminism

A Chicana feminist epistemology can validate and address experiences that are intertwined with issues such as immigration, migration, generational status, bilingualism and limited English proficiency (Bernal, 1998). The freedom to speak freely to teachers and students in Spanish, code switching and/or translanguage (purposefully speaking in more than one language simultaneously) in English/Spanish is somewhat limited within the context of the typical high school classroom. However, the mariachi classroom provided students the opportunity to express themselves culturally via their instrument and/or voice through the use of Spanish. The languages people learn from infancy has a direct connection to identity formation and the use of it should be encouraged both inside and outside of school. Relatedly, culture is interconnected with language and also needs to be valued.

The notion of Anzaldua's (1987) *mestizaje* can be used as a guide to understand how the mariachi students at STHS were able to navigate their daily lives while negotiating their identities both inside and outside of school. This included their identities within their families and communities. The negotiation of identities occurs nebulously; there are no distinct borders or boundaries in the spaces in which the students' identities are expressed. Both within and outside of the school day, many of the students in the STHS mariachi were involved in many other clubs and/or activities and had to negotiate and adapt themselves to their respective communities and environments within each space. Depending on the dynamics within each space, several forms of identity may be expressed in different ways by each student. It is important to note that in concordance with Anzaldua's *mestizaje*, these expressions are not always being expressed individually or in a turn-taking manner. Some expressions may even occur concurrently and depend on the context of the interactions between the students themselves as well as between the students and the mariachi director.

In choosing to study this particular high school and the Latinx students in the mariachi class, the intent was not to generalize their experiences, but rather to go beneath the surface of the mariachi as an icon of Mexican culture. Instead of simply recognizing the mariachi as a cultural music group that represents STHS and/or the larger community, I used characteristics of intersectional research analysis and to center on the Latina students' lived experiences by examining and exploring their identities both individually and within-group (Davis, Brunn-Bevel, & Olive, 2015).

5   Implications

The Latinx students' participation in the high school mariachi class may be seen as a form of transformational resistance, especially because the majority of the students in the mariachi band at STHS were female and engaged in social justice as well as care for each other. Transformational resistance (Bernal, 2001) is a "framework to understand some of the positive strategies used by Chicana and Chicano students to successfully navigate through the educational system" and graduate from high school.

As acts of resistance, according to Sandoval (2000), there are 6 ways to counter the effects of dominant forms as ideology: (1) the ability to speak outside the terms of ideology (speech of the oppressed), (2) language of "revolution" that is linked to the simultaneous destruction and transformation of the world, (3) the method of semiotic-mythology to read and deconstruct signs of power and to breakdown dominant ideology, (4) silence as a form of resistance that refuses to engage ideology at all, (5) "contemporary poetry" that leads back to the sign itself to find the "meaning of things" beyond their inscription in language, and (6) "meta-ideologizing" in order to prove the original dominant ideology as naïve and no longer natural and to reveal, transform, or disempower its signification in some other way (pp. 107–108). These types of manipulations have been essential for survival by those who have been oppressed and marginalized, such as the Latinas profiled in this chapter.

Freire (2005) believed that language of the dominant culture should be taught to lower-class students in order to give them the tools necessary to fight against injustice and discrimination. He also felt that they should be taught to recognize their own language as just as important and they should not be ashamed to use it. By utilizing a dialogical model of communication, conditions can be created for students of color in which they can find their voice through opportunities to reflect, critique, and act on their world to transform it (Darder, 1991). Freire "perceives dialogue as a helpful way to challenge social and ideological constructions used to oppress a social self" (p. 134), which is a reason why highlighting a group predominantly made up of to with strong Latina students is important. The profiles presented in this chapter provide more examples and evidence as to how students can be positively valued in their need for care, advocacy, and encouragement.

Anzaldúa (1987) speaks for all those who feel marginalized by others because of their language: "If you really want to hurt me, talk badly about my language. Ethnic identity is twin skin to linguistic identity – I am my language. Until I can take pride in my language, I cannot take pride in myself" (p. 81). Language acceptance is critical for all those who interact with children regularly, whether it be a student, parent, guardian, or teacher. Language acceptance fosters self-awareness, self-confidence, and self-identity within each student, especially those who are marginalized by the educational system as a whole. Too often, educators perceive Chicana/o students' culture and language as deficits to overcome instead of strength to cultivate (Yosso, 2006). If more teachers, parents and administrators understood that language is an integral part of one's identity, perhaps they would reconsider before telling students that Spanish or languages other than English are not allowed in the classroom. In addition, if Latinx students were made to feel their culture was valued, they would not be in such a hurry to acculturate and assimilate. They would be more likely to retain their first language and self-identity and become more adept to navigating between cultures.

Freire (1974) explains that education either conditions the younger generation into acceptance of society's status quo or becomes "the practice of freedom" through which people deal critically and creatively with reality to transform their worlds (p. 34). In order to achieve critical consciousness, one must have the ability to perceive social, political, and economic oppression and to take action against the oppressive elements of society. Therefore, "education is a political act" (Freire, 2005, p. 40). If more teachers engaged in critical study, especially those who teach in lower socioeconomic areas with disenfranchised students, perhaps more students can gain increased self-confidence and have opportunities to have their voices heard and make a difference in their communities.

In order for this to happen, teachers need to be able to provide a nurturing and accepting environment where the teacher and the students feel comfortable expressing their ideas and emotions, such as the mariachi directors provided for their students. Challenging power relations is central to critical pedagogy (Freire, 1970) which is based on an analysis of structural as well as cultural power. By teaching Latina students how they can participate in critical pedagogy, teachers are empowering them with the idea that together with the community, they can promote change in the future.

6   Conclusion

One day after the November 2016 presidential election, many racially charged and xenophobic incidents occurred in schools across the nation. There was one incident in particular in a middle school cafeteria outside of Detroit, Michigan. A Latina student video recorded students chanting, "BUILD A WALL! BUILD A WALL!" repeatedly, similar to what was chanted throughout the president elect's campaign (Wallace & LaMotte, 2016). According to the student, she decided to record the incident in order to gather evidence to show her parents, because she and others witnessed racism previously at this predominately White middle school (Wallace & LaMotte, 2016). Her mother shared the video privately with other parents at the school, and one parent posted it on social media. The video went viral quickly and prompted significant negative feedback to the school district. As a result, parents are now "advocating for diversity training for teachers and students and a review of the curriculum" (Wallace & LaMotte, 2016). However, because of the backlash the student received at the school, she has withdrawn and is now attending a private school and has managed to regain a sense of normalcy (Wallace & LaMotte, 2016).

As educators and teacher educators, we must ask ourselves, where were the teachers in this story? Was there any intervention by a teacher or administrator? Was there any support for the students immediately after this event occurred? What messages did viewing this video send to other Latinx students While this is a very unfortunate situation, it is something that should be discussed school-wide and district-wide to ensure that our schools, and not just particular classrooms, are safe spaces.

To address and prevent such situations, we must begin to build a community in which dialogue among all students, teachers and administrators is the norm. As Angela Davis (2016) remarked after the 2016 presidential election at a lecture at the University of Chicago, "Community is the answer...Whatever we are already doing, we need to do more. We need to accelerate our activism" (1:27:36) It is time that teachers and teacher educators begin learning to advocate in culturally appropriate and caring ways for their Latinx students.

References

Anzaldúa, G. (1987). *Borderlands/la frontera: The new mestiza.* San Francisco, CA: Aunt Lute Books.

Bernal, D. (1998). Using a Chicana feminist epistemology in educational research. *Harvard Educational Review, 68*(4), 555–582.

Bernal, D. D. (2001). Learning and living pedagogies of the home: The mestiza consciousness of Chicana students. *International Journal of Qualitative Studies in Education (QSE), 14*(5), 623–639.

Cummins, J. (1986). Empowering minority students: A framework for intervention. *Harvard educational review, 56*(1), 18–37.

Darder, A. (1991). *Culture and power in the classroom: A critical foundation for bicultural education*. Westport, CT: Bergin & Garvey.

Davis, A., & Taylor, K. Y. (2016, November 21). *Freedom is a constant struggle* [Video]. Retrieved from https://www.chicagoreader.com/Bleader/archives/2016/11/21/watch-angela-daviss-entire-postelection-lecture-at-the-university-of-chicagos-rockefeller-chapel

Davis, D. J., Brunn-Bevel, R. J., & Olive, J. L. (Eds.). (2015). *Intersectionality in educational research*. Sterling, VA: Stylus.

Diaz, E., & Flores, B. (2001). Teacher as sociocultural, sociohistorical mediator: Teaching to the potential. In M. D. Reyes & J. J. Halcón (Eds.), *The best for our children: Critical perspectives on literacy for Latino students* (pp. 29–47). New York, NY: Teachers College Press.

Freire, P. (1974). *Pedagogy of the oppressed*. New York, NY: Seabury.

Freire, P. (2005). *Letters to those who dare to teach*. Boulder, CO: Westview Press.

Gaytán, M. S., & de la Mora, S. (2016). Queening/queering mexicanidad: Lucha Reyes and the Canción Ranchera. *Feminist Formations, 28*(3), 196–221.

Holland, D., Lachicotte, Jr. W., Skinner, D., & Cain, C. (1998). *Identity and agency in cultural worlds*. Cambridge, MA: Harvard University Press.

Jáuregui, J. (2007). *El mariachi: Símbolo musical de México*. México: Instituto Nacional de Antropología e Historia.

Menken, K., & Kleyn, T. (2010). The long-term impact of subtractive schooling in the educational experiences of secondary English language learners. *International Journal of Bilingual Education and Bilingualism, 13*(4), 399–417.

Nasir, N. S., & Saxe, G. B. (2003). Ethnic and academic identities: A cultural practice perspective on emerging tensions and their management in the lives of minority students. *Educational Researcher, 32*(5), 14–18.

Nieto, S. (2000). *Affirming diversity, the sociopolitical context of multicultural education*. New York, NY: Longman.

Sandoval, C. (2000). *Methodology of the oppressed*. Minneapolis, MN: University of Minnesota Press.

Sheehy, D. E. (2006). *Mariachi music in America: Experiencing music, expressing culture*. New York, NY: Oxford University Press.

Solorzano, D. G., & Yosso, T. J. (2000). Toward a critical race theory of Chicana & Chicano education. In C. Tejada, C. Martinez, & Z. Leonardo (Eds.), *Charting new terrains Chicana(o)/Latina(o) education* (pp. 35–66). Creskill, NJ: Hampton Press.

Texas Education Agency. (2009). *2007–2008 school report card* (Data file). Retrieved from http://tea.texas.gov/perfreport/src/index.html

Texas Education Agency. (2010). *2008–2009 school report card* (Data file). Retrieved from http://tea.texas.gov/perfreport/src/index.html

Texas Education Agency. (2017). *2015–2016 school report card* (Data file). Retrieved from http://tea.texas.gov/perfreport/src/index.html

Valenzuela, A. (1999). *Subtractive schooling*. Albany, NY: State University of New York Press.

Vygotsky, L. (1978). *Mind in society*. Cambridge, MA: Harvard University Press.

Wallace, K., & LaMotte, S. (2016, December 28). The collateral damage after students' 'build a wall' chant goes viral. *CNN*. Retrieved from http://edition.cnn.com/2016/12/28/health/build-a-wall-viral-video-collateral-damage-middle-school/

Yosso, T. J. (2006). *Critical race counterstories along the Chicana/Chicano educational pipeline*. New York, NY: Routledge.

CHAPTER 12

Intersecting Histories in the Present: Deconstructing How White Preservice Teachers at Rural South African Schools Perceive Their Black Supervising Teacher and Students

Warren L. Chalklen

Ainscow and Sandill (2010) argue that the establishment of equity is the biggest challenge facing school systems throughout the world today. Whereas some teacher preparation programs use a mainstream human relations model that emphasizes "getting along with others," other programs use a social justice oriented approach that addresses oppression, injustice and inequity in education (O'Grady, 2000, p. 11). Education in South Africa has historically been a major site of social justice resistance to colonialism and apartheid. Post-apartheid South African education aims to address the legacy of racism, economic exploitation and social division by preparing teachers to teach diverse students. Fostering a culturally relevant disposition can be challenging when working with White, middle class preservice teachers who have grown up in urban environments with limited experience of diversity. As such, preservice teachers are often placed in programs designed to expose them to diverse teaching and learning environments as a mechanism to promote their culturally relevant competence.

Previous studies have explored South African preservice teachers' perceptions of diverse students and teachers in a higher education course (Vandeyar, 2008). Other studies scrutinized culturally relevant teaching practices at the university level (Coleman, 2013). While these studies focused on higher education settings, they omitted preservice teacher perceptions of teachers and students of color in rural settings. Discussed later in this chapter is a study I conducted that helps to fill this gap by exploring preservice teachers' perceptions of their Black supervising teacher and students in a rural setting.

1   Historical and Educational Perspectives

Before focusing on the study of White South African teacher candidates, the following sections provide brief overviews of South African history and

© KONINKLIJKE BRILL NV, LEIDEN, 2018 | DOI 10.1163/9789004365209_012

educational perspectives related to culturally responsive pedagogy and deficit thinking.

1.1   Educational Legacy of Colonialism and Apartheid

Like the community in this study, schools, need to be examined through a pre-colonial, colonial, apartheid, and post-apartheid lenses. Pre-colonial education in South Africa was based upon Indigenous learning systems. These learning systems were intertwined with the social, cultural, artistic, religious and recreational life of the people (Funteh, 2015). This shifted dramatically with the official arrival of European colonial settlers in 1652 who began to establish segregated missionary schools for the education of Black African students. Luthuli (1981) described how missionaries throughout the European occupation of South Africa became embedded in African society and used their allegiance with the Dutch and then the British Empire to disregard Indigenous education.

In 1948 the Nationalist government attained power and immediately implemented apartheid, which segregated South Africans across racial lines. Apartheid (1948–1994) was a hegemonic government system designed to enforce racial segregation through institutionalized White supremacy (Biko, 2002). Central to apartheid's project of White supremacy was the strangulation of Black African people's education, violent land dispossession, and systematic economic exploitation. The Bantu Education Act of 1953 halted funding for missionary schools and forced the education of Black African students into state-sponsored primary schools. These schools were severely underfunded and designed to prepare students for low-paying industrial and service jobs. Hartshorne (1992) explained, "Bantu Education epitomizes the use of education to reproduce social, economic and political power of the White minority over the Black majority" (p. i). Bantu Education dominated South African education policy in various forms until the advent of democracy in 1994.

Hyslop (1993) argues that the introduction of Bantu Education has to be understood in the context of the restructured urban environment (i.e., the collapse of subsistence agriculture and mass migration) and the need of the apartheid government for stability to implement grand apartheid (p. 294). South Africa's economic boom in the 1940's increased mass migration to urban areas and increased industrial influence on government education policy. In 1948, the Eiselen Commission led by Werner Eiselen, the former commissioner for Black education between 1936 and 1947 and the Secretary of Native Affairs in 1949, argued that the state, rather than mission schools, should control the education of Black students in order to prepare them for industrial jobs. The commission's recommendations included: (1) transferring educational control to the state; (2) establishing three types of schools: Bantu Community Schools,

State Aided schools, and provincial government schools; (3) abolishing unregistered schools; (4) forming school boards and committees appointed by the Minister of Bantu Affairs; (5) bringing all teachers under control of the board; and (6) increasing the powers of the Minister of Bantu Affairs to regulate school curriculum (Eiselen, 1948, p. 8). These recommendations were pushed through parliament and passed into law as the Bantu Education Act of 1953.

The damaging effects of Bantu Education on the educational outcomes of Black students demanded a pointed policy response. Post-apartheid reconstruction of the country prioritized dismantling the effects of the sustained educational inequalities through the South African Schools Act of 1996 (SASA). The broad goal of SASA was "to provide for a uniform system for the organization, governance, and funding of schools; to amend and repeal certain laws relating to schools; and to provide for matters connected therewith" (South African Schools Act, 1996, p. 2) and was in direct response to the Bantu Education Act 1953 and its subsequent weak reforms. SASA envisioned an integrated, humane, and high quality education system for all students.

1.2   *Culturally Relevant Pedagogy*

Research by Howard (2002) concluded that culturally relevant pedagogy is a clear example of a teaching practice that is effective with African American students. Considered a form of multicultural education, culturally relevant pedagogy has not only been effective with African American students, but it has also been successful with other minority and poor students (Banks, 1994). Preservice teaching preparation programs have traditionally emphasized technical pedagogical skills. But, more effective programs recognize the importance of culturally relevant behavior to prepare students to teach in increasingly diverse classrooms. For example, Ladson-Billings (2001) conceptualized a culturally relevant pedagogy that comprises 3 criteria: (1) teachers must demonstrate the ability to develop students academically, (2) teachers should exhibit a willingness to nurture and support cultural competence, and (3) teachers must nurture the development of a sociopolitical consciousness.

1.3   *Deficit Thinking*

Giroux (1980) argued that the educational system – schools, policy, staff and curriculum – is often perceived as a sorting mechanism to maintain and reproduce the status quo for different subgroups and communities in society. Building on the notion of education as social reproduction, Valencia (2010) described how the notion of deficit thinking is embedded in dominant education discourse. Deficit thinking theory refers to the labeling of low-income minority students and their families as disadvantaged, at risk, and uninvolved (Johnson, 1994). The deficit perspective is underpinned by the idea that the student themselves and not the social, economic, and political systems which institutionalize barriers to mobility are to be blamed for their "underperformance." This perspective has implications for preservice teacher preparation programs.

Mckenzie and Sheurich (2004) conducted a qualitative study that explored habits and perceptions of 8 White teachers at a low-income urban school. Their findings outlined 4 "equity traps": "The Deficit View," "Racial Erasure," "Employment and Avoidance of the Gaze," and "Paralogic Beliefs and Behaviors" (p. 619). The concept of equity traps explores the conscious and unconscious thinking patterns and behaviors that trap teachers, administrators, and others, preventing them from creating schools that are equitable, particularly for students of color. Marshall and Case (2010) explored the deficit view through scrutinizing discourses in a South African higher education institution. They argue that university pedagogy, especially curriculum discourse, should reflect student's cultural background while also confronting deficit perspectives.

2   Research Perspective and Context

The primary focus of this research was to analyze preservice teachers' perceptions of their Black supervising teacher and students. In this study, the teacher candidates' perceptions were defined as the lens through which they viewed or evaluated their own ideas or behaviors (Ladson-Billings, 1994). Intersectionality offered an useful tool to explore how the teacher's identities shaped their perceptions of students and supervising teachers. Collins (2000) outlines four characteristics of intersectionality theory: (1) Centering the lived experience, and specifically those of people of color and other marginalized groups, (2) complicating identity and examining both individual and group identities, (3) exploring identity salience as influenced by systems of power and privilege and unveiling power in interconnected structures of inequality, and (4) advancing larger goal of promoting social justice and social change (Collins, 2000, p. 3). Based on intersectionality, the following research questions were investigated in this study:

1 What are teachers' perceptions of their cultural competence in the classroom?
2 How do preservice teachers perceive their Black supervising teacher?
3 How do preservice teachers perceive their Black students?

2.1   *Participants and Pedagogical Context*
The participants of this study were 18 White female preservice teachers engaged in their teaching practicum from a prominent public South African university. All participants self-identified as middle to upper class English first language speakers from Johannesburg. Participants ranged in age from 22–26 years old and were all enrolled in their final year of a Bachelor's of Education degree. By specialization, a majority of the group was Foundation Phase (K-3), two focused on Intermediate Phase (grades 4–9) and two were Senior Phase (grades 10–12) majors. The teaching practicum was designed to immerse White preservice teachers in diverse rural schools. As such, participants worked closely with a Black supervising teacher and lead faculty member throughout their practicum. All teacher candidates in this study entered their respective practicum with a minimum of 18 weeks of prior student teaching experience. The teaching practical program was divided into two 3-week sections. The first section occurred in March and the second section in September of the same year. All participants completed both sections of the 6-week program.

2.2   *Overview of Researcher*
As the researcher, I was uniquely posited in this study. My research paradigm is intrinsically linked to my lived experience as a White, English-speaking, upper middle-class, male from Johannesburg, South Africa, who has received postgraduate education from a university in the United States. Because of my position in a socially constructed dominant group (Berghe, 1963), I actively negotiated and worked to recognize how my own biases can shape a research design, inform implementation of methodology and influence data interpretation. Particular attention was given to how my unearned advantages in the form of White privilege (Du Bois, 1903), gender dominance (Pascale, 2013), and class power (Pease, 2010) impacted this study. Failure to recognize power and privilege can become problematic when it leads White male researchers to believe they can write about the worlds of those in non-dominant groups without recognizing the privilege embedded in this decision (Dyson, Roediger, McIntosh, Meigs, & Suarez, 2007).

2.3   *Overview of the School-Community Context*
The geographical context of the study is a rural farming community in the province of Mpumalanga, South Africa. As of 2016, the community comprised 863 people in 263 households. By population group, 90.7% identified as Black African, 8.9% as White, 0.2% as Coloured,[1] and 0.2% as Indian/Asian. By first language, 43% spoke SePedi, 22% Siswati, 13% isiZulu, 8% Afrikaans, and 2% English. The average income disparity was immense. Of the 568 working aged population between 15 and 64 years of age, 17% received no income. Based

on per month earning of those who receive an income, 55% earned less than R400 (US$142), 24% earned up to R7,890 (US$579), and the remaining 4% (23) earned up to R204,800 (US$14,842) (Statistics South Africa, 2016). This compared to the national minimum wage of R4,084 (US$296) per month (World Bank, 2016). By living conditions, 84% of the people indicated that they had no access to electricity and 61.5% had no sewage pipes connected to their homes. Educationally, 7.8% of the population had received no formal schooling, 18.4% received some primary education, 44.3% some secondary education, 22% had passed matric (i.e., senior year of high school) and 3.5% enrolled in higher education (Statistics South Africa, 2016).

Hall Combined School (pseudonym) was built in the early 1900s to exclusively educate the children of White farmers and settlers. In the apartheid era, the school was reclassified to Model C, a designation that signified its exclusive White status. As such, it comprises six classrooms, a head office, sports field, school hall, flush toilets, electricity and running water. In the early post-apartheid era, surrounding schools reserved exclusively for students of color were closed and integrated into this school. Hall Primary School was renamed Hall Combined School, serving grades K-12 with over 100 students. In the early years of integration, the school's staff and student population was multiracial but later became predominantly Black African.

On a "private" farm not far from Hall Combined School was Blue Primary School (pseudonym). Blue Primary School was built during the apartheid era by the White farm owner to educate the children of the Black African workers on whose land the farmer occupied. As such it was classified as a Bantu school. In the post-apartheid era, the designation changed to Quintile one. Quintile one schools are fully government funded no-fee schools designated to support the education of children in low-income communities (Hall & Giese, 2009). Despite Blue Primary School's status changing from Bantu under apartheid to Quintile one in the post-apartheid era, the school architecture has not changed since its inception. It had four rooms, a small makeshift sports field, no electricity, and no running water. The school's 4 staff and more than 100 students were spread across grades 1–7 and were exclusively Black African.

Fire Pot Primary School (pseudonym) was built in the post-apartheid era to serve students who travelled significant distances to get to their closest school. Despite also being classified as a Quintile one school, Fire Pot Primary has six classrooms, electricity, running water, toilets and a small sports field. Seven teachers served around 150 students across grades K-7. The student population was exclusively Black African and all but one teacher identified as Black African.

3   Data Collection and Analysis

In order to pursue my research questions, I designed an interpretive study because "interpretive research seeks to perceive, describe, analyze, and interpret features of a specific situation or context, preserving its complexity and communicating the perspectives of the actual participants" (Borko, Whitcomb, & Byrnes, 2008, p. 1025). In order to provide credibility for the study, I utilized methodological triangulation (Creswell & Miller, 2000). My sources of data included semi-structured interviews, focus groups, and observations. I had specific questions to ask each interviewee to support the analysis but I allowed the conversation to flow (see Rubin & Rubin, 1995). The interview protocol asked participants to reflect on what they were learning from their experience, to describe their supervising teacher, and what they learned from working with diverse students. The focus groups comprised groups of 4–5 participants. These sessions were used to delve deeper into themes that had emerged from the interviews and observations. Additional data was collected by observing teacher candidates' interactions with students and teachers and at various events.

Major themes emerged from an open coding process. My analysis used an epistemological approach proposed by Cole (2009) that explored the intersections of identity. As I worked through the data I asked: (1) Who is included in this category? (2) What role does inequality play? (3) What are the similarities across social categories? Using Charmaz (2006) process of axial coding I grouped themes which allowed me to see overarching categories and themes. For example, some prominent codes that emerged included "undermine supervising teacher" and "unequal teacher and preservice teacher relationship." These codes were grouped into the overall category of "deficit framing." As a form of member checking, the transcribed interviews were sent to the participants to determine accuracy before coding took place. Pseudonyms were also assigned to each participant and schools to protect their identity. In addition, after coding and analysis, the findings were shared with the university tutor in charge of the preservice teachers' experience.

4   Findings

This study sought to explore how White preservice teachers perceived their Black supervising teacher and diverse students. All the data collected demonstrated that many of the preservice teachers perceived their supervising teacher and students through a deficit paradigm. Three broad themes emerged: (1) supervising teacher and student framing, (2) perceptions and expectations, and (3) lesson preparation and language differences. I interpreted the data using Ladson-Billings (1994) four indicators of cultural competences:

- teacher understands culture and its role in education,
- teacher takes responsibility for learning about the students and the community,
- teacher uses student culture as a basis for learning, and
- teacher promotes flexible use of students local and global culture.

4.1   *Supervising Teacher and Student Framing*

When describing their supervising teacher and students, the White teacher candidates overwhelmingly used deficit discourse. The discourse mainly described the competence and feelings of support from the supervising teacher. Preservice teacher Tatum perceived her supervising teacher as detrimental to student learning. Her reflections also implicitly indicated her belief that contextual factors were to blame for student learning. She wrote:

> I have felt that sometimes I don't want my teacher to teach my grade [level] because I'm afraid she won't teach them the right thing. I feel like the teacher doesn't teach properly...I have seen so much progress in the learners [and] I wish I could take them all home on a bus and teach them.

The framing of this statement aligns with Johnson's (1994) notion of deficit thinking theory when teacher and students are labeled as disadvantaged, at risk, and uninvolved. In addition to framing their supervising teachers as incompetent and unsupportive, Tatum also described her supervising teacher as unenthusiastic. Rose, another participant, described at length how she tried to encourage her supervising teacher to be involved in her lessons in order to "teach her how to teach." Rose expressed frustration when the supervising teacher resisted. Rose's actions were contrary to Ladson-Billings (1994) envisaged cultural competency which scrutinizes the extent to which teachers take responsibility for learning about the students' culture and community. In this instance, rather than Rose seeking to learn from the teacher, she instead tried to teach the supervising teacher.

When asked to describe their perceptions of the student's cultural backgrounds, many participants discussed student culture, discipline, and interpersonal boundaries. Jean, Sam and Kate often described the students as "disrespectful" and "uncaring." In one interview Jean elaborated on her perceptions of the students:

> The kids [students] have been so restless...I feel like there are no boundaries...I feel insulted when kids don't care...this is just so emotionally demanding...I sometimes feel so excited and other times so frustrated because I can't get through to the kids...they show absolute disrespect...how can I relate to them...is it in their culture?

Understanding culture and its role in education is one of the indicators of cultural competence (Ladson-Billings, 1994). When Jean described the students as uncaring and disrespectful, she revealed a lack of depth and understanding of the student's cultural context. Furthermore, when Jean cited the student's culture, she framed it as a barrier to learning rather than a resource. This aligns with Weiner's (2006) proposal that educators who operate within the deficit paradigm believe that unless students of color change background factors such as their culture, values, and family structures, they encounter minimal or no opportunities to have successful outcomes in school.

Applebaum (2005) argued that it is common for those in power – as a consequence of their dominant position – to have the ability and power to claim what is right and what is valuable. By discarding that what is considered deviant, dominant ideologies pathologize historically marginalized and subordinate populations. At the same time a dominant worldview is presented as normal, unbiased and neutral (Lukes, 2005). Instead of adopting a culturally relevant pedagogy that sought to use the student's culture as the basis of learning, Jean imposed her own cultural value system onto the children and community.

4.2   *Perceptions and Expectations*

Participants entered this program with perceptions and expectations. In the beginning of the program the participants described how they "wanted to make a difference." Claire stated, "I wanted a challenge...I thought the children didn't have enough and I wanted to help the teacher in a big way in sorting the children out." This statement largely captures the teacher candidates' sentiment early on in the program. It also aligns with Walker (2011) who described how preservice teachers who enter urban schools often perceive themselves as bringing change.

As the practicum proceeded, however, the participants began to reflect on being out of their comfort zones. Jenny captured her experience of cultural dissonance when she described herself as an alien:

> I have felt like an alien...first day I felt confident...the language barrier has been very difficult, lessons are not flowing, battling with basic language concepts and I feel so frustrated...I wanted to walk out of class...I feel [situation is] mind-boggling yet rewarding, [this is a] rollercoaster ride.

Ladson-Billings (1995) conceptualized culturally relevant pedagogy to ameliorate cultural dissonance in schools by helping educators become more sensitive to culturally influenced behaviors. In the above example, Jenny was grappling with cultural difference and reflecting on her emotions of teaching and learning in a cultural context different than hers.

4.3   Lesson Preparation and Language Differences

Participants who felt motivated to teach in a culturally relevant way reflected at length about the importance of preparing lessons with the students in mind. For example, interviews with and observations of Sarah consistently demonstrated a teacher candidate who was continually thinking about her students when she prepared her lessons. Sarah reflected,

> In Johannesburg I know where I'm going with my lessons but here I have to adapt my preparation and think about units. I am thinking about my lesson more deeply…it [lesson preparation] is more detailed and simpler…I am starting to think of individual learners in my class and I find myself asking: "How can I reach Thembi?"

Language as a site of cultural competence intersected with lesson preparation. When asked to describe their greatest teaching challenge, participants overwhelmingly described what they termed the "language barrier." The majority of the students spoke English as a third or fourth language whereas all the participants spoke English as their first language. Therefore, language became a site to explore culturally relevant pedagogy. Participants such as Lilah, Beth, and Kerry explored culturally relevant methodologies such as using body language, researching core terms, and code-switching between English and isiZulu. Each of these descriptions aligned with the cultural competency that calls for teachers to take responsibility for student learning. Ladson-Billings (1995) describes code-switching pedagogies as aligned with a culturally relevant pedagogy when it employs the use of home language to facilitate informal and formal contexts for writing and speaking.

5   Implications

My primary goal for exploring how White preservice teachers perceived both Black students and teachers was to gain a deeper insight into how to prepare preservice teachers who have internalized and demonstrated expectations for becoming culturally relevant teachers. This study illustrated overall that immersion of White preservice teachers into diverse environments is not enough to foster culturally relevant knowledge, skills, and dispositions. While some of the teacher candidates began to adapt their preparation and methodologies to respond to the students, the overwhelming majority perceived their supervising teacher and students in deficit terms. Because language is not neutral and needs to be understood as a historically and culturally contextualized tool to construct reality (Freire, 1970), a dichotomy of teaching practice and personal bias emerged.

Preservice teachers in this study demonstrated a genuine desire to teach their students and showed shifts in their teaching practice. Nevertheless, they simultaneously perceived their students as "poor," "disrespectful," and "uncaring." Some of the teacher candidates also saw themselves as teachers to their supervising teachers. These perceptions unmasked the intersection between the White teachers' position in a socially dominant group and the cultural competencies they still needed to teach culturally diverse students. The White preservice teachers in this study also used deficit language to describe their diverse supervising teacher and students. The context of colonialism and apartheid in South Africa suggests that deficit ideology cannot not exist in a vacuum. When the preservice teachers demonstrated deficit perceptions, they unmasked their socially constructed political, historical, social and economic power. This power is inextricably linked to their race and class status. Therefore, the preservice teachers cannot fully transform their practice to reflect culturally relevant teaching until they confront their personal biases.

6   Conclusion

This study highlights the need for further scrutiny of preservice teacher education curriculum in relation to equity-based practice. As South Africa seeks to develop culturally relevant teachers to transform the society towards equity and justice, it is necessary to closely analyze how personal bias intersects with teaching practice. Intersectionality theory offered a useful framework to unearth how South Africa's history of colonialism and apartheid, especially given the legacy of Bantu education that underpinned perceptions of race and class in this study. As preservice teachers framed students and teachers in deficit terms, they revealed the limitation of immersion teaching programs as tools to foster culturally responsive practice. Programs that seek only to expose White preservice teachers to difference without confronting their role in reproducing unequal power may in fact reinforce deeply held stereotypes and negative perceptions of culturally, racially, and economically diverse students and teachers. Programs integrating immersion in communities of color with active culturally responsive practice are better suited to truly realize the vision of equity centered teaching practice.

Note

1   "Coloured" is a colonial name ascribed to an ethnic group comprised primarily of people with mixed race heritage.

References

Ainscow, M., & Sandill, A. (2010). Developing inclusive education systems: The role of organizational cultures and leadership. *International Journal of Inclusive Education, 14*(4), 401–416.

Applebaum, B. (2005). In the name of morality: Moral responsibility, Whiteness and social justice education. *Journal of Moral Education, 34*(3), 277–290.

Banks, J. A. (1994). *An introduction to multicultural education.* Needlam Heights, MA: Allyn & Bacon.

Berghe, P. (1965). *South Africa: A study in conflict.* Berkeley, CA: University of California Press.

Biko, S. (2002). *I write what I like.* Chicago, IL: University of Chicago Press.

Borko, H., Whitcomb, J., & Byrnes, K. (2008). Genres of research in teacher education. In M. Cochran-Smith, S. Feiman-Nemser, & J. McIntyre (Eds.), *Handbook of research on teacher education: Enduring issues in changing contexts* (3rd ed., pp. 1017–1049). Mahwah, NJ: Lawrence Erlbaum Associates.

Charmaz, K. (2006). *Constructing grounded theory: A practical guide through qualitative analysis.* London: Sage.

Cole, E. R. (2009). Intersectionality and research in psychology. *American Psychologist, 64*(3), 170–180.

Coleman, L. (2013). *Avoiding deficit conceptualizations of students and their learning: Methodological considerations.* Paper presented at the Symposium: Higher Education in a Shifting Landscape: Emergence, Fragmentation and Convergence, Cape Peninsula University of Technology, Cape Town. Retrieved from http://heltasa.org.za/wp-content/uploads/2014/07/Avoiding-deficit-conceptualisations-of-students-and-their-learning.pdf

Collins, P. H. (2000). Gender, Black feminism, and Black political economy. *Annals of the American Academy of Political and Social Science, 568*, 41–53.

Creswell, J. W., & Miller, D. L. (2000). Determining validity in qualitative inquiry. *Theory into Practice, 39*(3), 124–130.

Du Bois, W. E. B. (1903). *The souls of Black folks.* New York, NY: Bantam Classic.

Dyson, M., Roediger, D., McIntosh, P., Meigs, A., & Suarez, R. (2007). Membership has its privileges. In M. Dyson (Ed.), *Debating race* (pp. 125–128). New York, NY: Basic Civitas Book.

Eiselen, W. (1948). *Report on the commission on native education*. Pretoria: Union Government.

Freire, P. (1970). *Pedagogy of the oppressed*. London: Continuum.

Funteh, M. (2015). Dimensioning Indigenous African educational system: A critical theory divide discourse. *International Journal of Humanities and Social Science, 5*, 139–140.

Giroux, H. A. (1980). Beyond the correspondence theory: Notes on the dynamics of educational reproduction and transformation. *Curriculum Inquiry, 10*(3), 225–247.

Hall, K., & Giese, S. (2008). Addressing quality through school fees and school funding. In S. Pendlebury, I. Lake, & C. Smith (Eds.), *South African child gauge 2008/2009* (pp. 37–40). Cape Town: Children's Institute, University of Cape Town.

Hartshorne, K. (1992). *Crisis and challenge: Black education 1910–1990*. Cape Town: Oxford University Press.

Howard, T. C. (2002). Hearing footsteps in the dark: African American students' descriptions of effective teachers. *Journal of Education for Students Placed at Risk, 7*, 425–444.

Hyslop, J. (1993). *A destruction coming in: Bantu education as a response to social crisis*. Johannesburg: Raven Press.

Johnson, G. M. (1994). An ecological framework for conceptualizing educational risk. *Urban Education, 29*(1), 34–49.

Ladson-Billings, G. (1994). *The dreamkeepers: Successful teachers of African American children*. San Francisco, CA: Jossey-Bass.

Ladson-Billings, G. (1995). Toward a theory of culturally relevant pedagogy. *American Educational Research Journal, 32*, 465–491.

Ladson-Billings, G. (2001). *Crossing over to Canaan: The journey of new teachers in diverse classrooms*. San Francisco, CA: Jossey-Bass.

Lukes, S. (2005). *Power: A radical view*. New York, NY: Palgrave Macmillan.

Luthuli, P. (1981). *The philosophical foundations of Black education in South Africa*. Durban: Butterworths.

Marshall, D., & Case, J. (2010). Rethinking 'disadvantage' in higher education: A paradigmatic case study using narrative analysis. *Studies in Higher Education, 35*(5), 491–504.

McKenzie, K., & Sheurich, J. (2004). Equity traps: A useful construct for preparing principals to lead schools that are successful with racially diverse students. *Educational Administration Quarterly, 40*(5), 601–632

O'Grady, C. (2000). Integrating service learning and multicultural education: An overview. In C. O'Grady (Ed.), *Integrating service learning and multicultural education in colleges and universities* (pp. 1–19). Mahwah, NJ: Lawrence Erlbaum Associates.

Pascale, C. M. (2013). *Making sense of race, class and gender: Commonsense, power, and privilege in the United States*. New York, NY: Routledge.

Pease, B. (2010). *Undoing privilege: Unearned advantage in a divided world*. London: Zed Books.

Rubin, H. J., & Rubin, I. S. (1995). *Qualitative interviewing: The art of hearing data*. Thousand Oaks, CA: Sage Publications.

South African Schools Act of 1996, 34620 C.F.R. (1996).

Statistics South Africa. (2016). *Mid year population estimates*. Pretoria: Statistics South Africa. Retrieved from http://www.statssa.gov.za/?s=mid+year+population+estimates&sitem=publications

Valencia, R. R. (2010). *Dismantling contemporary deficit thinking: Educational thought and practice*. New York, NY: Routledge.

Vandeyar, S. (2008). The attitudes, beliefs and anticipated actions of student teachers towards difference in South African classrooms. *South African Journal of Higher Education, 22*(3), 692–707.

Walker, K. (2011). Deficit thinking and the effective teacher. *Education & Urban Society, 43*(5), 576–597.

Weiner, L. (2006). Challenging deficit thinking. *Educational Leadership, 64*(1), 42–45.

World Bank. (2016). Price level ratio of PPP conversion factor (GDP) to market exchange rate. *International Comparison Program database*. Retrieved from http://data.worldbank.org/indicator/pa.nus.pppc.rf

CHAPTER 13

Afterword: Movement toward a "Third Reconstruction" and Educational Equity

Michael Vavrus

From the August 2014 police killing of an unarmed Black adolescent in the St. Louis suburb of Ferguson and the June 2015 murders of nine African Americans, including a state representative, in Charleston, South Carolina, to the 2016 presidential primaries and the eventual 2017 promotion of White nationalism within the governing circle of the president of the United States (Ganim, Welch, & Meyersohn, 2017; Harkinson, 2017), the U.S. witnessed a countervailing rise of a new civil rights movement (Taylor, 2016). As more deaths of unarmed Blacks at the hands of police surfaced, "Black Lives Matter" became a tagline for international protests as an expression of institutional racism experienced globally by historically marginalized populations (Tharoor, 2016). In this context Angela Davis (2016) reminds us that "the Black radical tradition is related not simply to Black people but to all people who are struggling for freedom" (p. 39).

Framing these collective actions as a historical movement toward a "Third Reconstruction" facilitates "thinking about moments in the past where there has been a combination of grassroots radicalism and political leadership" (Foner, 2015, p. 141). Although grassroots activism was visible during the composition of this book, overt and consistent political leadership for completing the freedom goals of the Civil Rights Movement and self-determination efforts by Indigenous groups has been missing. In fact, the world has witnessed an uptake in xenophobia and nativist nationalism, according to the United Nations (2016): "We still live in a world where we witness politicians and leaders using hateful and divisive rhetoric to divide instead of unite societies" (para. 2). In light of the damning documentation within this book about inequities a disproportionate number of children and youth of color suffer daily in public schools, we first briefly review previous efforts at reconstruction for social justice and educational equity.

© KONINKLIJKE BRILL NV, LEIDEN, 2018 | DOI 10.1163/9789004365209_013

1   Reconstruction(s) and White Backlash(es)

Reconstruction historically refers to the period of 1865–1877 when the U.S. set conditions for the South to return to the Union. Davis (2016) calls Reconstruction "one of the most hidden eras of U.S. history" (p. 70). She notes how "former slaves fought for the right to public education" and that "poor white children who had not had an education gained access to education as a direct result of former slaves" (p. 71). The removal of federal troops from the South and political normalization of racial discrimination in the North signaled, however, Reconstruction's end and an acceleration of White terrorism (Foner, 1990). The U.S. Supreme Court in *Plessy v. Ferguson* (1896) solidified the practice of White supremacist segregation by declaring in effect that public facilities could be "separate but equal" based on the phenotype of skin color. In the opinion of the court, racial segregation was "merely a legal distinction between the white and colored races – a distinction which is founded in the color of the two races and which must always exist so long as white men are distinguished from the other race by color" (para. 20). Using public education as an example, the court observed that the "most common instance of this is connected with the establishment of separate schools for white and colored children" (para. 23).

A half century after *Plessy*, the U.S. was in the midst of a Civil Rights Movement, which is considered a Second Reconstruction that extended from after World War II to 1968 (U.S. House of Representatives, n.d.; also, Woodward, 1955). During this same era oppressed populations in Asia, Africa, and Latin America along with Native American Indigenous groups responded to colonialism through self-determination movements. *De jure* school segregation on the basis of race was overturned by *Brown v. Board* in 1954. However, 20 years later the courts had abandoned enforcement at a time when racial segregation between and within schools was increasing (Irons, 2002). Hence, by the 1970s the federal government effectively withdrew support for the completion of a Second Reconstruction.

As the 2020s approach, we hear a resonance with former slave Frederick Douglas's (1881) description of a racialized "color line" of discrimination and W.E.B. Du Bois's (1903/2007) well-known observation that "the problem of the Twentieth Century is the problem of the color line" ("Forethought" n.p.). In 2015 a *Richmond Times-Dispatch* editorial called for a national "truth and reconciliation commission" because "*the color line persists*" and "accounting has not occurred" ("Virginia must lead," 2015, para. 4, 7, emphasis added). With little hope for such a national reconciliation, grassroots social justice activist Reverend Dr. William Barber II (2016) contends, "Nothing less than a Third Reconstruction holds the promise of healing our nation's wounds and birthing a better future for all" (p. xiii). In his home state of North Carolina Barber helped to create a movement that fused various social justice movements: *"Within the framework of a Third Reconstruction*, we see how our movements are flowing together, recognizing that *our intersectionality* creates the opportunity to *fundamentally redirect America"* (p. 122, emphasis added; also, Goodstein, 2017).

A growing body of research, some of which is contained within the chapters in this collection, applies intersectionality to document that conditions of racial discrimination and acts of resistance by people of color do not occur in isolation. Movement toward a Third Reconstruction signals an ever-increasing public and scholarly consciousness of a confluence of demographic and institutional categories that intersect with aspirations for equity and justice. A movement toward a Third Reconstruction provides a historical descriptor for critical educators to place their scholarship and teaching in a context of Black Lives Matter and other social justice movements led by historically marginalized groups (also, see Mann, 2006; Salazar & Rios, 2016). As teachers, teacher educators, and researchers join in a movement toward a Third Reconstruction, a conceptual framework to consider intersectional approaches emerges from this collection of chapters.

2   A Critical Multicultural Framework

The intersectional research of chapter authors collectively revealed complex matrices of race, ethnicity, class, and gender. *Critical multiculturalism* can serve as a theoretical framework for this work as it brings to the forefront such concepts as resistance, power, knowledge construction, class, cultural politics, and emancipatory actions (May, 2012; McLaren, 1994; Vavrus, 2015). Through "educational criticism" that "is not only deconstructive but reconstructive," the standpoint of critical multiculturalism actively "build[s] possibilities" that are disregarded by dominant ideologies (Leonardo, 2009, p. 147).

Critical multiculturalism incorporates intersectionality. As chapter authors demonstrated, intersectionality located within critical race theory helps to complicate commonsense, one-dimensional notions of race, ethnicity, class, and gender and subvert assertions of essentialized identities and categories. Intersectionality as "an analytic sensibility" (Cho, Crenshaw, & McCall, 2013, p. 795) includes *historical inquiry* that can reveal *political economy patterns* to inform our current historical moment. During the nearly three decades of intersectionality scholarship across a variety of disciplines, studies have ranged from the variability among individuals within categories of race, ethnicity, class, and gender to the interaction of such classifications with normative institutions. In other words, intersectionality claims indicate that some categories interact to produce novel effects, that is, that there are effects associated with occupying the intersection of multiple categories that are not present for individuals 'outside' the intersection (individuals who occupy only some of the categories but not all of them). (Bright, Malinsky, & Thompson, 2016, p. 71)

Complicating this is intersectionality with institutions of power, be they schools, police, or legislative bodies.

This chapter offers a critical multicultural overview of possible intersectional categories of oppression, some of which were presented in individual chapters in this book, that generally exist outside the schooling process yet affect access to an equitable education. A movement toward a Third Reconstruction fits within a broad critical multicultural conceptual umbrella to fuse such actions as (a) advancing a critical decolonial teacher education and school curriculum (Vavrus, 2017), (b) ending a racially discriminatory school-to-prison pipeline (Koon, 2013), (c) preparing teachers with a critical consciousness or *conscietização* to support equity needs of historically marginalized learners (Freire, 1970), and (d) honoring the gender and sexual identities of all students (Vavrus, 2015). Such a movement can reveal for teachers and teacher educators elements of structural violence that limit educational equity, elements that must be critiqued as part of the continuing development of theory, research, and practice for emancipatory schooling effects for *all* children.

3   Structural Violence

"Cultural violence leads to structural violence when it is incorporated into the formalized legal and economic exchanges of the society," explain Pilisuk and Rountree (2015, p. 81). Whereas direct violence by an individual is more visible, structural violence can be more difficult to recognize: "The invisibility of the structure of violence is frequently the result of our inability – or refusal – to see below the surface" (p. 82). For example, increasing wealth and income inequalities as a form of economic structural violence create additional barriers for poor students and those of color to access an equitable public education. Intersectionality research helps make visible normalized structural violence in relation to its impact on educational equity.

The following sections provide a sample of possible categories and issues that can conceptually fit within research and teaching for a movement toward a Third Reconstruction. Categories are conceptualized in a causal and symbiotic relationship that contain various intersections which in turn enable institutional discrimination on the basis of race, gender, sexuality, and economic status.

3.1   *Foundational Exclusion of People of Color from "The People"*

To analyze who constitutes "the people" of a nation-state, we consider the example of the U.S. and intersections embedded in the dispossession of Indigenous lands and culture, the modern invention of race, White supremacist nationalism, and colorblind/post-racial mythologies. Throughout this telling, intersections of class interests and racial and gender identity narratives evolved into tightening structures of racial and gender oppression that have had devastating schooling consequences for a disproportionate number of children of color. This perspective suggests that youth identified as Black, Latinx, and Indigenous along with those who are poor and hold nonconforming gender and sexual identities are perceived as not fully included within "the people," especially in regards to educational opportunities and support.

European settlers and the U.S. military forcibly removed Indigenous people from their ancestral lands, and *White* as a racial category signaled who "the people" would eventually be for the new nation, the United States of America. The story of *Whiteness* is one in which skin color and geographic origins were markers that determined status ranking and eventual property rights. Whiteness identified who "the people" were, a privileged group with various advantages over people of color. To disrupt labor and class solidarity in the late 1600s, the plantation and colonial aristocracy invented the modern notion of "race" to undermine alliances and revolts among imported African slaves, English indentured servants, and other poor English immigrants. Two races were invented – "White" and "Negro" – to separate the English from the Africans through legal means and sanctioned terrorism (Baum, 2006). Nearly 350 years later, social psychologists note how strong in-group loyalty exhibited by a White majority remains correlated with racial intolerance, nationalism, and ethnocentrism (Haidt & Kesebir, 2010). The intersection of 21st century hierarchies of "race" with "the people" highlights the lingering effects of racially labeling bodies in relation to degrees of educational access and inclusiveness for students of color, a condition negatively affected by White supremacist nationalism (see Zeskind, 2009).

Intersections of immigration policies with institutional governing power serve as a barometer to the influence of White supremacist nationalism. Contemporary resistance to immigration reform can be traced to intersections of xenophobia and nativist construction of immigrant cultures and languages in threatening terms (Behdad, 2005). Tropes that circulated since the Founding continue to find nationalistic traction for an "American" citizenship exclusively equated as White and Christian.

Despite claims that the U.S. is somehow a post-racial, colorblind society, skin color identification continues to materially favor Whites over people of color (Hall, 2008). Whereas evidence exists that numerous schools continue historical patterns of explicit and implicit racial discrimination, Supreme Court Chief Justice John Roberts simply argued that public policies should use a colorblind strategy to eliminate racial discrimination in public schools (*Parents Involved,* 2007). In kinship with Supreme Court colorblindness, post-racialism attempted to signal that "bad things had happened in the past, but that was long ago, and by electing a black president the country had forcefully and forever broken with bygone days" (López, 2014, p. 194). In educational settings, intersectionality research compares institutional claims of colorblindness and anti-discrimination to school disciplinary policies and practices and disparities in access to curricular and extra-curricular opportunities. A critical multicultural social justice framework makes clear that racial and economic discrimination and violence directed at millions of people of color contradicts the trope of a post-racial society (see Aja & Bustillo, 2015).

3.2   *Historical Constraints*

From British colonialism to the present, people of color experienced institutional constraints on their freedom through forms of structural violence. Black and Brown lives have been constrained by racialized employment, racialized residential housing, and racialized policing. Any of these factors can negatively affect the mobility of parents and their children, which reduces educational opportunities for children of color.

3.2.1   Racialized Employment

Despite the Civil Rights Act of 1964 that ended legalized job discrimination and increased the racial diversity of workplaces, racial discrimination remains. By 1980, for example, the "progress for black Americans in the workplace came to an abrupt stop" (Stainback & Tomaskovic-Devey, 2012, p. 177). Lack of access to living wage jobs negatively affects parental mobility and material resources in ways that can shape a child's access to equitable educational resources, especially in schools located in low-income communities (U.S. Department of Education, 2013). The same discrimination that a parent of color finds in employment is often what awaits their children.

3.2.2   Racialized Housing

Even where workplaces have some degree of racial integration, when the work day is over, the majority of Whites retreat to their historically racially isolated communities and social events. Notwithstanding various efforts by the U.S. Justice Department, Frankenberg (2013) notes, "Enforcement of the

Fair Housing Act has never been seriously monitored" (p. 563). For young, low-income adults of color, housing discrimination results in disproportional restrictions on their mobility and life opportunities (Britton & Goldsmith, 2013). A former administrator for the U.S. Department of Housing and Urban Development explained that practices of racial housing segregation intersects with a broad pattern of discrimination and social obstacles: "It's about everything that goes with it: joblessness, crime, drugs, *underperforming schools*, crumbling infrastructure, inadequate public services – the list goes on" (Goldfarb, 2015, p. A22, emphasis added).

Despite what the United Nations (2009) has identified as persistent racial profiling in police actions, the continuing disproportional arrest and incarceration of parents of color affects their job and housing options, all of which limit the quality of education their own children will receive.

3.2.3   Racialized Policing
From its colonial heritage, the U.S. government has a pattern of allowing the infliction of legal and extralegal violence on populations of color. For example, in the policing of Blacks from private slave patrols to the rise of modern urban police departments, Hahn and Jefferies (2003) explained, "The primary objective of white voters and politicians was to prevent both slave and free black persons from disrupting a segregated social structure, and the police served as an essential instrument of that policy" (p. 124) – all of which provided impunity for police in their use of violence on Black populations.

Comparatively, African Americans along with other populations of color are overly surveilled through policing (Cyril, 2015). Intersections among a history of underreported instances of punishment given to both children and adults by governmental authorities such as police, teachers, and administrators stem from *neo-Confederate narratives* of Black criminality (Vavrus, 2015). This history was empowered by the suppression of data on institutionalized physical abuse and the creation of a racialized perception as to who is inherently prone to criminal behavior.

3.2.4   As If It "Had Never Happened"
The 1705 Virginia Slave code noted that a murder of a slave by a White person would be as if it "had never happened" (General Assembly of Virginia, 1705, p. 459). More than two centuries later when Ferguson police detained journalists in violation of the First Amendment to the U.S. Constitution (Bomboy, 2014), Wesley Lowery, a Pulitzer Prize-winning *Washington Post* reporter, eerily echoed the 1705 Virginia Slave Code: "Apparently, in America, in 2014, police can manhandle you, take you into custody, put you in cell &

then open the door *like it didn't happen*" (as cited in Hartman, 2014, para. 18, emphasis added). The *Guardian*'s national security editor Spence Ackerman (2015) helped expose Chicago's Homan Square, a decades-old "secret" detention center where city police literally tortured local Black residents. Despite an unprecedented $5.5 million reparations agreement, the police officially continue to act "*as if that has never happened* in Chicago, that there's no history there, there's no legacy there" (para. 41, emphasis added). From the Virginia Slave Code to a school-to-prison pipeline, police shield abusive colleagues from criminal charges, actions that led an Ohio prosecutor to compare police defendants to an "organized crime syndicate" (McGinty, as cited in Queally, 2015, para. 4).

3.2.5   Criminalization of Bodies of Color

After the Civil War the Southern White political class sent propaganda warnings to the North about supposed criminal Blacks migrating to the North. Reiterating the ideology of the Confederate of States of America, African Americans were portrayed ideologically as "*domestic enemies*" that allowed states to adopt "a posture of self-protection" (McCurry, 2010, p. 219, emphasis added). The propaganda of Black criminality was very successful and was openly perpetuated by Woodrow Wilson, U.S. president during WWI and a long-time defender of Ku Klux Klan terrorism as necessary to maintain social order (see Wilson, 1902).

Murakawa (2014) documents that U.S. presidents for the past 65 years have considered the "first civil right" to be keeping a White public free from violence. This particular perception of civil rights was a pitch to Whites who feared people of color demanding equal rights in all aspects of public life. The assertion of a first civil right served as the backdrop for continuing governmental regimes spouting slogans of law-and-order to cast the source of crime primarily upon Black and Brown communities while turning poor urban schools into hostile learning environments (Fabricant & Fine, 2013). In effect, schools with a high population of students of color have gone "from rehabilitation and services to criminalization" (Koon, 2013, p. 3). Furthermore, the presence of police in schools is associated with "a surge in arrests or misdemeanor charges for essentially non-violent behavior...that sends children into criminal courts" (Eckholm, 2013, p. A1). For adolescents released from incarceration, the return to society is difficult because incarceration disrupted a high school education necessary for gainful employment. Returning to unstable social environments without a diploma and with possible learning challenges along with an arrest and conviction record intersect to make it nearly impossible to secure a living wage job and transition into civic life.

3.2.6   Gendered Oppression

Gender intersectionality captures the extreme oppression experienced by poor women of color. Cho, Crenshaw, and McCall (2013) note, "Although Black male and white female narratives of discrimination were understood to be fully inclusive and universal, Black female narratives were rendered partial, unrecognizable, something apart from the standard claims of race discrimination or gender discrimination" (pp. 790–791). Black women historically have been blamed for the poverty of African American communities, stereotyped in behavior, and had their academic potential and lived experiences and knowledge marginalized – all of which intersect to lower teacher expectations for achievement by Black girls, expectations that also extend to Latinx and Indigenous girls (Crenshaw, 2015; Epstein, Blake, & González, 2017).

A history of marginalizing and scapegoating African American women was reinforced during the 1960s War on Poverty. *The Negro Family: The Case for National Action* (U.S. Department of Labor, 1965) contended that poverty was a cultural feature of Black "family pathology" (p. 19). The identified cultural source was the Black female head-of-household because "a matriarchal structure...seriously retards the progress of the group as a whole, and imposes a crushing burden on the Negro male" (p. 29). The trope of the Black female parent as a cause of social problems would later become prominent in President Ronald Reagan's 1980s racializing discourse of mythic welfare queens and by the 2010s expanded into a "cultural commonsense created by rightwing race-baiting: lazy nonwhites abuse welfare, while hardworking whites pay for it" (López, 2014, p. 73).

Stereotypes of the Black female exist beyond the negativity projected upon their role in families and communities. Since the era of slavery, White men in particular constructed their female slaves as hypersexualized to justify rapes by Whites and the mixed race off-springs from these violent encounters. Collins (2000) notes how contemporary schools socialize females to express themselves "within a context where Black womanhood remains routinely derogated" (p. 100). In 21st century popular culture and public schools, an assertive African Americans female is often singled out as a socially inappropriate "angry Black woman" (e.g., Harris-Perry, 2016).

Despite a history of discrimination, African American women have been central to the theory and practice of Black resistance and civil rights activism. During the late 1800s and into the 20th century, for example, "Colored Women's Club" formed in every state in the western U.S. to create supportive environments in hostile societies. These organizations often were specifically created in response to lynchings (Taylor, 2003). The Civil Rights Movement of the Second Reconstruction era was propelled by the nearly invisible but tireless work of African American women in the relative freedom available through Black churches (Olson, 2001). More recently, it was three Black women who created the Black Lives Matter movement that spurred a movement toward a Third Reconstruction (see Garza, 2014) – and a formerly incarcerated 65-year old Black woman has become a leading advocate for incarcerated women (Burton & Lynn, 2017).

4   Moving Forward with Praxis

By briefly outlining examples of key issues of material consequences through intersecting categories of oppression and structural violence, this chapter offered a critical multicultural framework with both historical and contemporary perspectives. Freire (1970) claimed, however, that the discovery of oppressive conditions "cannot be purely intellectual but must involve *action*; nor can it be limited to mere activism, but must include *serious reflection*: only then will it be a *praxis*" (p. 52, emphasis added). Such actions involve applying aspects of the collective knowledge of social justice research by working and organizing across school districts and colleges of education along with grassroots community groups committed to equity (Associated Press & Romero, 2017; Au & Hagopian, 2017). Collaborative community organizing can result in publicly advancing electoral platforms – be it for local school boards or state offices – that offer policies and candidates committed to remedying inequities. Teachers and teacher educators can teach the history of activism and civil disobedience that has advanced equity and includes contemporary examples (Minsberg, 2017). Furthermore, educators can participate directly with contemporary social justice movements such as Black Lives Matter that "encourages purposely disruptive protests, peaceful civil disobedience, mainstream political activism, and mass demonstrations" (Linscott, 2017, p. 76) and endeavors to be an independent force in electoral politics (McClain, 2017). Hence, in order to expand a movement toward a Third Reconstruction, teachers, teacher educators, and researchers with a critical multicultural commitment will need to embrace praxis by engaging in scholarship, teaching, *and* actions that contribute to the advancement of educational equity for all our children.

References

Ackerman, S. (2015, May 15). As Chicago pays victims of past torture, police face new allegations of abuse at Homan Square (interview). *Democracy Now*. Retrieved from http://www.democracynow.org/2015/5/15/as_chicago_pays_victims_of_past

Aja, A. A., & Bustillo, D. (2015). Judicial histories and racial disparities: Affirmative action and the myth of the "post racial." *Hamline Journal of Public Law & Policy, 36*(1), 26–53.

Associated Press & Romero, N. (2017, October 13). DeVos fundraising visit draws about 1,000 protesters in Bellevue. *Q13 Fox*. Retrieved from http://q13fox.com/2017/10/13/devos-fundraising-visit-draws-about-1000-protesters-in-bellevue/

Au, W., & Hagopian, J. (2017). How one elementary school sparked a citywide movement to make Black students' lives matter. *Rethinking Schools, 32*(1). Retrieved from https://www-rethinkingschools-org.evergreen.idm.oclc.org/articles/how-one-elementary-school-sparked-a-citywide-movement-to-make-black-students-lives-matter

Barber, W. J. (2016). *The third Reconstruction: Moral Mondays, fusion politics, and the rise of a new justice movement.* Boston: Beacon Press.

Baum, B. (2006). *The rise and the fall of the Caucasian race: A political history of racial identity.* New York, NY: New York University Press.

Behdad, A. (2005). *A forgetful nation: On immigration and cultural identity in the United States.* Durham, NC: Duke University Press.

Bomboy, S. (2014, August 20). More journalist arrests in Ferguson add to first amendment media debate. *Constitution Daily.* Retrieved from http://blog.constitutioncenter.org/2014/08/more-journalist-arrests-in-ferguson-add-to-first-amendment-media-debate/

Bright, L. K., Malinsky, D., & Thompson, M. (2016, January). Causally interpreting intersectionality theory. *Philosophy of Science, 83*, 60–81.

Britton, M. L., & Goldsmith, P. R. (2013). Keeping people in their place? Young-adult mobility and persistence of residential segregation in US metropolitan areas. *Urban Studies, 50*(14), 2886–2903. doi:10.1177/0042098013482506

Burton, S., & Lynn, C. (2017). *Becoming Ms. Burton: From prison to recovery to leading the fight for incarcerated women.* New York, NY: New Press.

Cho, S., Crenshaw, K. M., & McCall, L. (2013). Toward a field of intersectionality studies: Theory, application, and praxis. *Signs: Journal of Women in Culture and Society, 38*(4), 785–810.

Collins, P. H. (2000). *Black feminist thought: Knowledge, consciousness, and the politics of empowerment* (2nd ed.). New York, NY: Routledge.

Crenshaw, K. M. (2015). *Black girls matter: Pushed out, overpoliced, and underprotected.* New York, NY: The African American Policy Forum and Center for Intersectionality and Social Policies Studies. Retrieved from http://www.atlanticphilanthropies.org/app/uploads/2015/09/BlackGirlsMatter_Report.pdf

Cyril, M. A. (2015, April). Black America's state of surveillance. *The Progressive.* Retrieved from http://www.progressive.org/news/2015/03/188074/black-americas-state-surveillance

Davis, A. Y. (2016). *Freedom is a constant struggle: Ferguson, Palestine, and the foundations of a movement.* Chicago, IL: Haymarket Books.

Douglass, F. (1881, June). The color line. *The North American Review, 132*(295), 567–577. Retrieved from JSTOR database.

Du Bois, W. E. B. (2007). *The souls of Black folks.* Oxford: Oxford University Press. [Original work published 1903.]

Eckholm, E. (2013, April 12). With police in schools, more children in court. *New York Times,* pp. A1, A13.

Epstein, R., Blake, J., & González, T. (2017). *Girlhood interrupted: The erasure of Black girls' childhood.* Washington, DC: Center on Poverty and Inequality. Retrieved from http://www.law.georgetown.edu/academics/centers-institutes/poverty-inequality/ upload/girlhood-interrupted.pdf

Fabricant, M., & Fine, M. (2013). *The changing politics of education: Privatization and the dispossessed lives left behind.* Boulder, CO: Paradigm.

Foner, E. (1990). *A short history of reconstruction, 1863–1877.* New York, NY: Harper Perennial.

Foner, E. (2015, April 6). Toward a third reconstruction: From abolition to civil rights and beyond. *The Nation, 300*(14), 138–141.

Frankenberg, E. (2013). The role of residential segregation in contemporary school segregation. *Education and Urban Society, 45*(5), 548–570. doi:10.1177/ 0013124513486288

Freire, P. (1970). *Pedagogy of the oppressed* (M. B. Ramos, Trans.). New York, NY: Seabury Press.

Ganim, S., Welch, C., & Meyersohn, N. (2017, February 16). 'A resurgence of White nationalism': Hate groups spiked in 2016. *CNN Politics.* Retrieved from http://www.cnn.com/2017/02/15/politics/hate-groups-spiked-in-2016/

Garza, A. (2014, October 7). A herstory of the #Blacklivesmatter movement. *The Feminist Wire.* Retrieved from http://www.thefeministwire.com/2014/10/blacklivesmatter-2/

General Assembly of Virginia. (1705). *An act concerning servants and slaves* (Excerpts). Retrieved from www.encyclopediavirginia.org/_An_act_concerning_Servants_and_ Slaves_1705

Goldfarb, A. (2015, May 20). Moving to end housing segregation. *New York Times,* p. A22.

Goodstein, L. (2017, June 11). Liberals fighting for their faith. *New York Times,* pp. A1, A22.

Hahn, H., & Jefferies, J. L. (2003). *Urban America and its police: From the postcolonial era through the turbulent 1960s.* Boulder, CO: University of Colorado Press.

Haidt, J., & Kesebir, S. (2010). Morality. In S. Fiske, D. Gilbert, & G. Lindzey (Eds.), *Handbook of social psychology* (5th ed., pp. 797–832). Hoboken, NJ: Wiley.

Harkinson, J. (2017, January 30). The dark history of the White house aides who crafted Trump's "Muslim ban." *Mother Jones.* Retrieved from http://www.motherjones.com/ politics/2017/01/stephen-bannon-miller-trump-refugee-ban-islamophobia-white- nationalist

Harris-Perry, M. (2016, April 6). Melissa Harris-Perry on race, media, and the story behind this year's presidential race. *Democracy Now!* Retrieved from http://www.democracynow.org/2016/4/7/melissa_harris_perry_on_race_media

Hartmann, M. (2014, August 13). Washington Post, Huffington Post reporters arrested in Ferguson. *New York.* Retrieved from http://nymag.com/daily/intelligencer/2014/08/ferguson-reporters-arrested.html

Irons, P. (2002). *Jim Crow's children: The broken promise of the Brown decision.* New York, NY: Viking.

Koon, D. S. (2013, April). *Exclusionary school discipline: An issue brief and review of the literature* (The Chief Justice Earl Warren Institute on Law and Social Policy, University of California, Berkeley School of Law). Retrieved from www.boysandmenofcolor.org/wp-content/uploads/2013/04/Exclusionary-School-Discipline-Warren-Institute.pdf

Leonardo, Z. (2009). Afterword. In W. Au (Ed.), *Unequal by design: High-stakes testing and the standardization of inequality* (pp. 147–153). New York, NY: Routledge.

Linscott, C. P. (2017). #Blacklivesmatter and the mediatic lives of a movement. *Black Camera, 8*(2), 75–80. Retrieved from http://www.jstor.org/stable/10.2979/blackcamera.8.2.04

López, I. H. (2014). *Dog whistle politics: How coded racial appeals have reinvented racism and wrecked the middle class.* New York, NY: Oxford University Press.

Mann, E. (2006). *Katrina's legacy: White racism and Black reconstruction in New Orleans and the Gulf Coast.* Los Angeles, CA: Frontlines Press.

May, S. (2012). Critical multiculturalism and education. In J. A. Banks (Ed.), *Encyclopedia of diversity in education* (Vol. 1, pp. 472–478). Thousand Oaks, CA: Sage.

McClain, D. (2017, October 9). The future of BLM: Can the movement win in the Trump era? *The Nation, 305*(8), 12–16.

McCurry, S. (2010). *Confederate reckoning: Power and politics in the civil war south.* Cambridge, MA: Harvard University Press.

McLaren, P. (1994). White terror and oppositional agency: Towards a critical multiculturalism. In D. T. Goldberg (Ed.), *Multiculturalism: A critical reader* (pp. 45–74). Cambridge, MA: Blackwell.

Minsberg, T. (2017, September 28). How teachers are bringing Charlottesville to the classroom. *New York Times.* Retrieved from https://www.nytimes.com/2017/09/28/learning/lesson-plans/teachers-charlottesville-curriculim.html

Murakawa, N. (2014). *The first civil right: How liberals built prison America.* New York, NY: Oxford University Press.

Olson, L. (2001). *Freedom's daughters: The unsung heroines of the civil rights movement from 1830 to 1970.* New York, NY: Scribner.

Parents Involved in Community Schools v. Seattle School District, 551 U.S. 701 (2007). Retrieved from WestlawNext database.

Pilisuk, M., & Rountree, J. A. (2015). *The hidden structure of violence: Who benefits from global violence and war.* New York, NY: Monthly Review Press.

Plessy v. Ferguson, 163 U.S. 537 (1896). *Cornell law school legal information institute.* Retrieved from https://www.law.cornell.edu/supremecourt/text/163/537# writing-ZS

Quelly, J. (2015, May 17). Cleveland officers' silence frustrates prosecutor in police trial. *Los Angeles Times.* Retrieved from http://www.latimes.com/nation/la-na-cleveland-police-20150517-story.html#page=1

Salazar, M. D. C., & Rios, F. (2016). Just scholarship! Publishing academic research with a social justice focus. *Multicultural Perspectives, 18*(1), 3–11.

Stainback, K., & Tomaskovic-Devey, D. (2012). *Documenting desegregation: Racial and gender segregation in private-sector employment since the civil rights act.* New York, NY: Russell Sage Foundation.

Taylor, K.-Y. (2016). *From #Blacklivesmatter to Black liberation.* Chicago, IL: Haymarket Books.

Taylor, Q. (2006). *The urban frontier, 1875–1940: African Americans in the cities of the west* (Video lecture). *UWtv.* Retrieved from http://uwtv.org/series/african-american-west-1528-2000/watch/7KMY7KoJ1hA/

Tharoor, I. (2016, July 12). Black lives matter is a global cause. *Washington Post.* Retrieved from https://www.washingtonpost.com/news/worldviews/wp/2016/07/12/black-lives-matter-is-a-global-cause/

United Nations. (2009, April 28). *Racism, racial discrimination, xenophobia and related forms of intolerance, follow-up to and implementation of the Durban declaration and programme of action.* Retrieved from http://www2.ohchr.org/english/bodies/hrcouncil/docs/11session/A.HRC.11.36.Add.3.pdf

United Nations. (2016, November 1). *Racism, xenophobia increasing globally, experts tell third committee, amid calls for laws to combat hate speech, concerns over freedom of expression.* Retrieved from https://www.un.org/press/en/2016/gashc4182.doc.htm

United States Department of Education. (2013). *For each and every child: A strategy for education equity and excellence.* Retrieved from https://www2.ed.gov/about/bdscomm/list/eec/equity-excellence-commission-report.pdf

United States Department of Labor. (1965). *The Negro family: The case for national action.* Ann Arbor, MI: University of Michigan Library.

United States House of Representative. (n.d.). *The civil rights movement and the second reconstruction, 1945–1968* (History, art, and archives). Retrieved from http://history.house.gov/Exhibitions-and-Publications/BAIC/Historical-Essays/Keeping-the-Faith/Civil-Rights-Movement/

Vavrus, M. (2015). *Diversity and education: A critical multicultural approach.* New York, NY: Teachers College Press.

Vavrus, M. (2017). A decolonial alternative to critical approaches to multicultural and intercultural education. In D. J. Clandinin & J. Husu (Eds.), *The Sage handbook of research on teacher education* (Vol. 1, pp. 473–490). Thousand Oaks, CA: Sage Publications.

Virginia must lead on racial truth and reconciliation. (2015, July 11). *Richmond Times-Dispatch*. Retrieved from http://www.richmond.com/opinion/our-opinion/article_5fca16bd-63ec-5b64-9216-47b445b438b0.html

Wilson, W. (1902). *A history of the American people* (Vol. 5). New York, NY: Harper & Brothers.

Woodward, C. V. (1955). *The strange career of Jim Crow*. New York, NY: Oxford University Press.

Zeskind, L. (2009). *Blood and politics: The history of the white nationalist movement from the margins to the mainstream*. New York, NY: Farrar Straus Giroux.

Index

Printed in the United States
By Bookmasters